PREHISTORY AND THE FIRST CIVILIZATIONS

THE ILLUSTRATED
HISTORY OF THE WORLD

VOLUME 1

PREHISTORY AND THE
FIRST CIVILIZATIONS

J. M. ROBERTS

New York
Oxford University Press

The Illustrated History of the World

This edition first published in 1999 in the United States of America by
Oxford University Press, Inc.,
198 Madison Avenue, New York, N.Y. 10016
Oxford is a registered trademark of Oxford University Press

PREHISTORY AND THE FIRST CIVILIZATIONS
Copyright © Editorial Debate SA 1998
Text Copyright © J. M. Roberts 1976, 1980, 1983, 1987, 1988, 1992, 1998
Artwork and diagrams Copyright © Editorial Debate SA 1998
(for copyright of photographs and maps, see acknowledgments on page 192, which are to
be regarded as an extension of this copyright)

Art Direction by Duncan Baird Publishers.
Produced by Duncan Baird Publishers, London, England,
and Editorial Debate, Madrid, Spain.

Series ISBN 0-19-521529-X
Volume 1 ISBN 0-19-521519-2

DBP staff:
Senior editor: Joanne Levêque
Assistant editor: Georgina Harris
Senior designer: Steven Painter
Assistant designer: Anita Schnable
Picture research: Julia Ruxton
Sales fulfilment: Ian Smalley
Map artwork: Russell Bell
Commissioned artwork: Gillie Newman, Stephen Conlin
Decorative borders: Lorraine Harrison

Editorial Debate staff:
Editors and picture researchers:
Isabel Belmonte Martínez, Feliciano Novoa Portela,
Ruth Betegón Díez, Dolores Redondo
Editorial coordination: Ana Lucía Vila

Typeset in Sabon 11/15 pt
Color reproduction by Trescan, Madrid, Spain
Printed in Singapore by Imago Limited

NOTE
The abbreviations CE and BCE are used throughout this book:
CE Common Era (the equivalent of AD)
BCE Before Common Era (the equivalent of BC)

10 9 8 7 6 5 4 3 2

CONTENTS

INTRODUCTION

Pᴇᴏᴘʟᴇ ʜᴀᴠᴇ very varied ideas not only over what actually happened in history, but over what historians should say about it, and universal agreement about what a history of the world should contain is too much to hope for. All history has to be a selection, and here that is very evident. There is nothing alarming about that. To specify every fact that shaped our past would be to relive it, a logical impossibility. At best, history can only be what one generation thinks important about the past. Sometimes the state of the evidence determines the selection; making the selection is usually the historian's business, though.

Among the things which have helped shape the particular viewpoint from which this book has been written is a certain criterion of historical importance. In one sense, it could be thought a very democratic one, for I have tried to set out the events, movements, determining facts and circumstances which have shaped most human lives. Some people might have preferred a criterion based on something else, but I have chosen to write about the things which seem to me to have had the greatest effect on human behaviour in the long run. One result has been my decision to tell the story of the great civilizations

Eᴺᴛɪᴛʟᴇᴅ *Cognoscenti in a Room hung with Pictures*, this 17th-century painting from the Flemish School probably depicts European art experts, historians and scholars of the day, although the collection of pictures, instruments and *objets d'art* is likely to be imaginary.

which laid down the foundations of human beliefs and institutions in different parts of the world for many centuries, rather than (for example) to list all countries and their rulers for their own sake. The proper place for such factual detail is an encyclopedia or historical dictionary, not a narrative history. That word "narrative" is another clue to my criteria: it has always seemed to me that chronology is the foundation of history and that historians should extract a story from the welter of fact. The story of this history is of an evolving humanity. It tries to set out interconnexions and relationships between places and individuals often distant from one another in both time and space, so that their contribution to the whole becomes apparent.

That meaningful story is one of the gradual assertion of humanity's ability to manage nature. Nowadays we are often told that human beings have failed; history, some people say, is a catalogue of follies – or worse. Because of it, they go on, we now face over-population, the destruction of the natural environment and barely contained violence. There is, indeed, a case to be made for such views, but they are easily overdone. Gloom and pessimism are not justified by a considered look backward at humanity's immense achievements. History reveals an increasing and astonishing display of human power to overcome obstacles and bring about conscious change (which is not to say that all the resultant changes have been wise or desirable). Our species has shown a unique ability; other living creatures have survived with more or less success by finding their niche in nature, but humanity has from the start adapted nature to suit itself. From its tiny beginnings in repeated struggles to master nature, for instance, by shaping a stone or an antler into a tool, or by striving to light or merely keep alive a fire, human history is a story of change brought about by human

manipulation of the natural world. Such a success story is just as impressive as that of many disasters encountered *en route*.

The great Swiss historian Burckhardt once pointed out, very wisely, that in history you can never begin at the beginning. World history is about human beings, but we do not know who the first human being was. In the usual sense the era of history is the era of literacy, where there are documents for us to use as sources, but we have to start before that, with what we call "prehistory". We must not spend too much precious space on it, but most of humanity's existence has been lived in prehistoric times. For tens of thousands of years before civilization was possible, people much like ourselves in physique were exploiting the earth and changing it slowly. Earlier still, for hundreds of thousands, even millions, of years when nothing like a human being existed on earth, things were happening which shaped our later development and much of later history in very broad and important ways. So we must start there. But the main body of what follows is the story of civilization, a unique achievement, and a very rich and varied one. To tell its story in a way which puts it in a perspective which illuminates our own situation and difficulties has been my deepest ambition in writing this book. I now welcome with enthusiasm the possibility of presenting it to an even wider audience than hitherto. The original text has been thoroughly revised and up-dated, and enhanced by the wealth of illustrations, feature boxes, time charts and maps now made available by its imaginative publishers.

J. M. Roberts

BEFORE HISTORY

WHEN DOES History begin? It is tempting to reply "In the beginning", but like many obvious answers, this soon turns out to be unhelpful. As a great Swiss historian once pointed out, history is the one subject where you cannot begin at the beginning. We can trace the chain of human descent back to the appearance of vertebrates, or even to the photosynthetic cells and other basic structures which lie at the start of life itself. We can go back further, to almost unimaginable upheavals which formed this planet and even to the origins of the universe. Yet this is not "history".

Commonsense helps here: history is the story of humankind, of what it has done, suffered or enjoyed. We all know that dogs and cats do not have histories, while human beings do. Even when historians write about a natural process beyond human control, such as the ups and downs of climate, or the spread of a disease, they do so only because it helps us to understand why people have lived (and died) in some ways rather than others.

This suggests that all we have to do is to identify the moment at which the first human beings step out from the shadows of the remote past. It is not quite as simple as that, though. First, we have to know what we are looking for, but most attempts to define humanity on the basis of observable characteristics prove in the end arbitrary and cramping, as long arguments about "ape-men" and "missing links" have shown. Physiological tests help us to classify data but do not identify what is or is not human. That is a matter of a definition about which disagreement is possible. Some people have suggested that human uniqueness lies in language, yet other primates possess vocal equipment similar to our own; when noises are made with it which are signals, at what point do they become speech? Another famous definition is that man is a tool-maker, but observation has cast doubt on our uniqueness in this respect, too, long after Dr Johnson scoffed at Boswell for quoting it to him.

What is surely and identifiably unique about the human species is not its possession of certain faculties or physical characteristics, but what it has done with them – its achievement, or history, in fact. Humanity's unique achievement is its remarkably intense level of activity and creativity, its cumulative capacity to create change. All animals have ways of living, some complex enough to be called cultures. Human culture alone is progressive; it has been increasingly built by conscious choice and selection within it as well as by accident and natural pressure, by the accumulation of a capital of experience and knowledge which humans have exploited. Human history began when the inheritance of genetics and behaviour which had until then provided the only way of dominating the environment was first broken through by conscious choice. Of course, human beings have always only been able to make their history within limits. These limits are now very wide indeed, but they were once so narrow that it is impossible to identify the first step which took human evolution away from the determination of nature. We have for a long time only a blurred story, obscure both because the evidence is fragmentary and because we cannot be sure exactly what we are looking for.

In the middle of the Sahara desert, there are thousands of images painted or etched onto the rock that portray a lost world of swollen river beds and fertile wooded plains. The most spectacular examples of prehistoric imagery from the central Sahara date from the period between 6000 and 1500 BCE, when the livestock farmers who inhabited the region painted scenes such as these onto the rocks of the Tassili ni'Ajjer mountains.

1 *THE FOUNDATIONS*

THE ROOTS OF HISTORY lie in the prehuman past and it is hard to grasp just how long ago that was. If we think of a century on our calendar as a minute on some great clock recording the passage of time, then white Europeans began to settle in the Americas only about five minutes ago. Slightly less than fifteen minutes before that, Christianity appeared. Rather more than an hour ago a people settled in southern Mesopotamia who were soon to evolve the oldest civilization known to us. This is already well beyond the furthest margin of written record; according to our clock people began writing down the past much less than an hour ago, too. Some six or seven hours further back on our scale and much more remote, we can discern the first recognizable human beings of a modern physiological type already established in western Europe. Behind them, anything from a fortnight to three weeks earlier, appear the first traces of creatures with some humanlike characteristics whose contribution to the evolution which followed is still in debate.

The continents, which were joined for a time as so-called Pangaea, began to drift around 200 million years ago. South America separated from Africa, as did India, which later moulded itself to Asia. Australia and the Antarctic slowly moved apart from one another.

THE ORIGINS OF HUMANKIND

HOW FAR BACK into a growing darkness we need go in order to understand human origins is debatable, but it is worth considering for a moment even larger tracts of time simply because so much happened in them which, even if we cannot say anything very precise about it, shaped what followed. This is because humanity was to carry forward into historical times certain possibilities and limitations, and they were settled long ago, in a part even more remote than the much shorter period of time – three or four million years or so – in which creatures with at least some claim to human qualities are known to have existed. Though it is not our direct concern, we need to try to understand what was in the baggage of advantages and disadvantages with which humans alone among the primates emerged after these huge tracts of time as changemakers. Virtually all the physical and much of the mental formation we still take for granted

The evolution of the hominids

The evolution of hominids – the superfamily in which zoologists classify both humans and their closest relations (chimpanzees, gorillas, orang-utans and gibbons) – started at the beginning of the Miocene era, some 24 million years ago. The first known members of our family (the hominids) lived 4 million years ago and have been classified as the *Australopithecus* genus. The first members of our genus (*Homo*) lived 2 million years ago and have been classified in the species *Homo habilis*. Our own species (*Homo sapiens*) appeared some 200,000 years ago. Although some of its earliest members, such as the Neanderthals, had features which distinguished them from us, the skeletons of those who lived in Cro-Magnon 30,000 years ago could easily be mistaken for ours.

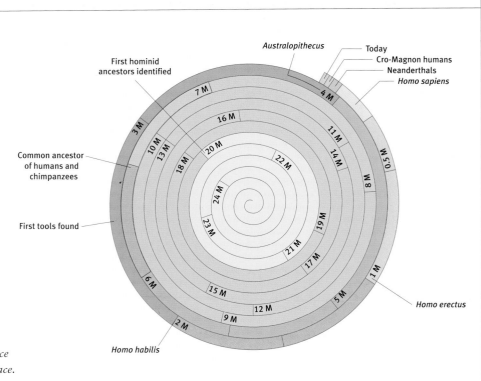

This spiral shows the number of millions of years since the main events in the evolution of hominids took place.

was by then determined, fixed in the sense that some possibilities were excluded and others were not. The crucial process is the evolution of creatures resembling humans as a distinct branch among the primates, for it is at this fork in the line, as it were, that we begin to look out for the station at which we get off for History. It is here that we can hope to find the first signs of that positive, conscious, impact upon environment which marks the first stage of human achievement.

THE CHANGING EARTH

The bedrock of the story is the earth itself. Changes recorded in fossils of flora and fauna, in geographical forms and geological strata, narrate a drama of epic scale lasting hundreds of millions of years. The shape of the world changed out of recognition many times. Great rifts opened and closed in its surface, coasts rose and fell; at times huge areas were covered with a long-since vanished vegetation. Many species of plants and animals emerged and proliferated. Most died out. Yet these "dramatic" events happened with almost unimaginable slowness. Some lasted millions of years; even the most rapid took centuries. The creatures who lived while they were going on could no more have perceived them than could a twentieth-century butterfly, in its three weeks or so of life, sense the rhythm of the seasons. Yet the earth was taking shape as a collection of habitats permitting different strains to survive. Meanwhile, biological evolution inched forwards with almost inconceivable slowness.

THE CHANGING CLIMATE

Climate was the first great pace-maker of change. About forty million years ago – an

The development of animals

Vertebrates appeared in the Cambrian, the first period of the primary or Palaeozoic era. They were water animals, from which amphibians would later emerge, the first vertebrates to venture out onto dry land. Many species of fish and amphibians became extinct at the end of the Permian period. After this the secondary or Mesozoic era began, characterized by a predominance of reptiles, including dinosaurs. Birds evolved from dinosaurs and began to frequent the skies during the Cretaceous period. Mammals, however, did not become widespread until the Cenozoic era (Tertiary and Quaternary periods).

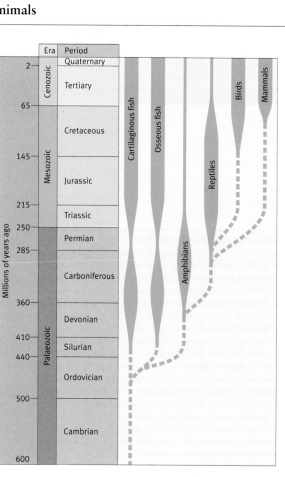

This chart represents the development of animals from the Palaeolithic to Cenozoic eras.

earlier. They now inherited the earth, or a considerable part of it. With many breaks in sequence and accidents of selection on the way, these strains were themselves to evolve into the mammals which occupy our own world – ourselves included.

Crudely summarized, the main lines of this evolution were probably determined for millions of years by astronomical cycles. As the earth's position changed in relation to the sun, so did climate. A huge pattern emerges, of recurrent swings of temperature. The extremes which resulted, of climatic cooling on the one hand and aridity on the other, choked off some possible lines of development. Conversely, in other times, and in certain places, the onset of appropriately benign conditions allowed certain species to flourish and encouraged their spread into new habitats. The only major sub-division of this immensely long process which concerns us comes very recently (in prehistoric terms), slightly less than four million years ago. There then began a period of climatic changes which we believe to have been more rapid and violent than any observed in earlier times. "Rapid", we must again remind ourselves, is a comparative term; these changes took tens of thousands of years. Such a pace of change, though, looks very different from the millions of years of much steadier conditions which lay in the past.

THE ICE AGES

SCHOLARS HAVE LONG talked about "Ice Ages", each lasting between fifty and a hundred thousand years, which covered big areas of the northern hemisphere (including much of Europe, and America as far south as modern New York) with great ice sheets, sometimes a mile or more thick. They have now distinguished some seventeen to nineteen

early enough point at which to begin to grapple with our story – a long warm climatic phase began to draw to a close. It had favoured the great reptiles and during it Antarctica had separated from Australia. There were no ice-fields then in any part of the globe. As the world grew colder and the new climatic conditions restricted their habitat, the great reptiles disappeared (though some have argued that other factors than environmental change were decisive). But the new conditions suited other animal strains which were already about, among them some mammals whose tiny ancestors had appeared two hundred million years or so

(there is argument about the exact number) such "glaciations" since the onset of the first, over three million years ago. We live in a warm period following the most recent of them, which came to an end some ten thousand years ago. Evidence about these glaciations and their effects is now available from all oceans and continents and they provide the backbone for prehistoric chronology. To the external scale which the Ice Ages provide we can relate such clues as we have to the evolution of humanity.

THE EFFECTS OF GLACIATION

The Ice Ages make it easy to see how climate determined life and its evolution in prehistoric times, but to emphasize their dramatic direct effects is misleading. No doubt the slow onset of the ice was decisive and often disastrous for what lay in its path. Many of us still live in landscapes shaped by its scouring and gougings thousands of centuries ago. The huge inundations which followed the retreat

of the ice as it melted must also have been locally catastrophic, destroying the habitats of creatures which had adapted to the challenge of arctic conditions. Yet they also created new opportunities. After each glaciation new species spread into the areas uncovered by the thaw. Beyond regions directly affected, though, the effects of the glaciations may have been even more important for the global story of evolution. Changes in environment followed cooling and warming thousands of miles from the ice itself; and the outcome had its own determining force. Both aridification and the spread of grassland, for instance, changed the possibilities of spreading themselves open to existing species. Some of those species form part of the human evolutionary story, and all the most important stages in that evolution so far observed have been located in Africa, far from the ice-fields.

Climate can still be very important today, as contemplation of the disasters brought by drought can show. But such effects, even when they affect millions of people, are not so

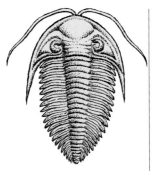

The origins of many of the types of animals that would later inhabit the planet were already present around 550 million years ago, even though animal life at that time was completely aquatic. The Trilobites, a subtype of marine arthropods of which more than 1,000 genera have been classified, were characteristic of such animal groups.

Glaciation

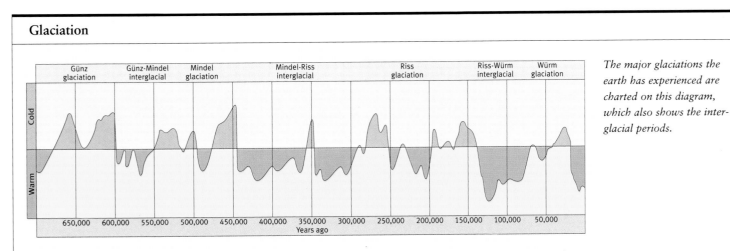

The major glaciations the earth has experienced are charted on this diagram, which also shows the interglacial periods.

A number of studies have managed to determine heat variations in the Quaternary (the last period of the Cenozoic era), which began two million years ago. During the coldest stages, there was an increase in the number of glaciers covering large areas of land. This was accompanied by a decrease in sea-level due to the retention of water masses, in the form of ice, on the continents. The last glaciations that occurred in the Alps have been named Günz, Mindel, Riss and Würm. Each glaciation was followed by a warmer period, known as an interglacial. Glaciations and interglacial periods can only be dated approximately.

fundamental as the slow transformation of the basic geography of the world and its supplies of food which climate wrought in prehistoric times. Until very recently climate determined where and how people lived. It made technique very important (and still does): the possession in early times of a skill such as fishing or fire-making could make new environments available to branches of the human family fortunate enough to possess such skills, or able to discover and learn them. Different food-gathering possibilities in different habitats meant different chances of a varied diet and, eventually, of progressing from gathering to hunting, and then to growing. Long before the Ice Ages, though, and even before the appearance of the creatures from which humanity was to evolve, climate was setting the stage for humanity and thus

shaping, by selection, the eventual genetic inheritance of humanity itself.

PROSIMIANS INTO PRIMATES

ONE MORE BACKWARD GLANCE is useful before plunging into the still shallow (though gradually deepening) pool of evidence. Fifty-five million or so years ago, primitive mammals were of two main sorts. One, rodent-like, remained on the ground; the other took to the trees. In this way the competition of the two families for resources was lessened and strains of each survived to people the world with the creatures we know today. The second group were the prosimians. We are among their descendants, for they were the ancestors of the first primates.

The genealogical tree of mammals

Mammals first appeared in the Triassic period, at the beginning of the Mesozoic era, but there were relatively few of these animals in existence during the great age of dinosaurs (Jurassic and Cretaceous periods). It was only after dinosaurs became extinct, around 65 million years ago, that mammals became dominant. In the Jurassic period they were divided into three large groups: prototherians (such as modern-day montotremes, which lay eggs), metatherians (such as modern-day marsupials, whose offspring continue to develop inside the mother's pouch after birth) and eutherians (which comprise all the other classes of modern-day mammals). The oldest fossils of most classes of modern-day mammals, including primates, date back to the beginning of the Tertiary period.

The division of mammals into three main groups is illustrated by this diagram.

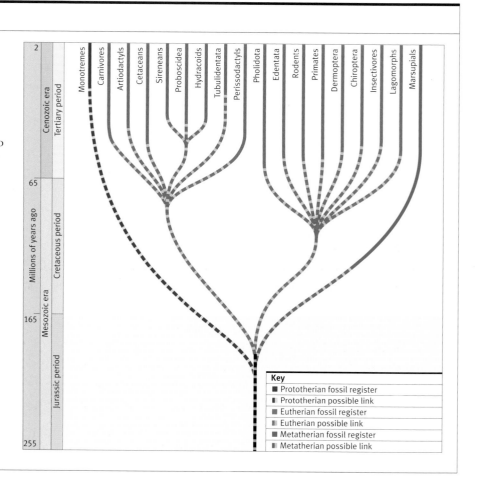

Key
- Prototherian fossil register
- Prototherian possible link
- Eutherian fossil register
- Eutherian possible link
- Metatherian fossil register
- Metatherian possible link

The savannah, a landscape characterized by the predominance of herbaceous plants, covers large areas of Africa today. It was one of the environments in which the first hominids evolved.

SUCCESSFUL GENETIC STRAINS

It is best not to be too impressed by talk about "ancestors" in any but the most general sense. Between the prosimians and ourselves lie millions of generations and many evolutionary blind alleys. It is important none the less that our remotest identifiable ancestors lived in trees because what survived in the next phase of evolution were genetic strains best suited to the special uncertainties and accidental challenges of the forest. That environment put a premium on the capacity to learn. Those survived whose genetic inheritance could respond and adapt to the surprising, sudden danger of deep shade, confused visual patterns, treacherous handholds. Strains prone to accident in such conditions were wiped out. Among those which prospered (genetically speaking) were some species with long digits which were to develop into fingers and, eventually, the oppositional thumb, and other forerunners of the apes already embarked upon an evolution towards three-dimensional vision and the decreasing importance of the sense of smell.

The prosimians were little creatures. Tree-shrews still exist which give us some idea of what they were like; they were far from being monkeys, let alone human beings. Yet for millions of years they carried the traits which made humanity possible. During this time geography counted for much in their evolution, by imposing limits on contact between different strains, sometimes effectively isolating them, and thus increasing differentiation. Changes would not happen quickly but it is likely that fragmentations of the environment caused by geographical disturbance led to the isolation of zones in which, little by little, the recognizable ancestors of many modern mammals appeared. Among them are the first monkeys and apes. They do not seem to go back more than thirty-five million years or so.

The more we study chimpanzees, the more similarities we discover between these intelligent creatures and human beings. Although anatomically chimpanzees have more in common with gorillas than they do with humans, genetically, they appear to be closer to us.

MONKEYS AND APES

Monkeys and apes represent a great evolutionary stride. Both families had much greater manipulative dexterity than any predecessor. Within them, species distinct in size or acrobatic quality began to evolve. Physiological

and psychological evolution blur in such matters. Like the development of better and stereoscopic vision, the growth of manipulative power seems to imply a growth of consciousness. Perhaps some of these creatures could already distinguish different colours. The brains of the first primates were already much more complex than those of any of their predecessors; they were bigger, too. Somewhere the brain of one or more of these strains became complex enough and its physical powers sufficiently developed for the animal to cross the line at which the world as a mass of undifferentiated sensations becomes at least in part a world of objects. Whenever this happened it was a decisive step towards mastering the world by using it, instead of reacting automatically to it.

Some twenty-five or thirty million years ago, as desiccation began to reduce the area of the forests, competition for diminishing forest resources became fiercer. Environmental challenge and opportunity

The Proconsul

The 18-million-year-old Proconsul is one of the first known hominids. A member of the *Dryopithecus* family, which originated in Africa, it probably lived in the trees. Some of its features, such as its large cranium, are similar to those of modern-day hominids, including chimpanzees and gorillas.

The cranium and skeleton of the Proconsul.

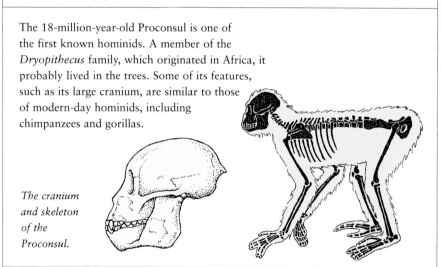

The evolution of anthropoids

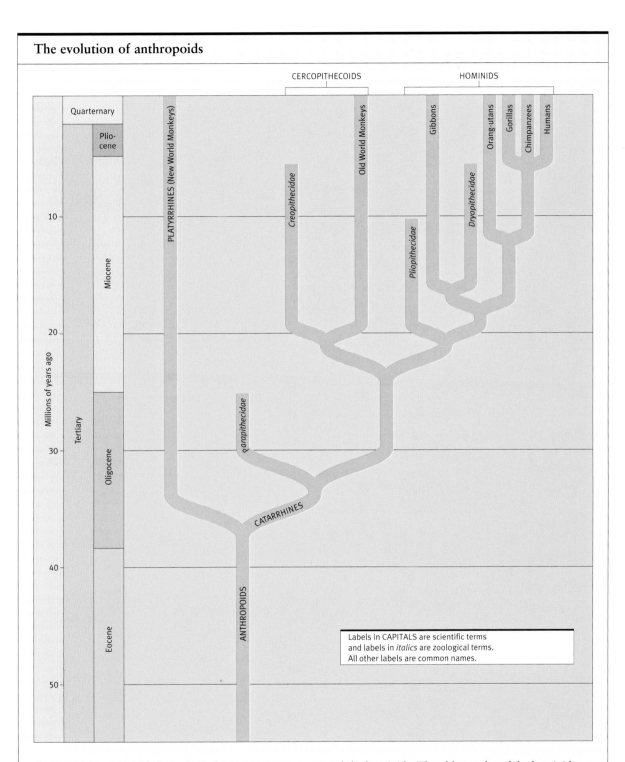

Labels in CAPITALS are scientific terms
and labels in *italics* are zoological terms.
All other labels are common names.

Anthropoids or apes (their zoological name is *Anthropoidea*) is one of the sub-classes into which primates are divided. In the Oligocene period, the second period of the Cenozoic era, they were divided into two branches: catarrhines, or Old World Monkeys, and platyrrhines, or New World Monkeys. At the beginning of the Miocene, the catarrhines were also divided into two branches, the cercopithecoids and the hominids. The oldest order of the hominid family to have been identified is the *Dryopithecus*, which became extinct at the end of the Miocene. Today there are four different hominid families: Hylobate (gibbon), Pongid (orang-utan), Pan (chimpanzee and gorilla) and Hominid (human). The separation between the ancestors of humans and chimpanzees is believed to have occurred five million years ago.

In 1970 CE a team of French and American investigators working in Hadar, Ethiopia, discovered this near-complete skeleton of a hominid female. Nick-named "Lucy", she is believed to have lived 3.2 million years ago. Lucy's pelvis shows that she walked upright, standing 3 ft 7 in (1.2 m) tall. She has been classified as a member of the species *Australopithecus afarensis.*

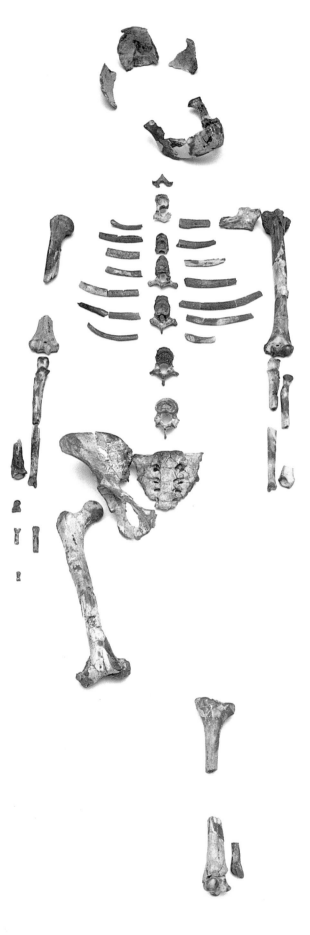

appeared where the trees and the grasslands met. Some primates not powerful enough to hold on to their forest homes were able, because of some genetic quality, to penetrate the savannahs in search of food and could meet the challenge and exploit the opportunities. Probably they had a posture and movement marginally more like that of humans than, say, that of the gorillas or chimpanzees. An upright stance and the capacity to move easily on two feet make it possible to carry burdens, among them food. The dangerous open savannah could then be explored and its resources withdrawn from it to a safer home base. Most animals consume their food where they find it; humans do not. Freedom to use the forelimbs for something other than locomotion or fighting also suggests other possibilities. We do not know what was the first "tool", but other primates than humans have been seen to pick up objects which come to hand and wave them as a deterrent, use them as weapons, or investigate and expose possible sources of food with their aid.

THE HOMINIDS

THE NEXT STEP in the argument is enormous, for it takes us to the first glimpse of a member of the biological family to which both humans and the great apes belong. The evidence is fragmentary, but suggests that some fifteen or sixteen million years ago a successful species was widespread throughout Africa, Europe and Asia. Probably he was a tree-dweller and certainly he was not very large – he may have weighed about 40 pounds. Unfortunately, the evidence is such as to leave him isolated in time. We have no direct knowledge of his immediate forebears or descendants, but some kind of fork in the road of primate evolution had occurred. While one branch was to lead to the great apes and chimpanzees, the other led to human beings. This line has been named "hominid". But the first hominid fossil (found in Kenya) is dated only some four and a half to five million years ago, so that for about ten million years the record is obscure. During that time big geological and geographical changes must have favoured and disfavoured many new evolutionary patterns.

Skull of a *Paranthropus boisei*, discovered in the Olduvai Gorge.

The first hominid fossil may not belong to it, but one evolutionary line which emerged from this upheaval was a small African hominid, subsequently named *Australopithecus*. The earliest fossil identified with this genus is more than four million years old and was found in Ethiopia. Evidence of other species of "australopithecines" (as they are usually termed) found as far apart as Kenya and the Transvaal can be dated to various periods over the next two million years and has had a great impact upon archaeological thinking. In the last quarter-century, something like three million years has been added to the period in which the search for human origins goes on, thanks to the australopithecine discoveries. Great uncertainty and much debate still surrounds them, but if the human species has a common ancestor it seems most likely that it belonged to a species of this genus. It is with *Australopithecus*, though, and with what, for want of a better word, we must call its "contemporaries" of other species, that the difficulties of distinguishing between apes, near-human apes and other creatures with some human characteristics first appear in their full complexity. The questions raised are still becoming in some ways more difficult to deal with. No simple picture has yet emerged and discoveries are still being made.

THE GENUS *HOMO*

We possess most evidence about *Australopithecus*. But there came to live contemporaneously with some australopithecine species other creatures, to whom the genus name *Homo* has been given. *Homo* was no doubt related to *Australopithecus*, but is first clearly identifiable as distinct about two million years ago on certain African sites; remains attributed to one of his species, though, have been dated by radioactivity to some million and a half years before that. Recently, to make confusion worse, the remains of an even bigger hominid have turned up near Lake Rudolf in northern Kenya. About five feet tall, with a brain about twice the size of a modern chimpanzee's, he has the undignified name of "1470 man", that being the number attached to his relics in the catalogue of the

Palaeontologist Louis Leakey (1903–1972 CE) is pictured with one of his major discoveries, the first remains of the species *Homo habilis*, which he found in the Olduvai Gorge in 1960. These bone fragments from the cranium, jaw and fingers provided proof that, 1.7 million years ago, a species of our own genus lived alongside the *Paranthropus boisei*.

The first hominids

All the oldest hominid remains have been discovered in eastern and southern Africa, which suggests that it was there that the evolution of the human family began. *Australopithecus afarensis* (the oldest species) and *Paranthropus robustus* lived in eastern Africa, whereas *Australopithecus africanus* and *Paranthropus boisei* lived in southern Africa. *Homo habilis* is known to have inhabited both regions. A number of experts believe that some of the fossil remains of African hominids should be classified in separate species from those mentioned above. However, because the above species are the most clearly identified at present, only they feature on this map.

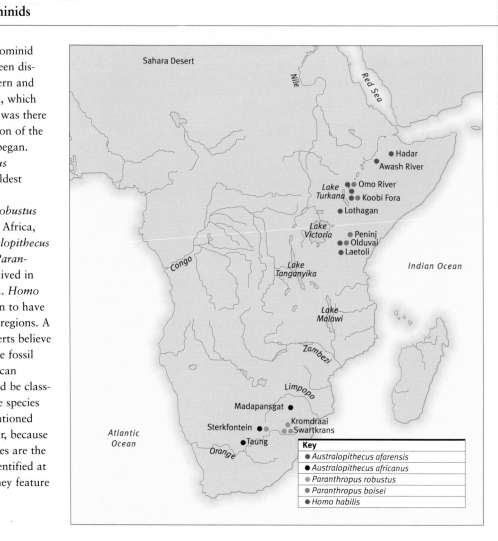

Key
- Australopithecus afarensis
- Australopithecus africanus
- Paranthropus robustus
- Paranthropus boisei
- Homo habilis

Kenya museum where they are to be found.

Where specialists disagree and may go on arguing about such fragmentary evidence as we have (all that is left of two million or so years of hominid life could be put on a big table), laymen had better not dogmatize. It is clear enough, though, that we can be fairly certain about the extent to which some characteristics later observable in humans already existed more than two million years ago. We know, for instance, that the australopithecines, though smaller than modern humans, had leg-bones and feet which resembled those of humans more than apes. They walked upright and could run and carry loads for long distances as apes could not. Their hands showed a flattening at the finger-tips characteristic of those of humans. These are stages far advanced on the road of human physique even if the actual descent of our species is from some other branch of the hominid tree.

THE FIRST TOOLS

It is to early members of the genus *Homo* (sometimes distinguished as *Homo habilis*) nonetheless, that we owe our first relics of tools. Tool-using is not confined to humans, but the making of tools has long been thought of as a human characteristic. It is a notable step in winning a livelihood from the environment. Tools found in Ethiopia are the oldest which we have (about two and a half million years old) and they consist of stones crudely fashioned by striking flakes off pebbles to give them an edge. The pebbles seem often to have been carried purposefully and perhaps selectively to the site where they were prepared. Conscious creation of implements had begun. Simple pebble choppers of the same type from later times turn up all over the Old World of prehistory; about one million years ago, for example, they were in use in the Jordan valley. In Africa, therefore, begins the flow of what was to prove the biggest single body of evidence about prehistoric human beings and their precursors and the one which has provided most information about their distribution and cultures. A site at the Olduvai Gorge in Tanzania has provided the traces of the first identified building, a windbreak of stones which has been dated 1.9 million years ago, as well as evidence that its inhabitants were meat-eaters, in the form of bones smashed to enable the marrow and brains to be got at and eaten raw.

THE OLDUVAI EVIDENCE

Olduvai prompts a tempting speculation. The bringing of stones and meat to the site combines with other evidence to suggest that the children of early hominids could not easily cling to their mother for long foraging expeditions as do the offspring of other primates. It may be that this is the first trace of the human institution of the home base. Among primates, only humans have them: places where females and children normally stay while the males search for food to bring back to them. Such a base also implies the shady outlines of sexual differentiation in economic

roles. It might even register the achievement already of some degree of forethought and planning, in that food was not devoured to gratify the immediate appetite on the spot where it was taken (as is the case with most primates), but reserved for family consumption elsewhere. Whether hunting, as opposed to scavenging, took place is another question, but the meat of large animals was consumed at a very early date at Olduvai.

Yet such exciting evidence only provides tiny and isolated islands of hard fact. It cannot be presumed that the East African sites were necessarily typical of those which sheltered and made possible the emergence of humanity; we know about them only because conditions there allowed the survival and subsequent discovery of early hominid remains. Nor, though the evidence may incline that way, can we be sure that any of these hominids is a direct ancestor of humanity;

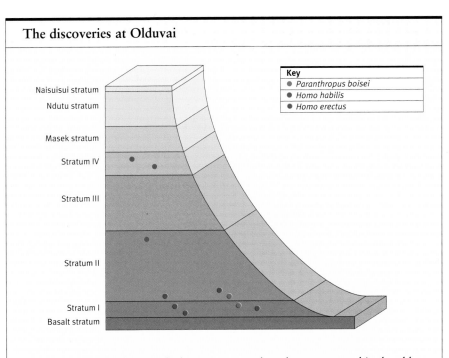

The discoveries at Olduvai

Key
- *Paranthropus boisei*
- *Homo habilis*
- *Homo erectus*

Naisuisui stratum
Ndutu stratum
Masek stratum
Stratum IV
Stratum III
Stratum II
Stratum I
Basalt stratum

The Olduvai Gorge has supplied a vast amount of information about human origins. As the diagram shows, fossils of both *Paranthropus boisei* and *Homo habilis*, who lived 1.5–2 million years ago, have been uncovered in the oldest layers (on the lower part of the hillside). In more recent layers (on the upper part of the hillside) remains of *Homo erectus* have been found.

they may all only be precursors. What can be said is that these creatures show remarkable evolutionary efficiency in the creative manner we associate with human beings, and suggest the uselessness of categories such as ape-men – and that few scholars would now be prepared to say categorically that we are not directly descended from *Homo habilis*, the species first identified with tool-using.

THE DIFFUSION OF THE GENUS *HOMO*

It is also easy to believe that the invention of the home base made biological survival easier.

It would have made possible brief periods of rest and recovery from the hazards posed by sickness and accident, thus sidestepping, however slightly, the process of evolution by physical selection. Together with their other advantages, it may help to explain how examples of the genus *Homo* were able to leave traces of themselves throughout most of the world outside the Americas and Australasia in the next million or so years. But we do not certainly know whether this was through the spread of one stock, or because similar creatures evolved in different places. It is generally held, though, that tool-making was carried to Asia and India (and perhaps to Europe) by migrants originally from East

The dispersion of *Homo erectus* beyond Africa

Homo erectus is the oldest species to definitely belong to the genus *Homo*. The earliest African remains of the species may be the ones found at Olduvai, which are known to be 1.2 million years old. (Remains found in Koobi Fora and Nariokotome, next to Lake Rudolf, which are 1.6 million years old, are also believed by some experts to belong to the species.) *Homo erectus* is the first species of hominids of which fossil remains have been discovered outside Africa. For a long time it was widely believed that *Homo erectus* began to spread beyond Africa around one million years ago. However, in 1989 CE a jaw was found in Dmanisi, Georgia, which may be 1.6 million years old. As a result of this discovery, the debate has been reopened.

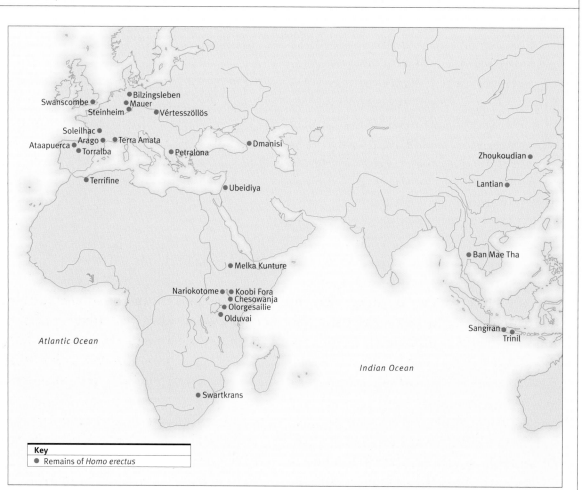

Key
● Remains of *Homo erectus*

Africa. The establishment and survival in so many different places of these hominids must show a superior capacity to grapple with changing conditions, but in the end we do not know what was the behavioural secret which suddenly (speaking once more in terms of prehistoric time) released that capacity and enabled them to spread over the landmass of Africa and Asia. No other mammal settled so widely and successfully before our own branch of the human family, which was eventually to occupy the whole planet, a unique biological achievement.

HOMO ERECTUS

THE NEXT CLEAR STAGE in the evolution of the human race is nothing less than a revolution in physique. After a divergence between hominids and more apelike creatures which may have occurred more than four million years ago, it took rather less than two million years for one successful family of hominids to increase its brain size to about twice that of *Australopithecus*. One of the most important stages of this process and some of the most crucial in the evolution of humanity were already reached in a species called *Homo erectus* which was widespread and successful a quarter of a million years ago. It had been in existence for at least half a million years and perhaps even longer (the oldest specimen so far identified may be about a million and a half years old). This species lasted much longer, that is to say, than has (so far) *Homo sapiens*, the branch of hominids to which we belong. Many signs once more point to an African origin and thence to a spread through Europe and Asia (where *Homo erectus* was first found). Apart from fossils, a special tool helps to plot the distribution of the new species by defining areas into which *Homo erectus* did not

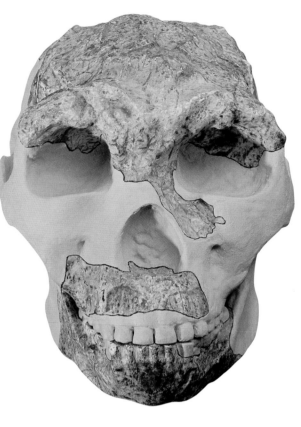

spread as well as those into which he did. This is the so-called "hand-axe" of stone whose main use seems to have been for skinning and cutting up large animals (its use as an axe seems unlikely, but the name is established). There can be no doubt of the success of *Homo erectus* as a genetic product.

PHYSIOLOGICAL CHANGE

When we finish with *Homo erectus* there is no precise dividing line (there never is in human prehistory, a fact it is only too easy to overlook or forget), but we are already dealing with a creature who has added to the upright stance of his predecessors a brain of the same order of magnitude as that of modern man. Though we still know little of the way in which the brain is organized, there is, allowing for body size, a rough correlation between size and intelligence. It is reasonable,

Cranial sizes

There can be no doubt that one of the fundamental landmarks in the evolution of the hominids has been the increase in cranial size needed to house the extraordinary human brain. As the illustration shows, *Australopithecus* had a larger cranial size, in relation to its body size, than either chimpanzees or gorillas. Examinations carried out on archaeological remains belonging to the species *Homo habilis* and *Homo erectus* also show, in this and in various other respects, progress towards the physiology of modern humans.

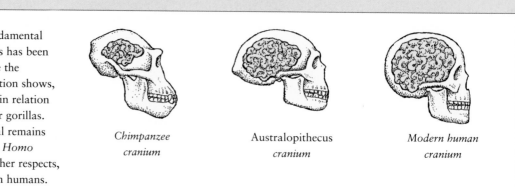

Chimpanzee cranium   Australopithecus *cranium*   *Modern human cranium*

therefore, to attribute great importance to the selection of strains with bigger brains and to reckon this a huge advance in the story of the slow accumulation of human characteristics.

PROLONGED INFANCY

Bigger brains meant bigger skulls and other changes, too. An increase in ante-natal size requires changes in the female pelvis to permit the birth of offspring with larger heads, and another consequence was a longer period of growth after birth; physiological evolution in the female was not sufficient to provide ante-natal accommodation to any point approaching physical maturity. Human children need maternal care long after birth. Prolonged infancy and immaturity in their turn imply prolonged dependency: it is a long time before such infants gather their own food. It may be with the offspring of *Homo erectus* that there began that long extension of the period of immaturity whose latest manifestation is the maintenance of young people by society during periods of higher education.

Biological change also meant that care and nurture came gradually to count for more than large litters in ensuring the survival of the species. This in turn implied further and

sharper differentiation in the roles of the sexes. Females were being pinned down much more by maternity at a time when food-gathering techniques seem to have become more elaborate and to demand arduous and prolonged cooperative action by males – perhaps because bigger creatures needed more and better food. Psychologically, too, the change may be significant. A new emphasis on the individual is one concomitant of prolonged infancy. Perhaps it was intensified by a social situation in which the importance of learning and memory was becoming more and more important and skills more complex. About this point the mechanics of what is going forward begin to slip from our grasp (if, indeed, they were ever in it). We are close to the area in which the genetic programming of the hominids is infringed by learning. This is the start of the great change from the natural physical endowment to tradition and culture – and eventually to conscious control – as evolutionary selectors, though we may never know where precisely this change occurs.

THE LOSS OF OESTRUS IN FEMALES

The loss of oestrus by the female hominid is another important physiological change. We do not know when this happened, but after it had been completed her sexual rhythm was importantly differentiated from that of other animals. Humans are the only animals in which the mechanism of the oestrus (the restriction of the female's sexual attractiveness and receptivity to the limited periods in which she is on heat) has entirely disappeared. It is easy to see the evolutionary connexion between this and the prolongation of infancy: if female hominids had undergone the violent disruption of their ordinary routine which the oestrus imposes, their offspring would have been periodically exposed to a neglect which would have made their survival impossible.

The selection of a genetic strain which dispensed with oestrus, therefore, was essential to the survival of the species; such a strain must have been available, though the process in which it emerged may have taken a million or a million and a half years because it cannot have been effected consciously.

Such a change has radical implications. The increasing attractiveness and receptivity of females to males make individual choice much more significant in mating. The selection of a partner is less shaped by the rhythm of nature; we are at the start of a very long

and obscure road which leads to the idea of sexual love. Together with prolonged infant dependency, the new possibilities of individual selection point ahead also to the stable and enduring family unit of father, mother and offspring, an institution unique to humanity. Some have even speculated that incest taboos (which are in practice well-nigh universal, however much the precise identification of the prohibited relationships may vary) originate in the recognition of the dangers presented by socially immature but sexually adult young males for long periods in close association with females who are always potentially sexually receptive.

Carefully placed rocks and the traces of holes in which posts had been set were discovered at the Terra Amata site in France in 1959 CE. The evidence seems to suggest that a hut of the kind shown in this illustration existed at the site 230,000 years ago. However, some experts question whether *Homo erectus* was capable of building such a dwelling.

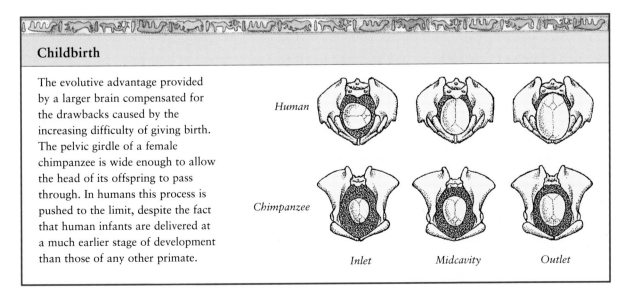

Childbirth

The evolutive advantage provided by a larger brain compensated for the drawbacks caused by the increasing difficulty of giving birth. The pelvic girdle of a female chimpanzee is wide enough to allow the head of its offspring to pass through. In humans this process is pushed to the limit, despite the fact that human infants are delivered at a much earlier stage of development than those of any other primate.

Human

Chimpanzee

Inlet   *Midcavity*   *Outlet*

Hand-axes such as this one were made in large areas of Africa, Europe and western Asia over a long period of time, lasting from 1.5 million to 150,000 years ago. Like this one, many axes were carved on both sides.

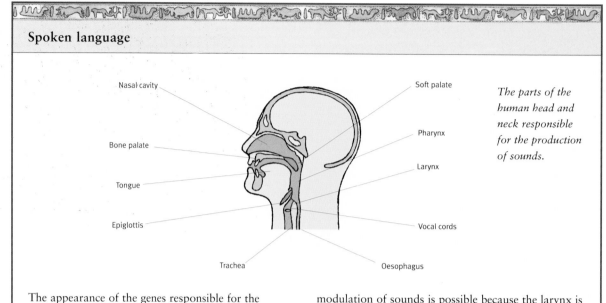

Spoken language

Nasal cavity

Bone palate

Tongue

Epiglottis

Trachea

Soft palate

Pharynx

Larynx

Vocal cords

Oesophagus

The parts of the human head and neck responsible for the production of sounds.

The appearance of the genes responsible for the structure of the larynx was a major development in human evolution. It allowed differentiation between dozens of different sounds instead of just a few and led to the creation of spoken language. In humans, the modulation of sounds is possible because the larynx is situated in a resonance chamber. In chimpanzees, the larynx is not capable of such sophisticated sound modulation and is therefore not able to produce the wide range of noises required for speech.

SIGNIFICANT ACHIEVEMENTS OF *HOMO ERECTUS*

In sexual matters it is best to be cautious. The evidence takes us only a very little way. Moreover, it is drawn from a very long span of time: examples of *Homo erectus* have been identified as active from at least a million and a half years ago, and to have continued to appear for another million. This would have given time for considerable physical, psychological and technological evolution. The earliest forms of *Homo erectus* may not have been much like the last, some of whom have been classified by some scientists as archaic forms of the next evolutionary stage of the hominid line. Yet all reflexions support the general hypothesis that the changes in hominids observable while *Homo erectus* occupies the centre of our stage were especially important in defining the arcs within which humanity was to evolve. He had unprecedented capacity to manipulate his environment, feeble though his handhold on it may seem to us. Besides the hand-axes which make possible the observation of his cultural traditions, late forms of *Homo erectus* left behind the earliest surviving traces of constructed dwellings (huts, sometimes fifty feet long, built of branches, with stone-slab or skin floors), the earliest worked wood, the first wooden spear and the earliest container, a wooden bowl. Creation on such a scale hints strongly at a new level of mentality, at a conception of the object formed before manufacture is begun, and perhaps an idea of process. Some have argued far more. In the repetition of simple forms, triangles, ellipses and ovals, in huge numbers of examples of stone tools, there has been discerned intense care to produce regular shapes which does not appear to be proportionate to any small gain in efficiency which may have been achieved. Can there perhaps be discerned in this the first tiny budding of the aesthetic sense?

Tools

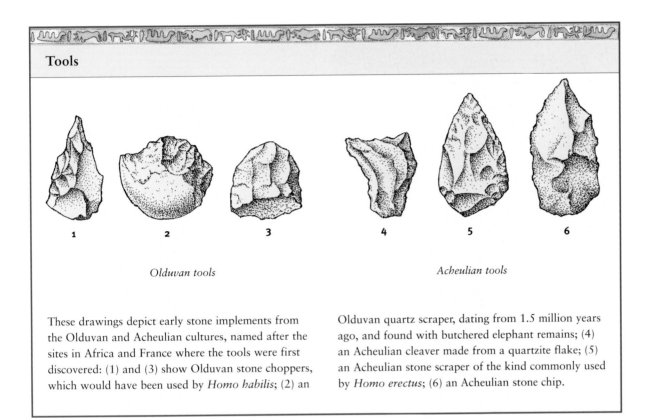

1   2   3   4   5   6

Olduvan tools   *Acheulian tools*

These drawings depict early stone implements from the Olduvan and Acheulian cultures, named after the sites in Africa and France where the tools were first discovered: (1) and (3) show Olduvan stone choppers, which would have been used by *Homo habilis*; (2) an

Olduvan quartz scraper, dating from 1.5 million years ago, and found with butchered elephant remains; (4) an Acheulian cleaver made from a quartzite flake; (5) an Acheulian stone scraper of the kind commonly used by *Homo erectus*; (6) an Acheulian stone chip.

FIRE

THE GREATEST OF PREHISTORIC technical and cultural advances was made when someone learnt how to manage fire. Until recently, the earliest available evidence of the use of fire had been found in China, and probably dated from between three and five hundred thousand years ago. But very recent discoveries in the Transvaal have provided evidence convincing to many scholars that hominids there were using fire well before that. It remains fairly certain that *Homo erectus* never learnt how to make fire and that even his successors did not for a long time possess this skill. That he knew how to use it, on the other hand, is indisputable. The importance of this knowledge is attested by the folklore of many later peoples; in almost all of them a heroic figure or magical beast first seizes fire. A violation of the supernatural order is implied: in the Greek legend Prometheus steals the fire of the gods. This is

suggestive, not solid, but perhaps the first fire was taken from outbreaks of natural gas or volcanic activity.

Culturally, economically, socially and technologically, fire was a revolutionary instrument, though we must again remember that a prehistoric "revolution" took thousands of years. It brought the possibility of warmth and light and therefore of a double extension of the human environment, into the cold and into the dark. In physical terms one obvious expression of this was the occupation of caves. Animals could now be driven out and kept out by fire (and perhaps the seed lies here of the use of fire to drive big game in hunting). Technology could move forward: spears could be hardened in fires and cooking became possible, indigestible substances such as seeds becoming sources of food and distasteful or bitter plants edible. This must have stimulated attention to the variety and availability of plant life; the science of botany was stirring without anyone knowing it.

The discovery of the use of fire by *Homo erectus* had a huge impact on all subsequent human communities and played a fundamental role in the communal activities of the Neanderthals, a later group depicted in this artist's impression.

SOCIAL CONSEQUENCES OF FIRE

Fire must have influenced mentality more directly, too. It was another factor strengthening the tendency to conscious inhibition and restraint, and therefore their evolutionary importance. The focus of the cooking fire as the source of light and warmth had also the deep psychological power which it still retains. Around the hearths after dark gathered a community almost certainly already aware of itself as a small and meaningful unit against a chaotic and unfriendly background. Language – of whose origins we as yet know nothing – would have been sharpened by a new kind of group intercourse. The group itself would be elaborated, too, in its structure. At some point, fire-bearers and fire specialists appeared, beings of awesome and mysterious importance, for on them depended, it might be, life and death. They carried and guarded the great liberating tool,

and the need to guard it must sometimes have made them masters. Yet the deepest tendency of this new power always ran towards the liberation of early humans. Fire began to break up the iron rigidity of night and day and even the discipline of the seasons. It thus carried further the breakdown of the great objective natural rhythms which bound our fireless ancestors. Behaviour could now be less routine and automatic. There is even a discernible possibility of leisure, as a direct result of the use of fire.

BIG-GAME HUNTING

BIG-GAME HUNTING was the other great achievement of *Homo erectus*. Its origins must lie far back in the scavenging which turned vegetarian hominids into omnivores. Meat-eating provided concentrated protein. It released meat-eaters from the incessant nibbling of so many vegetarian creatures, and so permitted economies of effort. It is one of the first signs that the capacity for conscious restraint is at work when food is being carried home to be shared tomorrow rather than consumed on the spot today. At the beginning of the archaeological record, an elephant and perhaps a few giraffes and buffaloes were among the beasts whose scavenged meat was consumed at Olduvai, but for a long time the bones of smaller animals vastly preponderate in the rubbish. By about three hundred thousand years ago the picture is wholly altered.

This may be where we can find a clue to the way by which *Australopithecus* and his relatives were replaced by the bigger, more efficient *Homo erectus*. A new food supply permits larger consumption but also imposes new environments: game has to be followed if meat-eating becomes general. As the hominids become more or less parasitic upon other species there follows further

At the Torralba and Ambrona sites in Spain, numerous elephant remains have been found in areas once inhabited by *Homo erectus*. The hominids may have hunted big game, although it is also possible that they were scavengers, taking meat from dead animals.

exploration of territory and new settlements, too, as sites particularly favoured by the mammoth or woolly rhinoceros are identified. Knowledge of such facts has to be learnt and passed on; technique has to be transmitted and guarded, for the skills required to trap, kill and dismember the huge beasts of

antiquity were enormous in relation to anything which preceded them. What is more, they were cooperative skills: only large numbers could carry out so complex an operation as the driving – perhaps by fire – of game to a killing-ground favourable because of bogs in which a weighty creature would flounder, or

San people in the Kalahari desert, Botswana, Africa. Their living conditions are similar to those of their ancestors, who inhabited Africa 10,000 years ago.

Only meticulous excavation work, involving successive campaigns over several years, can reveal most of the information that an archaeological site contains. The excavations shown here are at Atapuerca, Spain, an exceptionally important site at which the remains of numerous hominids have been uncovered.

because of a precipice, well-placed vantage points, or secure platforms for the hunters. Few weapons were available to supplement natural traps and, once dead, the victims presented further problems. With only wood, stone and flint, they had to be cut up and removed to the home base. Once carried home, the new supplies of meat mark another step towards the provision of leisure as the consumer is released for a time from the drudgery of ceaselessly rummaging in his environment for small, but continuously available, quantities of nourishment.

CULTURE AND TRADITION

It is difficult not to feel that this is an epoch of crucial significance. Considered against a background of millions of years of evolution, the pace of change, though still unbelievably slow in terms of later societies, is quickening. These are not humans as we know them, but they are beginning to be approximate to

them: the greatest race of predators is stirring in its cradle. Something like a true society, too, is dimly discernible, not merely in the complicated cooperative hunting enterprises, but in what this implies in passing on knowledge from generation to generation. Culture and tradition are slowly taking over from genetic mutation and natural selection as the primary sources of change among the hominids. It is the groups with the best "memories" of effective techniques which will carry forward evolution. The importance of experience was very great, for knowledge of methods which were likely to succeed rested upon it, not (as increasingly in modern society) on experiment and analysis. This fact alone would have given new importance to older men and women. They knew how things were done and what methods worked and they did so at a time when the home base and big-game hunting made their maintenance by the group easier. They would not have been very old, of course. It is unlikely that many lived more than forty years.

EARLY LANGUAGE

Selection also favoured those groups whose members not only had good memories, but the increasing power to reflect upon it given by speech. We know very little about the pre-history of language. Modern types of language can only have appeared long after *Homo erectus* disappeared. Yet some sort of communication must have been used in big-game hunting, and all primates make meaningful signals. How early hominids communicated may never be known, but one plausible suggestion is that they began by breaking up calls akin to those of other animals into particular sounds capable of rearrangement. This would give the possibility of different messages and may be the remote taproot of grammar. What is certain is that a great acceleration of evolution would follow the appearance of groups able to pool experience, to practise and refine skills, to elaborate ideas through language. Once more, we cannot separate one process from others: better vision, an increased physical capacity to deal with the world as a set of discrete objects and the multiplication of artifacts by using tools were all going on simultaneously over the hundreds of thousands of years in which language was evolving. Together they contributed to a growing extension of mental capacity until one day conceptualization became possible and abstract thought appeared.

WAS *HOMO ERECTUS* HUMAN?

It remains true, though, that if nothing very general can be confidently said about the behaviour of hominids before humans, still less can anything very precise. We move in a fog, dimly apprehending for a moment creatures now more, now less, like human beings.

These are fragments of the cranium of a 780,000-year-old hominid – the oldest ever found in Europe. The cranium was discovered in Atapuerca, Spain, by a team of Spanish palaeontologists.

Their minds, we can be sure, are almost inconceivably unlike our own as instruments for the registration of the outside world. Yet when we look at the range of the attributes of *Homo erectus* it is his human, not pre-human, characteristics which are most striking. Physically, he has a brain of an order of magnitude comparable to our own. He makes tools (and does so within more than one technical tradition), builds shelters, takes over natural refuges by exploiting fire, and sallies out of them to hunt and gather his food. He does this in groups with a discipline which can sustain complicated operations; he therefore has some ability to exchange ideas by speech. The basic biological units of his hunting groups probably prefigure the human nuclear family, being founded on the institutions of the home base and a sexual differentiation of activity. There may even be some complexity of social organization in so

Various techniques are used to ascertain the age of archaeological remains. Stratigraphy, for example, involves the analysis of the order in which the strata in the ground and rock within a specific region are found. There are also several physical and biological techniques available to researchers, but the most commonly used dating methods involve chemical techniques, which are based on the radioactive properties of elements such as carbon 14, potassium and uranium. Of these chemical methods, the most widely employed, and often the most reliable, is the carbon dating method. The element carbon 14 converts to nitrogen 14 at a constant rate and is not affected by fluctuations in temperature. It takes 5,730 years for the number of atoms in a sample to be reduced by half, which means that carbon dating provides a relatively accurate means of measuring time.

A researcher extracts a sample from an archaeological find – the sample will be tested by the carbon dating method to determine the object's age.

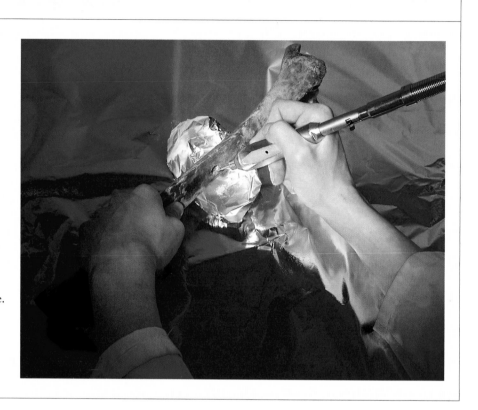

far as fire-bearers and gatherers or old creatures whose memories made them the data banks of their "societies" could be supported by the labour of others. There has to be some social organization to permit the sharing of cooperatively obtained food, too. There is nothing to be usefully added to an account such as this by pretending to say where exactly can be found a prehistorical point or dividing line at which such things had come to be, but subsequent human history is unimaginable without them. When a sub-species of *Homo erectus*, perhaps possessing slightly larger and more complex brains than others, evolved into *Homo sapiens* it did so with an enormous achievement and heritage already secure in its grasp. Whether we choose to call it human or not hardly matters.

A team of archaeologists at work at the La Brea site in Los Angeles, USA. Excavations carried out at the site uncovered the world's richest fossil deposits.

2 HOMO SAPIENS

THE APPEARANCE of *Homo sapiens* is momentous: here, at last, is recognizable humanity, however raw in form. Yet this evolutionary step is another abstraction. It is the beginning of the main drama and the end of the prologue, but we cannot usefully ask precisely when this happens. It is a process, not a point, and it is not a process occurring everywhere at the same rate. All we have to date it are a few physical relics of early humans of types recognizably modern or closely related to the modern. Some of them may well overlap by thousands of years the continuing life of earlier hominids. Some may represent false starts and dead ends, for human evolution must have continued to be highly selective. Though much faster than in earlier times, this evolution is still very slow: we are dealing with something that took place over perhaps two hundred thousand years in which we do not know when our first true "ancestor" appeared (though the place was almost certainly Africa). It is not ever easy to pose the right questions; the physiological and technical and mental lines at which we leave *Homo erectus* behind are matters of definition.

EARLY HUMAN REMAINS

The few early human fossils have provoked much argument. Two famous European skulls seem to belong to the period between two Ice Ages about two hundred thousand years ago, an age climatically so different from ours that elephants browsed in a semi-tropical Thames valley and the ancestors of lions prowled in what would one day be Yorkshire. The "Swanscombe" skull, named after the place where it was found, shows its possessor to have had a big brain (about 1300 cc) but in other ways not much to resemble modern humans: if "Swanscombe man" was *Homo sapiens*, then he represents a very early version. The other skull, that of "Steinheim man", differs in shape from that of *Homo sapiens* but again held a big brain. Perhaps they are best regarded as the forerunners of early prototypes of *Homo sapiens*, though creatures still living (as their tools show) much like *Homo erectus*.

The next Ice Age then brings down the curtain. When it lifts, a hundred and thirty thousand or so years ago, in the next warm period, human remains again appear. There has been much argument about what they show but it is indisputable that there has been a great step forward. At this point we are entering a period where there is a fairly dense

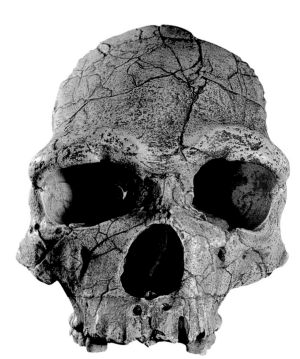

This cranium, found in the French Pyrenees, is more than 200,000 years old and shows the intermediate features of a stage between *Homo erectus* and *Homo sapiens neanderthalis*. The existence of intermediate fossils adds strength to the generally accepted theory that *Homo sapiens* evolved from colonies of *Homo erectus*.

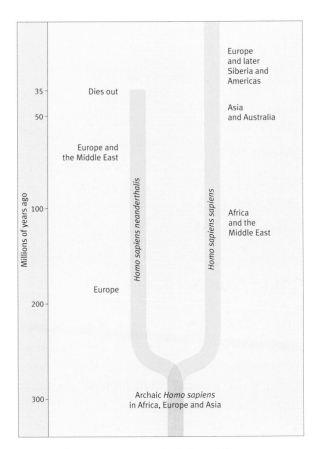

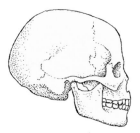

Homo sapiens

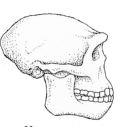

Homo erectus

Origins of Homo sapiens neanderthalis *and* Homo sapiens.

against what must have been great variation in the animal population and vegetation near these sites; to survive so long, such cultures must have been resourceful and adaptive.

THE NEANDERTHALS

FOR ALL THEIR ESSENTIAL SIMILARITY to ourselves, the peoples who created the early cultures in Europe are still physiologically distinguishable from modern humans. The first discovery of their remains was at Neanderthal in Germany (because of this, humans of this type are usually called Neanderthals) and it was of a skull so curiously shaped that it was for a long time thought to be that of a modern idiot. Scientific analysis still leaves much about it unexplained. But it is now thought that *Homo sapiens neanderthalis* (as the Neanderthal is scientifically classified) has its ultimate origin in an early expansion out of Africa of advanced forms of *Homo erectus*, possibly seven hundred thousand years ago. Across many intervening genetic stages, there emerged a population of pre-Neanderthals, from which, in turn, the extreme form evolved whose striking remains were found in Europe (and, so far, nowhere else). This special development has been interpreted by some as a Neanderthal sub-species, perhaps cut off by some accident of glaciation. Evidence of other Neanderthalers has turned up in Morocco, in the northern Sahara, at

These illustrations, which depict the craniums of a *Homo erectus* from Java and of a late Palaeolithic *Homo sapiens* from Europe, demonstrate the differences between the two species. *Homo sapiens* has a larger cranium, a higher forehead (without the marked supraorbital arch), a shorter jaw, smaller teeth and a pronounced chin.

though broken record. Its unravelling can begin in Europe. Creatures we must now call humans lived there just over a hundred thousand years ago. There are caves in the Dordogne area which were occupied on and off for some fifty thousand years. The cultures of these peoples therefore survived a period of huge climatic change; the first traces of them belong to a warm interglacial period and the last run out in the middle of the last Ice Age. This is an impressive continuity to set

Time chart (4,000,000 BCE–100,000 BCE)

					230,000–30,000 BCE Neanderthals	Modern *Homo sapiens*
4,000,000 BCE	3,000,000 BCE	2,000,000 BCE	1,000,000 BCE		100,000 BCE	
Appearance of *Australopithecus*		*Homo habilis*	1,000,000 BCE *Homo erectus*	250,000 BCE *Homo sapiens*		

TERTIARY   QUATERNARY

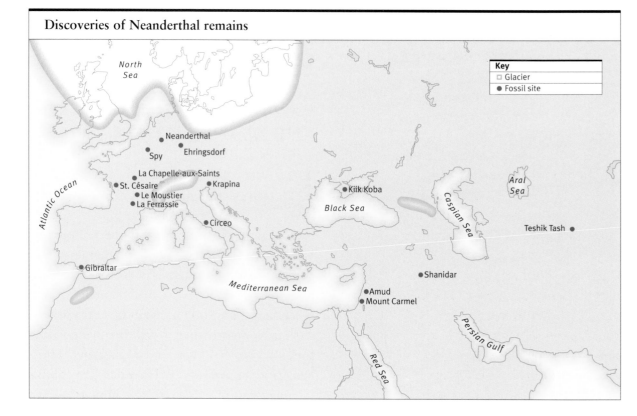

Discoveries of Neanderthal remains

The flint implements made by the Neanderthals have been called Mousterian tools, after the French site at Le Moustier where they were discovered. Large numbers of these tools have been found.

Mount Carmel in Palestine and elsewhere in the Near East and Iran. They have also been traced in Central Asia and China, where the earliest specimens may go back something like two hundred millennia. Evidently, it was for a long time a highly successful species.

Eighty thousand years ago, the artifacts of the Neanderthals had spread all over Eurasia. They show differences of technique and form. But technology from over a hundred thousand years ago and associated with other forms of "anatomically modern humans", as scholars term other creatures evolved from advanced forms of *Homo erectus*, has been identified in parts of Africa. Moreover, it was more widely spread than that of the Neanderthals. The primeval cultural unity had thus already fragmented, and distinct cultural traditions were beginning to emerge. From the start, there is a kind of provincialism within humanity.

The Neanderthals, like other species which specialists refer to as anatomically modern, walked erect and had big brains. Though in other ways more primitive than the sub-species to which we belong, *Homo sapiens sapiens* (as the guess about the first skull suggests), they represent none the less a great evolutionary stride and show a new mental sophistication we can still hardly grasp, let alone measure. One striking example is their use of technology to overcome environment: we know from the evidence of skin-scrapers they used to dress skins and pelts that Neanderthals wore clothes (though none have survived; the oldest clothed body yet discovered, in Russia, has been dated to about thirty-five thousand years ago). This was an important advance in the manipulation of environment.

RITUALIZED BURIAL

One of the most startling phenomena of the Neanderthal period was the appearance of formal burial. The act of burial itself is momentous for archaeology; graves are of enormous importance because of the artifacts of ancient society they preserve. Yet the Neanderthal graves provide more than this: they also contain the first evidence of ritual or ceremony.

This may mean a great deal and it is very difficult to control speculation. Perhaps some early totemism explains the ring of horns within which a Neanderthal child was buried near Samarkand. Conjecture is stimulated, too, by a fleeting vision of the primitive community in northern Iraq which went out one day to gather the masses of wild flowers and grasses which eventually lay under and surrounded the dead companion it wished so to honour. Some have suggested that careful burial may reflect a new concern for the individual which was one result of the greater interdependence of the group in the renewed Ice Ages. This could have intensified the sense of loss when a member died and might also point to something more. A skeleton of a Neanderthal man who had lost his right arm years before his death has been found. He

must have been very dependent on others, and was sustained by his group in spite of his handicap.

More hazardous still is the suggestion that ritualized burial implies some view of an after-life. If this were true, it would testify to a huge power of abstraction in the hominids and the origins of one of the greatest and most enduring myths, that life is an illusion, that reality lies invisible elsewhere, that things are not what they seem. Without going so far,

The skeleton of a Neanderthal man, who was found in the Shanidar Cave surrounded by traces of pollen. It is thought that flowers may have been buried with the man's body. However, it is also possible that the ceiling fell onto the body, showering it in earth containing pollen.

Comparison of cranium sizes

One of the first remains of the Neanderthal type to be found was a female cranium, which was discovered in a quarry in Gibraltar in 1848. In 1856, a find in the Neander river valley in Germany gave the Neanderthal variety of *Homo sapiens* its name. Palaeontologists did not immediately realize the significance of their discovery. The findings in La Chapelle-aux-Saints (1908) and La Ferrassie (1909), however, confirmed that the remains found in Neanderthal were not those of a deformed individual, as had been

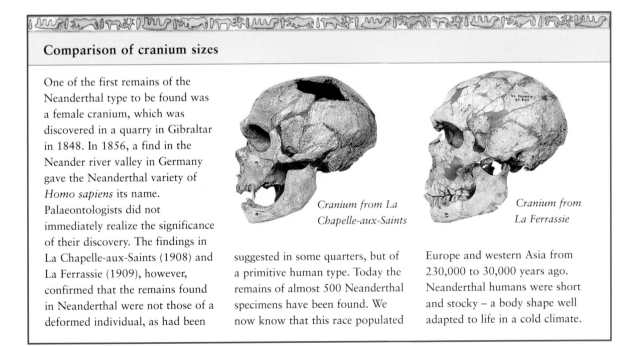

Cranium from La Chapelle-aux-Saints

Cranium from La Ferrassie

suggested in some quarters, but of a primitive human type. Today the remains of almost 500 Neanderthal specimens have been found. We now know that this race populated

Europe and western Asia from 230,000 to 30,000 years ago. Neanderthal humans were short and stocky – a body shape well adapted to life in a cold climate.

it is at least possible to agree that a momentous change is under way. Like the hints of rituals involving animals which Neanderthal caves also offer here and there, careful burial may mark a new attempt to dominate the environment. The human brain must already have been capable of discerning questions it wanted to answer and perhaps of providing answers in the shape of rituals. Slightly, tentatively, clumsily – however we describe it and still in the shallows though it may be – the human mind is afloat; the greatest voyage of exploration has begun.

THE NEANDERTHALS DISAPPEAR

Neanderthals provide our first evidence of another great institution, warfare. It may have been practised in connexion with cannibalism, which was directed apparently to the eating of the brains of victims. Analogy with later societies suggests that here again we have the start of some conceptualizing about

In the 1930s the remains of a number of *Homo sapiens* were discovered in the Skhul Cave, Mount Carmel, Israel. This photograph shows the reconstructed cranium and various bones of an adult male called Skhul 4. According to the latest research, the inhabitants of Skhul Cave lived 100,000 years ago, which means that their remains are three times older than those of the Cro-Magnon man and contemporaries of classic Neanderthals. However, these remains are anatomically modern.

a soul or spirit; such acts are sometimes directed to acquiring the magical or spiritual power of the vanquished. Whatever the magnitude of the evolutionary step which the Neanderthals represent, however, they failed in the end as a sub-species. After long and widespread success they were not in the end to be the inheritors of the earth. Effectively, Neanderthal survivors were genetically "vanquished" by the strain of *Homo sapiens* which was in the end to be dominant, and about the reasons for this we know nothing. Nor can we know to what extent, if at all, it was mitigated by some genetic transmission through the mingling of stocks.

HOMO SAPIENS SAPIENS

THE SUCCESSORS TO NEANDERTHALS had smaller faces, lighter skulls and straighter limbs. This was *Homo sapiens sapiens*, the outstandingly successful sub-species which was to spread world-wide in about twenty thousand years. To it we all belong. Scholars suggest that its origin is to be sought in another expansion out of Africa, about a hundred thousand years ago, which led to the establishment of anatomically modern humans over much of the Levant, the Near East and southeastern Europe in the next fifty thousand years. Why expansion should have taken this direction rather than another is not known, but it has been suggested that warm climates away from glacial environments had allowed hunters to develop their techniques to a high level, while tropical conditions put different sorts of obstacle in the way of these further south. However this may be, when a shift to drier climates becomes observable, the coastal corridor between the mountains and the sea in what is today Israel and the Lebanon seems especially significant in the appearance of modern humans.

Modern *Homo sapiens*

In 1868 CE the remains of an anatomically modern man (now thought to be 30,000 years old) were found in Cro-Magnon, France. More recent discoveries suggest that modern *Homo sapiens* emerged, probably in Africa, more than 100,000 years ago. The map shows some of the places where the earliest specimens of modern *Homo sapiens* were found, and the possible routes they took to spread to Europe. If this hypothesis is correct, the Neanderthals are not direct ancestors of modern humans, who descended from one ancient African community.

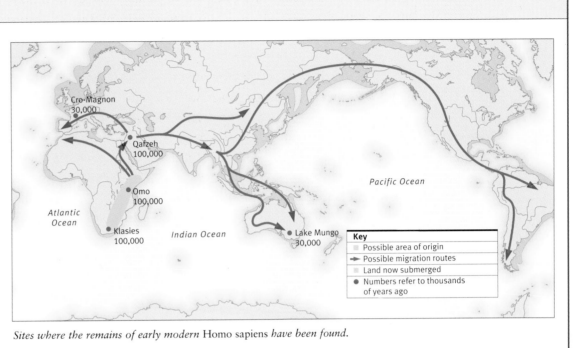

Sites where the remains of early modern Homo sapiens *have been found.*

THE PALAEOLITHIC

Palaeo-anthropologists are cautious. They do not like to assert that fossil remains more than thirty thousand or so years old are those of *Homo sapiens sapiens*. Nevertheless, it is clear that from about fifty thousand years ago to the end of the last Ice Age in about 9000 BCE we are at last considering plentiful evidence of humans of modern type. This period is normally referred to as the "Upper" Palaeolithic, a name derived from the Greek for "old stones". It corresponds, roughly, to the more familiar term "Stone Age", but, like other contributions to the terminology of prehistory, there are difficulties in using such words without careful qualification.

To separate "Upper" and "Lower" Palaeolithic is easy; the division represents the physical fact that the topmost layers of geological strata are the most recent and that, therefore, fossils and artifacts found among them are later than those found at lower

levels. The Lower Palaeolithic is therefore the designation of an age more ancient than the Upper. Almost all the artifacts which survive from the Palaeolithic are made from stone; none is made from metal, whose appearance makes it possible to follow a terminology used by the Roman poet Lucretius by labelling what comes after the Stone Age as the Bronze and Iron Ages.

These are, of course, cultural and technological labels; their great merit is that they direct attention to human activities. At one time tools and weapons are made of stone, then of bronze, then of iron. None the less, these terms have disadvantages, too. The obvious one is that within the huge tracts of time in which stone artifacts provide the largest significant body of evidence, we are dealing for the most part with hominids. They had, in varying degree, some, but not all, human characteristics; many stone tools are not made by human beings. Increasingly, too, the fact that this terminology originated

The colonization of America

Many of the facts about the colonization of America by humans remain unclear, but the evidence points towards the main migrations originating from north-east Asia. The first colonization is thought to have occurred during glacial periods, when the decrease in sea-level exposed a land bridge now named Beringia. Human communities travelled from Alaska deeper into the continent, either along the coast, or along a narrow ice-free passage between two glaciers. Some finds in South America seem to indicate that the arrival of *Homo sapiens* in America happened perhaps 40,000 years ago – much earlier than was previously believed.

Key
- Glacier in 10,000 BCE
- Land now submerged
- Possible entry route
- Settlement earlier than 10,000 BCE

Homo sapiens sapiens appears in Europe roughly at the beginning of the Upper Palaeolithic, somewhere about forty thousand years ago, although anatomically modern humans only shadowily distinct from him had appeared much earlier in Africa. It is in Europe, though, that the largest quantity of skeletal remains has been found, and it is on this evidence that the distinction of the species has been based.

CLIMATIC FLUCTUATIONS

The climate of human prehistory was not constant; though usually cold, there were important fluctuations, probably including the sharp onset of the coldest conditions for a million years somewhere about twenty thousand years ago. Such climatic variations still exercised great determinative force on the evolution of society. It was perhaps thirty thousand years ago that they made it possible for human beings for the first time to enter the Americas, crossing from Asia somewhere in the region of what is now the Bering Strait by a link provided by ice or, perhaps, by land left exposed because the ice-caps contained so much of what is now sea-water and sea-level was much lower. They moved southwards for thousands of years as they followed the game which had drawn them to the last uninhabited continent. The Americas were from the first peopled by immigrants. But the ice sheets also retreated and as they did huge transformations occurred to coasts, routes and food supplies. This was all as it had been for ages, but there was this time a crucial difference. Humans were present. A new order of intelligence was available to use new and growing resources in order to cope with environmental change. The change to history, when conscious human action to control environment will increasingly be effective, is under way.

in European archaeology created difficulties as more and more evidence accumulated about the rest of the world which did not really fit in. A final disadvantage is that it blurs important distinctions within periods even in Europe. The result has been its further refinement. Within the Stone Age scholars have distinguished (in sequence) the Lower, Middle and Upper Palaeolithic and then the Mesolithic and the Neolithic (the last of which blurs the division attributed by the older schemes to the coming of metallurgy). The period down to the end of the last Ice Age in Europe is also sometimes called the Old Stone Age, another complication, because here we have yet another principle of classification, simply that provided by chronology.

NEW IMPLEMENTS

For this period in Europe much has been done to classify cultures identified by their implements. To talk of a change to history may seem a big claim in the light of early humans' resources, judging by their tool kits and weaponry. Yet they already represent a huge range of capacities if we compare them with their predecessors'. The basic tools of *Homo sapiens* were stone, but they were made to serve many more precise purposes than earlier tools and were made in a different way, by striking flakes from a carefully prepared core. Their variety and elaboration are another sign of the growing acceleration of human evolution. New materials came into use in the Upper Palaeolithic, too, as bone and antler were added to the wood and flint of earlier workshops and armouries. These provided new possibilities of manufacture; the bone needle was a great step in the elaboration of clothing, pressure flaking enabled some skilled workmen to carry the refinement of their flint blades to a point at which it seems non-utilitarian, so delicately thinned have they become. The first man-made material, a mixture of clay with powdered bone, also makes its appearance. Weapons especially are improved. The tendency which can be seen towards the end of the Upper Palaeolithic for small flint implements to appear more frequently and for them to be more regularly geometrical suggests the making of more complex weapon points. In the same era come the invention and spread of the spear-thrower, the bow and arrow, and the barbed harpoon, used first on mammals and later to catch fish. The last shows an extension of hunting – and therefore of resources – to water. Long before this, perhaps six hundred thousand years ago, hominids had gathered molluscs for food in China and doubtless elsewhere. With harpoons and, perhaps, more

perishable implements such as nets and lines, new and richer aquatic sources of food (some created by the temperature changes of the last Ice Ages) could now be exploited, and this led to achievements in hunting, possibly connected with the growth of forests in post-glacial phases and with a new dependence on and knowledge of the movements of reindeer and wild cattle.

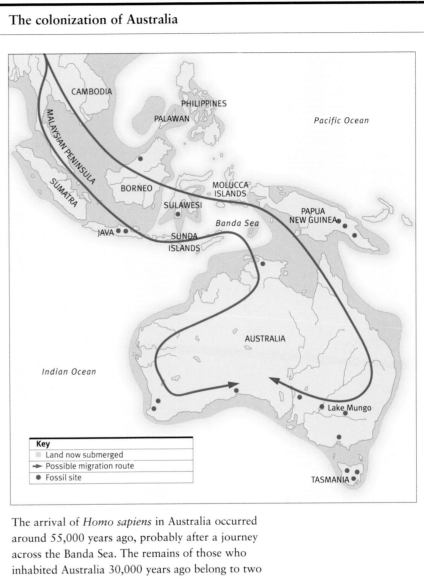

The colonization of Australia

Key
- Land now submerged
- → Possible migration route
- ● Fossil site

The arrival of *Homo sapiens* in Australia occurred around 55,000 years ago, probably after a journey across the Banda Sea. The remains of those who inhabited Australia 30,000 years ago belong to two kinds of *Homo sapiens*. This fact has led some experts to believe that there were two separate migrations to the continent. However, it is also possible that the difference between the two *Homo sapiens* groups was produced within Australia.

EARLY ART

The MOST REMARKABLE and mysterious evidence of all which has survived the peoples of the Upper Palaeolithic is their art. It is the first of whose existence we can be sure. Earlier humans or even humanoid creatures may have scratched patterns in the mud, daubed their bodies, moved rhythmically in dance or spread flowers in patterns, but of such things we know nothing, because of them, if they ever happened, nothing has survived. Some creature took the trouble to accumulate little hoards of red ochre some forty or sixty thousand years ago, but the purpose of doing so is unknown. It has been suggested that two indentations on a Neanderthal gravestone are the earliest surviving art, but the first plentiful and assured evidence comes in Europe thirty-five thousand years ago. It then swells dramatically until we find ourselves in the presence of a conscious art whose greatest technical and aesthetic achievements appear, without warning or forerunner, already almost mature. They continue so for thousands of years until this art vanishes. Just as it has no ancestor, it leaves no descendant, though it seems to have employed many of the basic processes of the visual arts still in use today.

These tools are characteristic of the late Palaeolithic. The flint point (left), which is finely carved, is typical of the Solutrean culture. The bone harpoon is from the Magdalenian culture.

Its isolation both in space and time must be ground for suspicion that there is more to be discovered. Caves in Africa abound with prehistoric paintings and carvings dated as far back as twenty-seven thousand years ago and continuing to be added to well into the reign of England's Queen Victoria; in Australia there was cave-painting at least twenty thousand years ago. Palaeolithic art is not, therefore, confined to Europe, but what has been discovered there has, so far, been studied much more intermittently. We do not yet know enough about the dating of cave paintings in other parts of the world, nor about the uniqueness of the conditions which led to the preservation in Europe of objects which may have had parallels elsewhere. Nor do we know what may have disappeared; there is a vast field of possibilities of what may have been produced in gesture, sound or perishable materials which cannot be explored. None the less, the art of western Europe in the Upper Palaeolithic, all qualifications made, has a colossal and solid impressiveness which is unique.

Flint (left) and bone tools from the Aurignacian tradition of the late Palaeolithic.

INTERPRETATION

Most early art has been found in a relatively small area of southwestern France and northern Spain and consists of three main bodies of material: small figures of stone, bone or, occasionally, clay (usually female), decorated objects (often tools and weapons) and the painted walls and roofs of caves. In these caves (and in the decoration of objects) there is an overwhelming preponderance of animal themes. The meaning of these designs, above all in the elaborate sequences of the cave paintings, has intrigued scholars. Obviously, many of the beasts so carefully observed were central to a hunting economy. At least in the French caves, too, it now seems highly probable that a conscious order exists in the sequences in which they are shown. But to go further in the argument is still very hard.

In December 1994 CE, explorers discovered the Chauvet Cave in the Ardèche valley. Inside the cave, more than 300 painted and engraved images of animals were found. Radio carbon tests show that the drawings are more than 30,000 years old. They are, therefore, the oldest paintings yet found and are remarkably well executed, as these beautiful horses' heads show.

This statuette from Lespugue, France, is 23,000 years old and possesses the characteristic features of Palaeolithic Venuses. It has been suggested that her buttocks reveal steatopygia – an accumulation of fat in the hips which acts as a calorie reserve during long periods without food.

Clearly, art in Upper Palaeolithic times has to carry much of a burden later carried by writing, but what its messages mean is still obscure. It seems likely that the paintings were connected with religious or magical practice: African rock painting has been convincingly shown to be linked to magic and shamanism and the selection of such remote and difficult corners of caves as those in which the European paintings have been traced is by itself strongly suggestive that some special rite was carried out when they were painted or gazed upon. (Artificial light, of course, was needed in these dark corners.) The origins of religion have been hinted at in Neanderthal burials and appear even more strongly in those of the Upper Palaeolithic peoples which are often elaborate; here, in their art, is something where inferences are even harder to resist. Perhaps it provides the first surviving relics of organized religion.

THE DEVELOPMENT OF EARLY ART

The birth, maturity and death of the earliest artistic achievement of humankind in Europe occupies a very long period, perhaps of thirty thousand years. Somewhere about thirty-five thousand years ago appear decorated and coloured objects, often of bone and ivory. Then, fifteen millennia or so later, we reach the first figurative art and, soon afterwards, the peak of the prehistoric aesthetic achievement, the great painted and incised cave "sanctuaries" (as they have been called), with their processions of animals and mysterious repeated symbolic shapes. This high phase lasted about five thousand years, a startlingly long time for the maintenance of so consistent a style and content. So long a period – almost as long as the whole history of civilization on this planet – illustrates the slowness with which tradition changed in ancient times and its imperviousness to outside influence. Perhaps it is an index, too, of the geographical isolation of prehistoric cultures. The last phase of this art which has been discerned takes the story down to about 9000 BCE; in it, the stag more and more replaces other animals as subject matter (no doubt thus reflecting the disappearance of the reindeer and the mammoth as the ice retreated) before a final burst of richly decorated tools and weapons brings Europe's first great artistic achievement to an end. The age which followed produced nothing approaching it in scale or quality; its best surviving relics are a few decorated pebbles. Six thousand years were to pass before the next great art.

THE DISAPPEARANCE OF EARLY ART

For all the splendour of this art, we know little about its collapse. The light is never more than dim in the Upper Palaeolithic and the darkness closes in rapidly – which is to say, of course, over thousands of years. Nevertheless,

The Palaeolithic Venuses

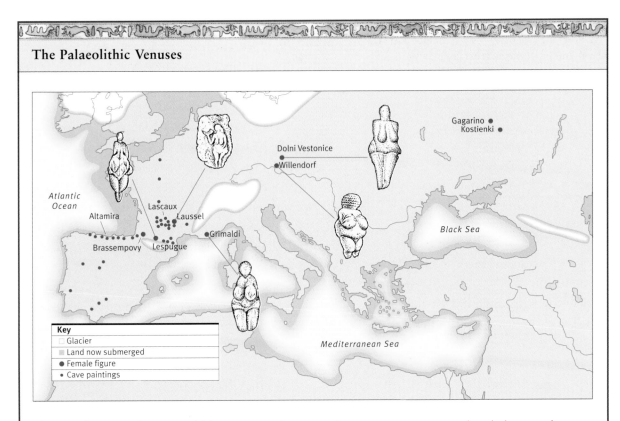

These small statues of women, which are commonly known as the Palaeolithic Venuses, have been discovered at sites all over Europe, from the Pyrenees to Russia, and are between 21,000 and 29,000 years old. They depict partially or completely naked women, with large breasts and buttocks, some of whom may be pregnant. The figures' heads and limbs are given only summary treatment, as though they were less interesting. The statues are thought to be associated with a fertility ritual. Their remarkably widespread geographical distribution demonstrates that they were cultural symbols shared by communities that lived for thousands of years in a territory which extended over a vast area.

the impression left by the violence of the contrast between what was before and what came after produces a sense of shock. So relatively sudden an extinction is a mystery. We have no precise dates or even precise sequences: nothing ended in one year or another. There was only a gradual closing down of artistic activity over a long time which seems in the end to have been absolute. Some scholars have blamed climate. Perhaps, they argue, the whole phenomenon of cave art was linked to efforts to influence the movements or abundance of the great game herds on which the hunting peoples relied. As the last Ice Age ebbed and each year the reindeer retreated a little, new and magical techniques were sought to manipulate them, but gradually as the ice sheets withdrew more and more, an environment to which earlier humans had successfully adapted disappeared. So did the hope of influencing nature. *Homo sapiens* was not powerless; far from it, it could adapt, and did, to a new challenge. But for a time one cultural impoverishment at least, the abandonment of the first art, was a consequence of adaptation.

It is easy to see much that is fanciful in such speculation, but difficult to restrain excitement over such an astonishing achievement. People have spoken of the great cave sequences as "cathedrals" of the Palaeolithic world and such metaphors are justified if the

Our ancestors

DNA studies of diverse human communities suggest that present-day humankind descends from one line. That line began to subdivide about 100,000 years ago and continued to do so throughout the late Palaeolithic

(Quaternary period). This diagram, based on studies carried out by Luigi Luca Cavalli-Sforza and his team, shows how the first division separates African communities from the rest of the world.

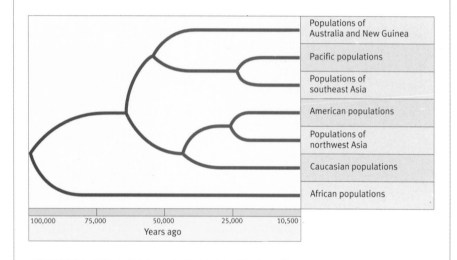

Populations of Australia and New Guinea

Pacific populations

Populations of southeast Asia

American populations

Populations of northwest Asia

Caucasian populations

African populations

100,000   75,000   50,000   25,000   10,500
Years ago

level of achievement and the scale of the work undertaken is measured against what evidence we have of the earlier triumphs of man. With the first great art, the hominids are now left far behind and we have unequivocal evidence of the power of the human mind.

RACIAL DIFFERENTIATION

Much that is known of the Upper Palaeolithic confirms the sense that the crucial genetic changes are behind and that evolution is now a mental and social phenomenon. The distribution of major racial divisions in the world which last down to early modern times is already broadly fixed by the end of the Upper Palaeolithic. Geographical and climatic divisions had produced specializations within *Homo sapiens* in skin pigment, hair characteristics, the shape of the skull and the bone structure of the face. In the earliest

Chinese relics of *Homo sapiens* the Mongoloid characteristics are discernible. All the main racial groups are established by 10,000 BCE, broadly speaking in the areas they dominated until the great resettlement of the Caucasian stocks which was one aspect of the rise of European civilization to world domination after 1500 CE. The world was filling up during the Old Stone Age. Human beings at last penetrated the virgin continents. Between thirty and fifteen thousand years ago Mongoloid peoples spread over the Americas; the earliest Australian Palaeolithic site has been dated about thirty-five thousand years ago and *Homo sapiens* probably reached that continent by water from southeast Asia.

POPULATION SIZE

The Upper Palaeolithic world was still a very empty place. Calculations suggest that twenty thousand humans lived in France in Neanderthal times, possibly fifty thousand millennia ago. There were then perhaps ten million humans in the whole world. "A human desert swarming with game" is one scholar's description of it. They lived by hunting and gathering, and a lot of land was needed to support a family.

However questionable such figures may be, if they are agreed to be of this order of magnitude it is not hard to see that they still mean very slow cultural change. Greatly accelerated though human beings' progress in

Many figures in a similar style to the Palaeolithic cave paintings have been discovered carved in bone, horn and stone. This carved shoulder blade, for example, comes from the Castillo Cave in Cantabria, Spain.

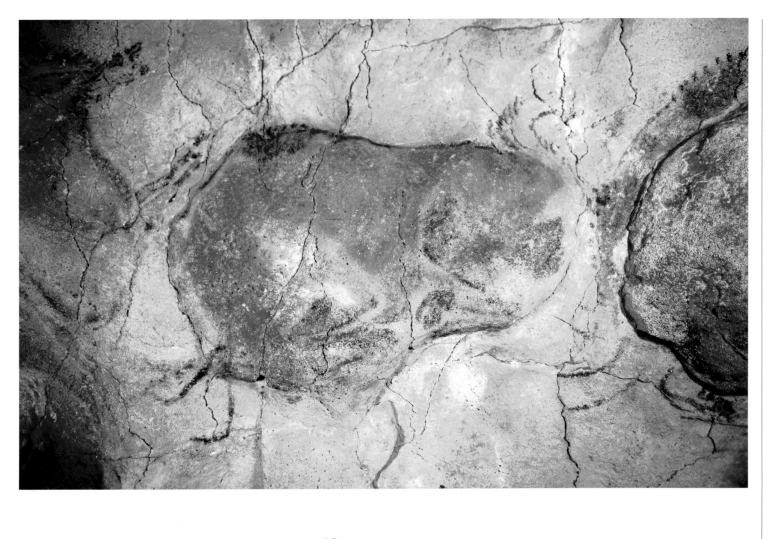

A plan of the paintings in the Altamira Cave.

The first Palaeolithic cave paintings were found in the Altamira Cave in Cantabria, Spain. Twelve thousand years ago, by the light of a flickering torch, someone painted the splendid bison shown above, probably as part of a ritual.

the Old Stone Age may be and much more versatile though they are becoming, they are still taking thousands of years to transmit learning across the barriers of geography and social division. A person might, after all, live all his or her life without meeting anyone from another group or tribe, let alone another culture. The divisions which already existed between different groups of *Homo sapiens* open a historical era whose whole tendency was towards the cultural distinction, if not isolation, of one group from another, and this was to increase human variety until reversed by technical and political forces in very recent times.

About the groups in which Upper Palaeolithic humans lived there is still much unknown. What is clear is that they were both larger in size than in former times and also more settled. The earliest remains of buildings come from the hunters of the Upper Palaeolithic who inhabited what are now the Czech and Slovak Republics and southern Russia. In about 10,000 BCE in parts of France some clusters of shelters seem to have contained anything from four to six hundred people, but judging by the archaeological record, this was unusual. Something like the tribe probably existed, therefore, though about its organization and hierarchies it is virtually impossible to speak. All that is clear

is that there was a continuing sexual specialization in the Old Stone Age as hunting grew more elaborate and its skills more demanding, while settlements provided new possibilities of vegetable gathering by women.

THE END OF THE PALAEOLITHIC

Cloudy though its picture is, none the less, the earth at the end of the Old Stone Age is in important respects one we can recognize. There were still to be geological changes (the English Channel was only to make its latest appearance in about 7000 BCE, for example) but we have lived in a period of comparative topographical stability which has preserved the major shapes of the world of about 9000 BCE. That world was already firmly humankind's world. The descendants of the primates who came out of the trees had, by the acquisition of their tool-making skills, by using natural materials to make shelters and by domesticating fire, by hunting and exploiting other animals, long achieved an important measure of independence of natural rhythms. This had brought them to a high enough level of social organization to undertake important cooperative works. Their needs had provoked economic differentiation between the sexes. Grappling with these and other material problems had led to the transmission of ideas by speech, to the invention of ritual practices and ideas which lie at the roots of religion, and, eventually, to a great art. It has even been argued that Upper Palaeolithic societies had a lunar calendar. Humans as they leave prehistory are already conceptualizing creatures, equipped with intellect, with the power to objectify and abstract. It is very difficult not to believe that it is this new strength which explains humanity's capacity to make the last and greatest stride in prehistory, the invention of agriculture.

At the Princevent site in the Seine valley, France, a number of circles have been found on the ground. The circles have a fireplace at one end and indications that they were inhabited by reindeer hunters, who lived some 10,000 years ago. There are no traces of any posts, which suggests that the hunters built lightweight tents similar to the ones in this drawing. A frame of sticks was probably covered with animal skins.

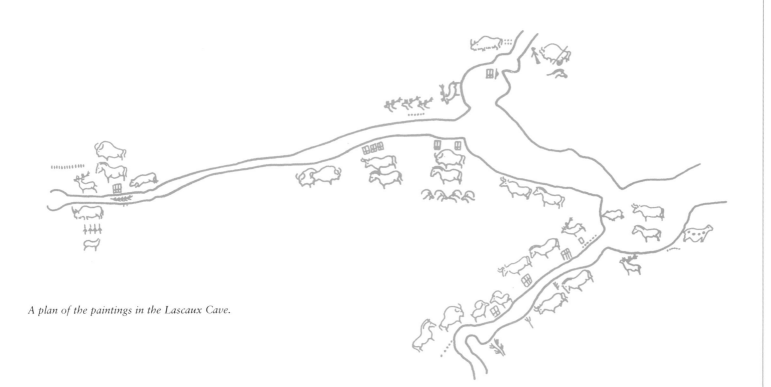

A plan of the paintings in the Lascaux Cave.

Currently, we know of the existence of more than 200 caves in Europe containing Palaeolithic paintings. Most of the images date from the Magdalenian cultural period, which lasted from 15,000 to 10,000 BCE, and 90 per cent of them can be found in France and Spain. This photograph shows one of the most impressive paintings ever discovered, from the Lascaux Cave, in the Dordogne, France.

3 *THE POSSIBILITY OF CIVILIZATION*

Many cave paintings from the Mesolithic cultural age have been found in eastern Spain. This scene, from the Roca del Moros in Cogull, depicts human figures.

THE SPECIES *Homo sapiens* has existed for at least ten and perhaps twenty times as long as the civilization it has created. The waning of the last Ice Age allowed the long march to civilization to be completed and is the immediate prelude to History. Within five or six thousand years a succession of momentous changes took place; the most important of them was an increase in food supply. Nothing so sharply accelerated human development or had such widespread results until the changes called industrial revolution which have been going on for the last two and a half centuries.

THE NEOLITHIC CULTURE

ONE SCHOLAR SUMMED UP these changes which mark the end of prehistory with a similar phrase, the "Neolithic revolution". Here is another little tangle of potentially

This painting of deer running at full speed was found on the rocks of the Gasullo ravine in the Castellón region. It is just one example of the many animal paintings that have been found in the east of Spain.

REGIONAL DIFFERENCES

Even in the narrowest technological sense, the Neolithic phase of human development does not begin, flower or end everywhere at the same time. In one place it may last thousands of years longer than in another and its beginnings are separated from what went before not by a clear line but by a mysterious zone of cultural change. Then, within it, not all societies possess the same range of skills and resources; some discover how to make pottery, as well as polished stone tools, others go on to domesticate animals and begin to gather or raise cereal crops. Slow evolution is the rule and not all societies had reached the same level by the time literate civilization appears. Nevertheless, Neolithic culture is the matrix from which civilization appears and provides the preconditions on which it rests, and they are by no means limited to the production of the highly finished stone tools

misleading terminology, though the last we need consider in prehistory. Archaeologists follow the Palaeolithic era by the Mesolithic and that by the Neolithic (some add a fourth, the Chalcolithic, by which they mean a phase of society in which artifacts of stone and copper are in simultaneous use). The distinction between the first two is really of moment only to the specialist, but all these terms describe cultural facts; they identify sequences of artifacts which show growing resources and capacities. Only the term "Neolithic" need concern us. It means, at its strictest, a culture in which ground or polished stone tools replace chipped ones (though other criteria are sometimes added to this). This may not seem so startling a change as to justify the excitement over the Neolithic which has been shown by some prehistorians, far less talk of a "Neolithic revolution". In fact, though the phrase is still sometimes used it is unsatisfactory because it has had to cover too many different ideas. None the less, it was an attempt to pin down an important and complex change which took place with many local variations. It is still worth while, therefore, to try to understand what made the Neolithic so important.

Spanish cave paintings provide the first evidence of the use of bows and arrows.

Neolithic cultures are characterized by the existence of polished stone tools, which were rubbed until they had a smooth surface. These polished Neolithic axeheads were used to cut down trees in order to make clearings in forests.

which gave the phase its name.

We must also qualify the word "revolution" when discussing this change. Though we leave behind the slow evolutions of the Pleistocene and move into an accelerating era of prehistory, there are still no clear-cut divisions. They are pretty rare in later history; even when they try to do so, few societies ever break with their past. What we can see is a slow but radical transformation of human behaviour and organization over more and more of the world, not a sudden new departure. It is made up of several crucial changes which make the last period of prehistory identifiable as a unity, whatever we call it.

PHYSIOLOGICAL CHANGE

At the end of the Upper Palaeolithic, humans existed physically much as we know them. They were, of course, still to change somewhat in height and weight, most obviously in those areas of the world where they gained in stature and life expectancy as nutrition

improved. In the Old Stone Age it was still unlikely that a man or a woman would reach the age of forty and if they did then they were likely to live pretty miserable lives, in our eyes prematurely aged, tormented by arthritis, rheumatism and the casual accidents of broken bones or rotting teeth. This would only slowly improve. The shape of the human face would go on evolving, too, as diet altered. (It seems to be only after 1066 CE that the edge-to-edge bite gave way among Anglo-Saxons to the overbite which was the ultimate consequence of a shift to more starch and carbohydrate, a development of some importance for the later appearance of the English.)

Human physical types differed in different continents, but we cannot presume that capacities did. In all parts of the world *Homo sapiens sapiens* was showing great versatility in adapting his heritage to the climatic and geographical upheavals of the ebbing phase of the last Ice Age. In the beginnings of settlements of some size and permanence, in the elaboration of technology and in the growth of language and the dawn of characterization in art lay some of the rudimentary elements of the compound which was eventually to crystallize as civilization. But much more than these were needed. Above all, there had to be the possibility of some sort of economic surplus to daily requirements.

This was hardly conceivable except in occasional, specially favourable areas of the hunting and gathering economy which sustained all human life and was the only one known to human beings until about ten thousand years ago.

EARLY AGRICULTURE

What made civilization possible was the invention of agriculture. The importance of this was so great that it does

This Neolithic flaked spearhead dates from between 4400 and 3300 BCE.

seem to justify a strong metaphor and the "farming revolution" or "food-gathering revolution" are terms whose meaning is readily clear. They single out the fact which explains why the Neolithic era could provide the circumstances in which civilizations could appear. Even a knowledge of metallurgy, which was spreading in some societies during their Neolithic phases, is not so fundamental. Farming truly revolutionized the conditions of human existence and it is the main thing to bear in mind when considering the meaning of Neolithic, a meaning concisely summarized by a leading archaeologist as "not a time phase falling between exact dates, but ... a period between the end of the hunting way of life and the beginning of a full metal-using economy, when the practice of farming arose and spread through most of Europe, Asia and North Africa like a slow-moving wave".

The essentials of agriculture are the growing of crops and the practice of animal husbandry. How these came about and at what places and times is more mysterious. Some environments must have helped more than others; while some peoples pursued game across plains uncovered by the retreating ice, others

In the western Sahara, which was far more humid a few thousand years ago than it is today, many small, engraved stone plaques depicting various animals have been found.
These provide evidence of the gradual change from hunting to the domestication of livestock. This plaque comes from the Saguia el-Hamra region.

were intensifying the skills needed to exploit the new, prolific river valleys and coastal inlets rich in edible plants and fish. The same must be true of cultivation and herding. On the whole, the Old World of Africa and Eurasia was better off in domesticable animals than what would later be called the Americas. Not surprisingly, then, agriculture began in more than one place and in different forms. It seems likely that the earliest instance, based on the cultivation of primitive forms of millet and rice, occurred in the Near East, somewhere about 10,000 BCE.

AGRICULTURE IN THE NEAR EAST

Because of what was to happen later and because of the accidents of historical survivals and the direction taken by scholarly effort, much more is known about early agriculture in the Near East than its possible precursors in the Far East. There are good reasons for continuing to regard it as a crucial zone, even if it is not given pride of place in terms of chronology. Both the predisposing conditions and the evidence point to the region later called the "Fertile Crescent" as especially significant,

Time chart (10,000 BCE–c.3500 BCE)					
	First Neolithic sculptures in western Asia			Beginning of the Bronze Age in western Asia	
10,000 BCE	8000 BCE	6000 BCE	4000 BCE		2000 BCE
	10,000–5000 BCE Mesolithic cultures in Europe		First Neolithic sculptures in Europe		

Agricultural tools from the Neolithic: a grinding stone (above) and flint blades (right), which may have been used for reaping.

Age seems to have presented a manageable challenge; population pressure might well have stimulated attempts to extend living-space by clearing and planting when hunting-gathering areas became over-crowded. From this region the new foods and the techniques for planting and harvesting them seem to have spread into Europe in about 6000 BCE. Within the region, of course, contacts were relatively easier than outside it; a date as early as 8000 BCE has been given to discoveries of bladed tools found in south-west Iran but made from obsidian which came from Anatolia. But diffusion was not the only process at work. Agriculture later appeared in the Americas, seemingly without any import of techniques from outside.

THE DOMESTICATION OF ANIMALS

The jump from gathering wild cereals to planting and harvesting them seems marginally greater than that from driving game for hunting to herding, but the domestication of animals was almost as momentous. The first traces of the keeping of sheep come from northern Iraq, in about 9000 BCE. Over such hilly, grassy areas the wild forebears of the Jersey cow and the Sussex White pig roamed untroubled for thousands of years except by occasional contact with their hunters. Pigs, it is true, could be found all over the Old World, but sheep and goats were especially plentiful in Asia Minor and a region running across much of Asia itself. From their systematic exploitation would follow the control of their breeding and other economic and technological innovations. The use of skins and wool opened new possibilities; the taking of milk launched dairying. Riding and the use of animals for traction would come later. So would domestic poultry.

the whole arc of territory running northward from Egypt through Palestine and the Levant, through Anatolia to the hills between Iran and the south Caspian to enclose the river valleys of Mesopotamia. Much of it now looks very different from the same area's lush landscape when the climate was at its best, five thousand or so years ago. Wild barley and a wheatlike cereal then grew in southern Turkey and emmer, a wild wheat, in the Jordan valley. Egypt enjoyed enough rain for the hunting of big game well into historical times, and elephants were still to be found in Syrian forests in 1000 BCE.

The whole region today is fertile by comparison with the desert which is its boundary, but in prehistoric times it was even more favoured. The cereal grasses which are the ancestors of later crops have been traced back furthest in these lands. There is evidence of the harvesting, though not necessarily of the cultivating, of wild grasses in Asia Minor in about 9500 BCE. There, too, the afforestation which followed the end of the last Ice

The beginnings of agriculture

The cultivation of plants and the domestication of animals, both of which brought about a radical transformation in the way human beings lived, did not begin in one place. There is a great deal of evidence to suggest that different agrarian traditions developed independently at different times from a number of distinct places of origin, at least eight of which have been identified (see map, right, above). The earliest of agricultural developments appear to have taken place in the Near East area, where farming villages are known to have existed some 10,000 years ago. Agriculture and livestock farming gradually spread from these early centres into new regions. The European farming tradition, for example, was probably disseminated from the Near East into Europe along two main routes: through the Balkans and along the River Danube (from around 6500 BCE) and along the Mediterranean coast (reaching southern France around 5000 BCE).

The map depicting the diffusion of agriculture in Europe (right, below) shows how closely the spread of farming was linked to the spread of pottery manufacture. The typical pottery found in the Mediterranean region is known as cardial pottery, after its *cardium*, or "cockle-shell", decoration. So-called band pottery, named after its incised linear decorations, has been found north of the Alps and across central Europe. Through the discovery of objects belonging to these two groups of pottery, it is possible to chart the locations of early farming communities.

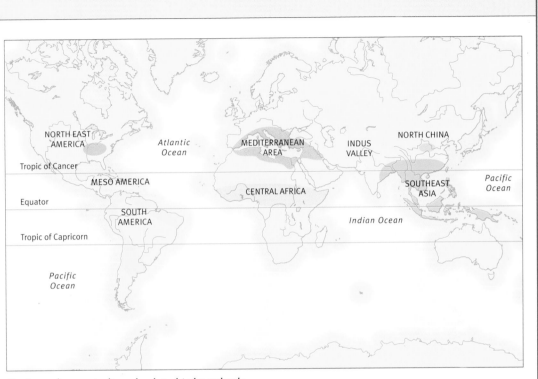

Regions where agriculture developed independently.

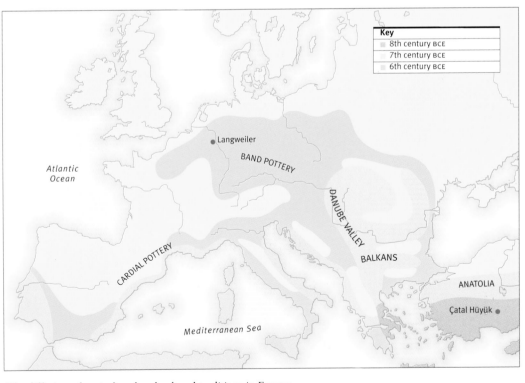

The diffusion of agricultural and cultural traditions in Europe.

THE IMPLICATIONS OF SURPLUSES

Various Neolithic cultural traditions can be identified by their distinct pottery styles. The object pictured above, found in Andalusia in Spain, is an example of the cardial pottery that was characteristic of the western Mediterranean region during the early Neolithic period.

THE STORY OF HUMANITY is now far past the point at which the impact of such changes can be easily grasped. Suddenly, with the coming of agriculture, the whole material fabric on which subsequent human history was to be based flashes into view, though not into existence. It began the greatest of humanity's transformations of the environment. In a hunting-gathering society thousands of acres are needed to support a family, whereas in primitive agricultural society about twenty-five acres is enough. In terms of population growth, a huge acceleration became possible.

An assured or virtually assured food surplus also meant settlements of a new solidity. Bigger populations could live on smaller areas and true villages could appear. Specialists not engaged in food production could be tolerated and fed more easily while they practised their own skills. Before 9000 BCE there was a

Basket-making is thought to have begun during the final stages of the Neolithic. These incredibly well-preserved grass baskets were found in Cueva de los Murciélagos in Granada, Spain.

village (and perhaps a shrine) at Jericho. A thousand years later it had grown to some eight to ten acres of mud-brick houses.

SOCIAL CHANGES

It is a long time before we can discern much of the social organization and behaviour of early Near Eastern communities. It seems possible that at this time, as much as at any other, local divisions were decisive. Physically, humans were more uniform than ever, but culturally they were diversifying as they grappled with different problems and appropriated different resources. The adaptability of different branches of *Homo sapiens* in the conditions left behind after the retreat of the last Ice Age is very striking and produced variations in experience unlike those following earlier glaciations. They lived for the most part in isolated, settled traditions, in which the importance of routine was overwhelming. This would give new stability to the divisions of culture and race which had appeared so slowly throughout Palaeolithic times. It would take much less time in the historical future which lay ahead for these local peculiarities to crumble under the impact of population growth, speedier communication and the coming of trade – a mere ten thousand years, at most. Within the new farming communities it seems likely that distinctions of role multiplied and new collective disciplines had to be accepted. For some people there must have been more leisure (though for others actually engaged in the production of food, leisure may well have diminished). It is likely that social distinctions became more marked. This may be connected with new possibilities as surpluses became available for barter which led eventually to trade.

Excavations at the Jericho site, West Bank, have revealed this spectacular circular stone tower. The tower is 30 ft (9 m) high and dates from 8000 BCE. This suggests that some of the earliest Neolithic farming communities were already using complex systems of fortification to defend themselves against enemy incursions.

NEW GROUNDS FOR CONFLICT

The surpluses may also have encouraged humanity's oldest sport after hunting, warfare. New prizes must have made raids and conquest more tempting. Perhaps, too, a conflict, which was to have centuries of vitality before it, finds its origins here – that between nomads and settlers. Political power may have its origin in the need to organize protection for crops and stock from human predators. We may even speculate that the dim roots of the notion of aristocracy are to be sought in the successes (which must have been frequent) of hunter-gatherers, representatives of an older social order, in exploiting the vulnerability of the settlers, tied to their areas of cultivation, by enslaving them. Hunting was long to be the sport of kings and

This plaster model of a human head was found in Jericho. Carved in bas-relief, it dates from the 7th millennium BCE.

mastery of the animal world was an attribute of the first heroes of whose exploits we have records in sculpture and legend. None the less, though much of the just prehistoric world must have been lawless and violent, it is worth remembering that there was an offsetting factor: the world was still not very full. The replacement of hunter-gatherers by farmers did not have to be a violent process. The ample space and thin populations of Europe on the eve of the introduction of farming may explain the lack of archaeological evidence of violent struggle. It was only slowly that growing populations and pressure on the new farming resources increased the likelihood of competition.

An early Bronze Age flat axe (far right) and a late Bronze Age axe (right). The high price of bronze restricted its use – it was mainly employed for making weapons.

EARLY METALLURGY

In the long run metallurgy changed things as much as did farming, but it was to be a very much longer run. Immediately, it made a less rapid and fundamental difference. This is probably because the deposits of ore first discovered were few and scattered: for a long time there was just not much metal around. The first of whose use we find evidence is copper (which rather weakens the attractiveness of the old term "Bronze Age" for the beginning of metal-using culture). At some time between 7000 and 6000 BCE it was being hammered into shape without heating at Çatal Hüyük, in Anatolia, though the earliest known metal artifacts date from about 4000 BCE and are beaten copper pins found in Egypt. Once the technique of blending copper with tin (which was in use in Mesopotamia soon after 3000 BCE) to produce bronze was discovered, a metal was available which was both relatively easy to cast and retained a much better cutting edge. On this much could be built; from it much derived, among other results the quite new importance of ore-bearing areas. In its turn, this was to give a new twist to trade, to markets and to routes. Further complications, of course, followed the coming of iron, which appeared after some cultures had indisputably evolved into civilizations – another reflexion of the way in which the historical and prehistoric eras run so untidily into one another. Its obvious military value springs to the eye, but it had just as much importance when turned into agricultural tools. This is looking a long way ahead, but it made possible a huge extension of living-space and food-producing soil: however successfully they burned woodland and scrub, Neolithic peoples could only scratch at heavy soils with an antler or wooden pick. Turning them over and digging deep began to be possible only when the invention of ploughing (in the Near East in about 3000 BCE) brought animal muscle-power to the assistance of human, and when iron tools became common.

CENTRES OF DEVELOPMENT

It is already clear how quickly – the term is legitimate against the background of earlier prehistory, even if it takes thousands of years in some places – interpenetration and interplay begin to influence the pace and direction of change. Long before these processes have exhausted their effects in some areas, too, the first civilizations are in being. Prehistorians used to argue whether innovations were diffused from a single source or appeared spontaneously and independently in different places, but so complex a background has made this seem a waste of time and energy. Both

Stone moulds were used to cast various bronze objects. This needle-casting mould was found in Switzerland.

views, if put forward in an unqualified way, seem somewhat implausible. To say that in one place, and in one place only, all the conditions for the appearance of new phenomena existed and that these were then simply diffused elsewhere is as implausible as saying that in widely differing circumstances of geography, climate and cultural inheritance exactly the same inventions could be thrown up, as it were, time and time again. What we can observe is a concentration of factors in the Near East which made it at one crucial moment immeasurably the most concentrated, active and important centre of new developments. It does not mean that similar individual developments may not have occurred elsewhere: pottery, it seems, was first produced in Japan in about 10,000 BCE, and agriculture evolved in America perhaps

as early as 5000 BCE in complete isolation from the Old World.

THE EVE OF CIVILIZATION

THE PROLOGUE to human history thus comes to a ragged, untidy end; once again, there is no neat dividing line. At the end of prehistory and on the eve of the first civilizations we can discern a world of human societies more differentiated than ever before and more successful than ever in mastering different environments and surviving. Some will continue into history. It is only within the last century or so that the Ainus of northern Japan have disappeared, taking with them a life that is said to have been very similar to one they lived fifteen thousand years ago. Englishmen and Frenchmen who went to North America in the sixteenth century CE found hunter-gatherers there who must have lived much as their own ancestors had done ten thousand years before. Plato and Aristotle were to live and die before prehistory in America gave way to the appearance of the great Mayan civilization of Yucatán, and prehistory lasted for Eskimos and Australian Aborigines until the nineteenth century.

THE PACE OF CHANGE

No crude divisions of chronology will help in unravelling so interwoven a pattern of peoples and cultures. But its most important feature is clear enough: by 6000 or 5000 BCE, there

This stone mould (below, left), found in Switzerland, was used to cast bronze needles such as the one shown below, right.

existed in one area of the Old World all the essential constituents of civilized life. Their deepest roots lay hundreds of thousands of years further back, in ages dominated by the slow rhythm of genetic evolution. Through the Upper Palaeolithic eras the pace of change had quickened by a huge factor as culture slowly became more important, but this was as nothing to what was to follow. Civilization was to bring conscious attempts on a quite new scale to control and organize humans and their environment. Civilization builds on a basis of cumulative mental and technological resources and the feedback from its own transformations further accelerates the process of change. Ahead lies faster

This figure, found at Çatal Hüyük, dates from 8000–7000 BCE.

development in every field, in the technical control of environment, in the elaboration of mental patterns, in the changing of social organization, in the accumulation of wealth, in the growth of population.

It is important that we get our perspective in this matter right. From some modern points of view the centuries of the European Middle Ages look like a long slumber. No medievalist would agree, of course, but a modern reader who is impressed by the rapidity of the change which encompasses him or her and the relative immobility of medieval society ought to reflect that the art which develops from the Romanesque of Charlemagne's Aachen to the Flamboyant of fifteenth-

An artist's reconstruction of part of the Çatal Hüyük Neolithic site, discovered in 1958 CE in Anatolia. The site's 1,000 dwellings date from around 6000 BCE. They had remarkably regular ground plans, were made of sun-dried bricks and mud and measured around 270 sq ft (25 sq m). The entrance to each house was through a low door from a roof terrace. Wall paintings, statues of a mother goddess and the figure of a bull were found inside some of the buildings, which suggests that they were used as sanctuaries.

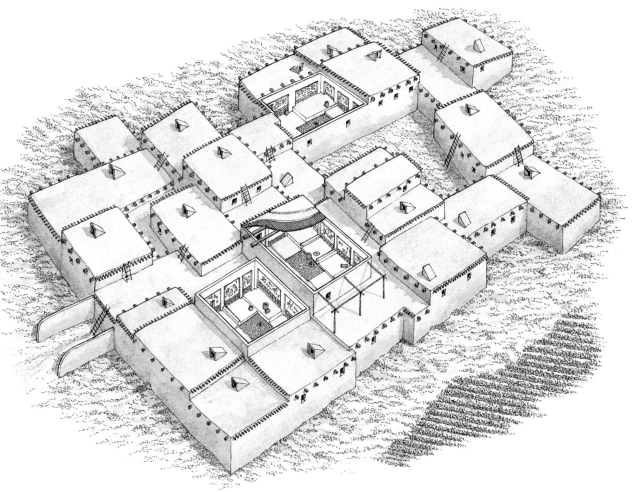

This building, 36 ft (11 m) x 33 ft (10 m), was erected in the 4th millennium BCE at the centre of a small village in Banpo, south of the Yellow River, China. This was the main building in the village, which was inhabited by people from the Yangshao Neolithic culture.

century France was revolutionized in five or six centuries; in a period about ten times as long, the first known art, that of Upper Palaeolithic Europe, shows, by comparison, insignificant stylistic change.

Further back, the pace is even slower as the long persistence of early tool types shows. Still more fundamental changes are even less easy to comprehend. So far as we know, the last twelve thousand years register nothing new in human physiology comparable to the colossal transformations of the early Pleistocene which are registered for us in a handful of relics of a few of nature's experiments, yet those took hundreds of thousands of years.

THE ROLE OF HUMAN CONSCIOUSNESS

In part, the contrast in the rate of change is the one with which we began, that between Nature and humanity as makers of change. Humans increasingly choose for themselves and even in prehistory the story of change is therefore increasingly one of conscious adaptation. So the story will continue into historical times, more intensively still. This is why the most important part of the story of humanity is the story of consciousness; when, long ago, it broke the genetic slow march, it made everything else possible. Nature and nurture are there from the moment that humans can first be discerned; perhaps they can never be quite disentangled, but man-made culture and tradition are increasingly the determinants of change.

Found at the Çatal Hüyük site, this terracotta sculpture dates from 6000 BCE and represents the Hittite mother goddess giving birth between two lions or leopards.

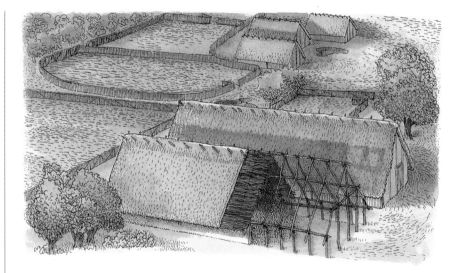

The Langweiler 2 site (above) is characteristic of the band pottery culture of the middle of the 6th millennium BCE. These early European farmers lived in villages that consisted of a few very large buildings of up to 483 sq ft (45 sq m), divided into three areas. The central area was used by the family, another space was set aside for livestock and a third probably served as a grain store. The villagers grew cereals and vegetables, bred cattle and pigs and hunted in the large forests nearby.

HUMANKIND'S INHERITANCE

Two reflexions ought to be made to balance the indisputable fact that humans have some control over their own destiny. The first is that they have almost certainly not shown any improvement in innate capacity since the Upper Palaeolithic. Their physique has not changed fundamentally in forty thousand years or so and it would be surprising if their mental capacity had done so. So short a time could hardly suffice for genetic changes comparable to those of earlier eras. The rapidity with which humanity has achieved so much since prehistoric times can be accounted for quite simply: there are many more of us upon whose talents humanity can draw and, more important still, human achievements are essentially cumulative. They

rest upon a heritage itself accumulating at, as it were, compound interest. Primitive societies had far less inherited advantage in the bank. This makes the magnitude of their greatest steps forward all the more amazing.

If this is speculative, the second reflexion need not be: our genetic inheritance not only enables us to make conscious change, to undertake an unprecedented kind of evolution, but also controls and limits us. The irrationalities of this century show the narrow limits of our capacity for conscious control of our destiny. To this extent, we are still determined, still unfree, still a part of a nature which produced our unique qualities in the first place only by evolutionary selection. It is not easy to separate this part of our inheritance, either, from the emotional shaping we have received from the processes through which we evolved. That shaping still lies deep at the heart of all our aesthetic and affective life. Humans must live with an inbuilt dualism. To deal with it has been the aim of most of the great philosophies and religions and the mythologies by which we still live, but they are themselves moulded by it. As we move from prehistory to history it is important not to forget that its determining effect still proves much more resistant to control than those blind prehistoric forces of geography and climate which were so quickly overcome. Nevertheless, human beings at the edge of history are already the creatures we know, change-makers.

A San man in the Kalahari desert in Africa quenches his thirst by extracting the sap from a root. Like today's traditional communities, our prehistoric ancestors managed to survive thanks to a wealth of knowledge about their environment.

THE FIRST CIVILIZATIONS

TEN THOUSAND YEARS AGO, the physical shape of the world was much what it is today. The outlines of the continents were broadly those we know and the major natural barriers and channels of communication have remained constant ever since. By comparison with the upheavals of the hundreds of millennia preceding the end of the last Ice Age, climate, too, was from this time stable; from this point the historian need only regard its short-term fluctuations. Ahead lay the age (in which we still live) in which most change was to be man-made.

Civilization has been one of the great accelerators of such change. It began at least seven times says one historian, meaning by that that he can distinguish at least seven occasions on which particular mixes of human skills and natural facts came together to make possible a new order of life based on the exploitation of nature. Though all these beginnings fall within a span of three thousand years or so – barely a moment by comparison with the vast scale of prehistory – they were neither simultaneous, nor equally successful. They turned out very differently, some of them racing ahead to lasting achievements while others declined or disappeared, even if after spectacular flowerings. Yet all of them signified an increase in the rate and scale of change dramatic by comparison with anything achieved in earlier times.

Some of these early civilizations are still real foundations of our own world. Some of them, on the other hand, now exercise little or no influence, except perhaps upon our imaginations and emotions when we contemplate the relics which are all that is now left of them. None the less, together they determined much of the cultural map of the world down to this day because of the power of the traditions which sprang from them even when their achievements in ideas, social organization or technology had long been forgotten. The establishment of the first civilizations took place between about 3500 BCE and 500 BCE and it provides the first of the major chronological divisions of world history.

Egypt's exceptional artistic heritage has captured the world's imagination since its rediscovery by the archaeologists and scholars who went there with Napoleon Bonaparte in 1798 CE. This remarkable temple in Luxor (the name given to the southern part of Thebes) was built by Amenhotep III (1411–1375 BCE) and was one of the most important temples in Egypt during the New Kingdom period.

1 EARLY CIVILIZED LIFE

FOR AS LONG AS WE KNOW there has been at Jericho a never-failing spring feeding what is still a sizable oasis. No doubt it explains why people have lived there on and off for about ten thousand years. Farmers clustered about it in late prehistoric times; its population may then have numbered two or three thousand. Before 6000 BCE it had great water tanks which suggest provision for big needs, possibly for irrigation, and there was a massive stone tower which was part of elaborate defences long kept in repair. Clearly its inhabitants thought they had something worth defending; they had property. Jericho was a considerable place. For all that, it was not the beginnings of a civilization; too much was still lacking.

THE FOUNDATIONS OF CIVILIZATION

It is worth considering for a moment at the outset of the era of civilization just what it is

Sites of the first civilizations

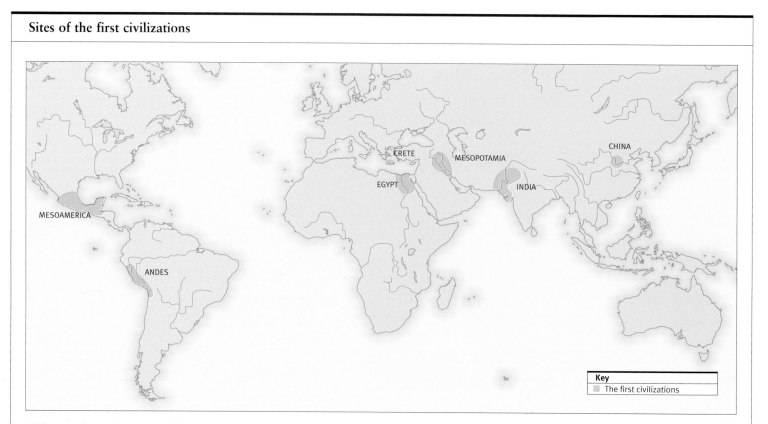

This map shows the areas of the world where ancient civilizations appeared. The fact that each civilization possesses distinguishing features suggests that they all had independent origins. However, those civilizations that were located close to each other, such as Mesopotamia and Egypt, soon came into contact as their respective rulers explored the land around them. Each civilization sought to learn as much as possible about the present or potential resources to be found in its neighbours' territories.

we are looking for. It is a little like the problem of pinning down in time the first human beings. There is a shaded area in which we know the change occurs, but we can still disagree about the point at which a line has been crossed. All over the Near East around 5000 BCE farming villages provided the agricultural surpluses on which civilization could eventually be raised. Some of them have left behind evidence of complex religious practice and elaborate painted pottery, one of the most widespread forms of art in the Neolithic era. Somewhere about 6000 BCE brick building was going on in Turkey at Çatal Hüyük, a

site only slightly younger than Jericho. But by civilization we usually mean something more than ritual, art or the presence of a certain technology, and certainly something more than the mere agglomeration of human beings in the same place.

WHAT IS CIVILIZATION?

Defining civilization is a little like speaking of "an educated man": everyone can recognize one when they see him, but not all educated men are recognized as such by all observers,

A page from the papyrus Book of the Dead of the ancient Egyptian scribe Ani. The larger figures represent the deceased and his wife.

Time chart (3500 BCE–c.1000 BCE)

	3100 BCE Egyptian civilization appears		Minoan civilization in Crete		Mesoamerican civilizations	
3500 BCE	3000 BCE	2500 BCE		2000 BCE	1500 BCE	
First recognizable civilization in Mesopotamia			Appearance of the first civilization in India		First Chinese civilization	

nor is a formal qualification (a university degree, for example) either a necessary or infallible indicator. Dictionary definitions are of no help in pinning down "civilization", either. That of the *Oxford English Dictionary* is indisputable but so cautious as to be useless: "a developed or advanced state of human society". What we have still to decide about is how far developed or advanced and along what lines.

Some have said that a civilized society is different from an uncivilized society because it has a certain attribute – writing, cities, monumental building have all been suggested.

But agreement is difficult and it seems safer not to rely on any such single test. If, instead, we look at examples of what everyone has agreed to call civilizations and not at the marginal and doubtful cases, then it is obvious that what they have in common is complexity. They have all reached a level of elaboration which allows much more variety of human action and experience than even a well-off primitive community. Civilization is the name we give to the interaction of human beings in a very creative way, when a critical mass of cultural potential and a certain surplus of resources have been built up. In civilization this releases human capacities for development at quite a new level and in large measure the development which follows is self-sustaining.

This earthenware female figurine with a reptile head was found in Ur in Mesopotamia and dates from the 5th millennium BCE.

EARLY CIVILIZATIONS

SOMEWHERE ABOUT 3500 BCE is the starting-point of the story of civilizations and it will be helpful to set out a rough overall chronology right at the start. We begin with the first recognizable civilization in Mesopotamia. The next example is in Egypt, where civilization is observable at a slightly later date, perhaps about 3100 BCE. Another marker in the Near East is Minoan civilization in Crete, appearing about 2000 BCE, and from that time we can disregard questions of priorities in this part of the world: it is already a complex of civilizations in interplay with one another. Meanwhile, by that time, and perhaps about 2500 BCE, another civilization has appeared in India and it is at least in a measure literate. China's first civilization starts later, towards the middle of the second millennium BCE. Later still come the Mesoamericans. Once we are past about 1500 BCE, though, only this last example is sufficiently isolated for interaction not to be a big part of explaining what happens. From that time, there are no civilizations to be explained which appear without the stimulus, shock or inheritance provided by others which have appeared earlier. For the moment, then, our preliminary sketch is complete enough at this point.

About these first civilizations (whose appearance and shaping is the subject matter of the next few chapters) it is very difficult to generalize.

Of course they all show a low level of technological achievement, even if it is astonishingly high by comparison with that of their uncivilized predecessors. To this extent their shape and development were still determined much more than those of our own civilization by their setting. Yet they had begun to nibble at the restraints of geography. The topography of the world was already much as it is today; the continents were settled in the forms they now have and the barriers and channels to communication they supplied were to be constants, but there was a growing technological ability to exploit and transcend them. The currents of wind and water which directed early maritime travel have not changed, and even in the second millennium BCE human beings were learning to use them and to escape from their determining force.

This suggests, correctly, that at a very early date the possibilities of human interchange were very considerable and this makes it very unwise to dogmatize about civilization appearing in any standard way in different places. Arguments have been put forward about favourable environments, river valleys for example: obviously, their rich and easily cultivated soils could support fairly dense populations of farmers in villages which would then grow to form the first cities. This was decisive in Mesopotamia, Egypt, the Indus valley and China. But cities and civilizations have also arisen away from river valleys, in Mesoamerica, Minoan Crete and,

The city of Tiahuanaco, located on the shores of Lake Titicaca in Peru, is one of the most impressive cities erected by the ancient Andean civilizations. The city's heyday lasted from 500 to 1000 CE and its monumental ruins, such as this monolithic statue, are still standing today.

later, in Greece. With the last two, there is the strong likelihood of important influence from the outside, but Egypt and the Indus valley, too, were in touch with Mesopotamia at a very early date in their evolution. Evidence of such contact led at one time to the view put forward a few years ago that we should look for one central source of civilization from which all others came. This is not now very popular. There is not only the awkward case of civilization in the isolated Americas to deal with, but great difficulty in getting the time-table of the supposed diffusion right as more and more knowledge of early chronology is acquired by the techniques of radio-carbon dating.

The Shang Dynasty, which appeared in the Yellow River valley in the 18th century BCE, gives its name to the first stage of Chinese civilization. Its important archaeological legacy includes bronze objects, such as this receptacle decorated with images of human faces.

DETERMINING FACTORS

The most satisfactory theory appears to be that civilization was likely always to result from the coming together of a number of factors predisposing a particular area to throw up something dense enough to be recognized later as civilization, but that different environments, different influences from outside and different cultural inheritances from the past mean that humanity did not move in all parts of the world at the same pace or even towards the same goals. The idea of a standard pattern of social "evolution" was discredited even before the idea of "diffusion" from a common civilizing source. Clearly, a favourable geographical setting was essential; in the first civilizations everything

rested on the existence of an agricultural surplus. But another factor was just as important – the capacity of the peoples on the spot to take advantage of an environment or rise to a challenge, and here external contacts may be as important as tradition. China seems at first sight almost insulated from the outside, but even there possibilities of contact existed. The way in which different societies generate the critical mass of elements necessary to civilization therefore remains very hard to pin down.

It is easier to say something generally true about the marks of early civilization than about the way it happened. Again, no absolute and universal statements are plausible. Civilizations have existed without writing, useful as it is for storing and using experience. More mechanical skills have been

Early systems of writing

Almost all early civilizations developed their own systems of writing, whose marked differences make the possibility of a common origin unlikely. The following examples are illustrated: (1) a 4,300-year-old inscription on a small stamp from Mohenjo Daro, in the undeciphered writing of the Indus valley civilization; (2) a 4,000-year-old Sumerian philosophical text on an earthenware tablet in cuneiform writing; (3) an example of Egyptian hieroglyphs from the temple of the pharaoh Mentuhotep II, in Deir el-Bahari, dating from the same period.

This oracle was engraved on a turtle's shell 3,300 years ago during the Shang period in ancient China.

very unevenly distributed, too: the Mesoamericans carried out major building operations with neither draught animals nor the wheel, and the Chinese could cast iron nearly fifteen hundred years before Europeans. Nor have all civilizations followed the same patterns of growth; there are wide disparities between their staying-power, let alone their successes.

URBANIZATION

Early civilizations, like later ones, seem to have a common positive characteristic in that they change the human scale of things. They bring together the cooperative efforts of more men and women than in earlier societies and usually do this by physically bringing them together in larger agglomerations, too. Our word "civilization" suggests, in its Latin roots, a connexion with urbanization. Admittedly, it would be a bold man or woman who was willing to draw a precise line at the moment when the balance tipped from a dense pattern of agricultural villages

clustered around a religious centre or a market to reveal the first true city. Yet it is perfectly reasonable to say that more than any other institution the city has provided the critical mass which produces civilization and that it has fostered innovation better than any other environment so far. Inside the city the surpluses of wealth produced by agriculture made possible other things characteristic of civilized life. They provided for the upkeep of a priestly class which elaborated a complex religious structure, leading to the construction of great buildings with more than merely economic functions, and eventually to the writing down of literature. Much bigger resources than in earlier times were thus allocated to something other than immediate consumption and this meant a storing of enterprise and experience in new forms. The accumulated culture gradually became a more and more effective instrument for changing the world.

CULTURAL DIFFERENCES

One of the changes resulting from the birth of civilization is quickly apparent: in different parts of the world human beings grew more rapidly more unlike one another. The most obvious fact about early civilizations is that they are startlingly different in style, but because it is so obvious we usually overlook it. The coming of civilization opens an era of ever more rapid differentiation – of dress, architecture, technology, behaviour, social forms and thought. The roots of this obviously lie in prehistory, when there already existed peoples with different life-styles, different patterns of existence, different mentalities, as well as different physical characteristics. With the emergence of the first civilizations this becomes much more obvious, but is no longer merely the product of the natural endowment of environment, but of the creative power of civilization itself. Only with the rise to dominance of Western technology in the twentieth century has this variety begun to diminish. From the first civilizations to our own day there have always been alternative models of society available even if they knew little of one another.

Much of this variety is very hard to recover. All that we can do in some instances is to be aware that it is there. At the beginning there is still little evidence about the life of the mind except institutions so far as we can recover them, symbols in art and ideas embodied in literature. In them lie presuppositions which are the great coordinates around which a view of the world is built – even when the people holding that view do not know they are there (history is often the discovery of what people did not know about themselves). Many of them are irrecoverable, and even when we can begin to grasp the

shapes which defined the world of the people living in the old civilizations, a constant effort of imagination must be made to avoid the danger of falling into anachronism which surrounds us on every side. Even literacy does not reveal very much of the minds of creatures who were so like and yet so unlike ourselves.

THE NEAR EAST

IT IS IN THE NEAR EAST that the stimulating effects of different cultures upon one another first become obvious and no doubt it is much of the story of the appearance of the earliest civilizations there. A turmoil of racial comings and goings for three or four thousand years both enriched and disrupted this area, where our history must begin. The Fertile Crescent was to be for most of historic times a great crucible of cultures, a zone not

---

The Fertile Crescent: birthplace of civilization

The oldest civilizations appeared more than 5,000 years ago in a region known as the Fertile Crescent. This consists of a succession of fertile, arable plains that spread out in the shape of a crescent moon from the mouth of the Tigris and Euphrates rivers to the mouth of the Nile, through Mesopotamia, Syria, Palestine and Egypt. To the north and the east of the Fertile Crescent lie mountainous areas. To the south and west lie the vast deserts of Arabia and Libya.

The northern part of the Fertile Crescent.

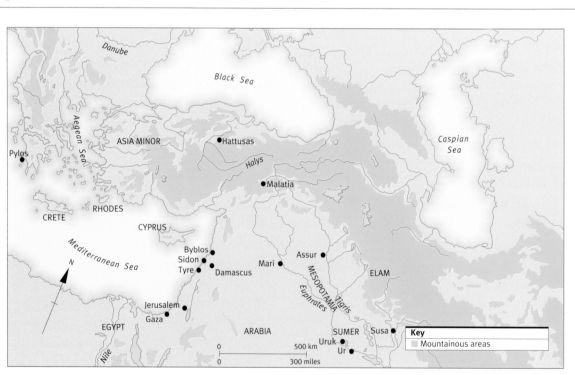

Key
Mountainous areas

only of settlement but of transit, through which poured an ebb and flow of people and ideas. In the end this produced a fertile interchange of institutions, language and belief from which stems much of human thought and custom even today.

THE EFFECTS OF OVER-POPULATION

Why so many people came to the Fertile Crescent cannot exactly be explained, but the overwhelming presumption must be that the root cause was over-population in the lands from which the intruders came. At first sight over-population is a curious notion to apply to a world whose total population in about 4000 BCE has been estimated only at between eighty and ninety millions. In the next four thousand years it grew by about fifty per cent to about one hundred and thirty millions; this implies an annual increase almost imperceptible by comparison with those we take for granted. It shows both the relative slowness with which our species added to its power and how much and how soon the new possibilities of civilization had already reinforced the human propensity to multiply and prosper

T his earthenware figurine, found at Mohenjo-Daro, may represent a mother goddess. It was produced by people of the Indus valley civilization.

by comparison with prehistoric times.

Such growth was still slight by later standards because it was always based on a very fragile margin of resources and it is this fragility which justifies talk of over-population. Drought or desiccation could dramatically and suddenly destroy an area's capacity to feed itself and it was to be thousands of years before food could easily be brought from elsewhere. The immediate results must often have been famine, but in the longer run there were others more important. The disturbances which resulted were the prime movers of early history; climatic change was still at work as a determinant, though now in much more local and specific ways. Droughts, catastrophic storms, even a few decades of marginally lower or higher temperatures, could force peoples to get on the move and so help to bring on civilization by throwing together peoples of different tradition. In collision and cooperation they learnt from one another and so increased the total potential of their societies.

NEAR EASTERN PEOPLES

The peoples who are the actors of early history in the Near East all belonged to the light-skinned human family (sometimes confusingly termed Caucasian) which is one of the three major ethnic classifications of the species *Homo sapiens* (the others being Negroid and

T his is an illustration of an ivory handle from Yebel el-Arak, in northern Egypt. Made around 3400 BCE, the handle clearly shows the Mesopotamian influence on the Nile valley. It depicts battles on land and sea; the ships at the base of the handle appear to be Egyptian in origin, while those shown in the centre are thought to be Mesopotamian.

Mongoloid). Linguistic differences make it possible to distinguish them further. All the peoples in the Fertile Crescent of early civilized times can be assigned either to the Hamitic stocks who evolved in Africa north and north-east of the Sahara, to the Semites of the Arabian peninsula, to the Indo-Europeans who, from southern Russia, had spread also by 4000 BCE into Europe and Iran, or to the true "Caucasians" of Georgia. These are the *dramatis personae* of early Near Eastern history. Their historic centres all lay round the zone in which agriculture and civilization appear at an early date. The wealth of as well-settled an area must have attracted peripheral peoples.

THE MOVEMENT OF PEOPLES IN THE NEAR EAST

By about 4000 BCE most of the Fertile Crescent was occupied by Caucasians. Probably Semitic peoples had already begun to penetrate it by then, too; their pressure grew until by the middle of the third millennium BCE (long after the appearance of civilization) they would be well established in central Mesopotamia, across the middle sections of the Tigris and Euphrates. The interplay and rivalry of the Semitic peoples with the Caucasians, who were able to hang on to the higher lands which enclosed Mesopotamia from the north-east, is one continuing theme scholars have discerned in the early history of the area. By 2000 BCE the peoples whose languages form part of what is called the Indo-European group have also entered on the scene, and from two directions. One of these peoples, the Hittites, pushed into Anatolia from Europe, while their advance was matched from the east by that of the Iranians. Between 2000 BCE and 1500 BCE branches of these sub-units dispute and mingle with the Semitic and Caucasian peoples in the Crescent itself, while the contacts of the Hamites and Semites lie behind much of the political history of old Egypt. This scenario is, of course, highly impressionistic. Its value is only that it helps to indicate the basic dynamism and rhythms of the history of the ancient Near East. Much of its detail is still highly uncertain (as will appear) and little can be said about what maintained this fluidity. None the less, whatever its cause, this wandering of peoples was the background against which the first civilization appeared and prospered.

This colossal statue of Ramses II with a princess at his feet was placed in the temple of Karnak 33 centuries ago. The statue still stands, but the inscription bearing the name of Ramses II has been replaced by that of another Egyptian pharaoh.

2 *ANCIENT MESOPOTAMIA*

THE BEST CASE for the first appearance of something which is recognizably civilization has been made for the southern part of Mesopotamia, the seven-hundred-mile-long land formed by the two river valleys of the Tigris and Euphrates. This end of the Fertile Crescent was thickly studded with farming villages in Neolithic times. Some of the oldest settlements of all seem to have been in the extreme south, where deposits from centuries of drainage from up-country and annual floodings had built up a soil of great richness. It must always have been much easier to grow crops there than elsewhere provided that the water supply could be made continuously and safely available; this was possible, for though rain was slight and irregular, the river bed was often above the level of the surrounding plain. A calculation has been made that in about 2500

BCE the yield of grain in southern Mesopotamia compared favourably with that of the best Canadian wheat-fields today. Here, at an early date, was the possibility of growing more than was needed for daily consumption, the surplus indispensable to the appearance of town life. Furthermore, fish could be taken from the nearby sea.

IRRIGATION AND RECLAMATION

The setting of southern Mesopotamia was a challenge, as well as an opportunity. The Tigris and Euphrates could suddenly and violently change their beds: the marshy, low-lying land of the delta had to be raised above flood level by banking and ditching and canals had to be built to carry water away. Thousands of years later, techniques could still be seen in use in Mesopotamia which were probably those first employed to form the platforms of reed and mud on which were built the first homesteads of the area. These patches of cultivation would be grouped where the soil was richest. The drains and irrigation channels they needed could be managed properly only if they were managed collectively. No doubt the social organization of reclamation was another result. However it happened, the seemingly unprecedented achievement of making land from watery marsh must have been the forcing house of a new complexity in the way human beings lived together.

This alabaster vase, dating from c.3000 BCE, was found in Uruk and depicts an offering ceremony to the goddess Inanna. The scene may be a reference to a sacred wedding during which the priest, representing the god Dumuzi, was united with the priestess, representing Inanna, in order to renew the fertility of the land.

An illustration of a Sumerian stamp from Uruk depicting a boat. Shipping played an important role in ancient Sumer, now southern Iraq.

COLLECTIVE ORGANIZATION

As the number of Mesopotamians increased, more land was taken to grow food. Sooner or later men of different villages would have come face to face with others intent on reclaiming marsh which had previously separated them from one another. Different irrigation needs may even have brought them into contact before this. There was a choice: to fight or to cooperate. Each meant further collective organization and a new agglomeration of power. Somewhere along this path it made sense for people to band together in bigger units than hitherto for self-protection or management of the environment. One physical result is the town, mud-walled at first to keep out floods and enemies, raised above the waters on a platform. It was logical for the local deity's shrine to be the place chosen: he stood behind the community's authority. It would be exercised by his chief priest, who became the ruler of a little theocracy competing with others.

Something like this explains the difference between southern Mesopotamia in the third and fourth millennia BCE and the other zones of Neolithic culture with which by then it had already long been in contact. There is plenty of evidence in the existence of pottery and characteristic shrines of links between Mesopotamia and the Neolithic cultures of Anatolia, Assyria and Iran. They all

Towering above the ruins of the city of Uruk are the remains of one of the oldest ziggurats (stepped temples) of Mesopotamia. The ziggurat was built in the 21st century BCE by Ur Nammu, King of Ur, in honour of Inanna, the goddess of fertility.

had much in common. But only in one relatively small area did a pattern of village life common to much of the Near East begin to grow faster and harden into something else. From that background emerges the first true urbanism, that of Sumer, and the first observable civilization.

THE SUMERIAN CIVILIZATION

SUMER IS AN ANCIENT NAME for southern Mesopotamia, which then extended about a hundred miles less to the south than it does

now. The people who lived there may have been Caucasians, unlike their Semitic neighbours to the south-west and like their northern neighbours the Elamites who lived on the other side of the Tigris. Scholars are still divided about when the Sumerians – that is, those who spoke the language later called Sumerian – arrived in the area: they may have been there since about 4000 BCE. But since we know the population of civilized Sumer to be a mixture of races, perhaps including the earlier inhabitants of the region, with a culture which mixed foreign and local elements, it does not much matter.

Time chart (3300 BCE–1154 BCE)

		2700 BCE Gilgamesh is King of Uruk		1700 BCE Beginning of the Hittite Empire	1415–1154 BCE Kassite domination of Babylonia
4000 BCE		3000 BCE		2000 BCE	1000 BCE
	3300 BCE Sumerian civilization appears		2400 BCE Empire of Sargon of Akkadia		1792–1750 BCE Hammurabi is King of Babylonia

EARLY CULT CENTRES

Sumerian civilization had deep roots. The people long shared a way of life not very different from that of their neighbours. They lived in villages and had a few important cult centres which were continuously occupied. One of these, at a place called Eridu, probably originated in about 5000 BCE.

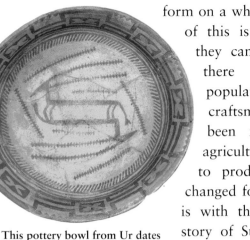

This pottery bowl from Ur dates from the 5th century BCE.

It grew steadily well into historic times and by the middle of the fourth millennium there was a temple there which some have thought to have provided the original model for Mesopotamian monumental architecture, though nothing is now left of it but the platform on which it rested. Such cult centres began by serving those who lived near them. They were not true cities, but places of devotion and pilgrimage. They may have had no considerable resident populations, but they were usually the centres around which cities later crystallized and this helps to explain the close relationship religion and government always had in ancient Mesopotamia. Well before 3000 BCE some such sites had very big temples indeed; at Uruk (which is called Erech in the Bible) there was an especially splendid one, with elaborate decoration and impressive pillars of mud brick, eight feet in diameter.

Pottery is among the most important evidence linking pre-civilized Mesopotamia with historic times. It provides one of the first clues that something culturally important is going forward which is qualitatively different from the evolutions of the Neolithic. The so-called Uruk pots (the name is derived from the site where they were found) are often duller, less exciting than earlier ones. They are, in fact, mass-produced, made in standard form on a wheel. The implication of this is strong that when they came to be produced there already existed a population of specialized craftsmen; it must have been maintained by an agriculture sufficiently rich to produce a surplus exchanged for their creations. It is with this change that the story of Sumerian civilization can conveniently be begun.

THE INVENTION OF CUNEIFORM

THE SUMERIAN CIVILIZATION lasts about thirteen hundred years (roughly from 3300 to 2000 BCE), which is approximately as much time as separates us from the age of Charlemagne. At the beginning comes the invention of writing, possibly the only invention of comparable importance to the invention of agriculture before the age of

The most important of the early Sumerian cities was Ur, home of the legendary hero Gilgamesh. Excavations have revealed the remains of enormous constructions that are more than 5,000 years old. These pillars, decorated with mosaics, were found in the sanctuary of the goddess Inanna and have been reconstructed at the Berlin Museum.

The origins of writing

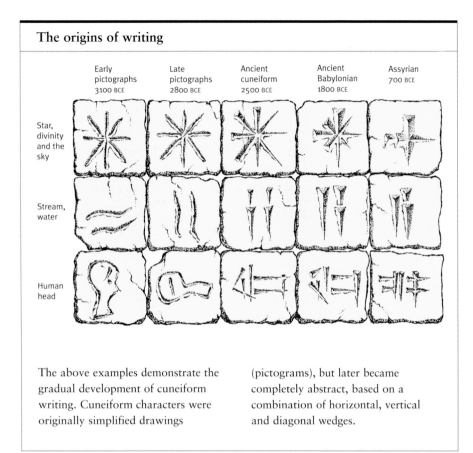

	Early pictographs 3100 BCE	Late pictographs 2800 BCE	Ancient cuneiform 2500 BCE	Ancient Babylonian 1800 BCE	Assyrian 700 BCE
Star, divinity and the sky					
Stream, water					
Human head					

The above examples demonstrate the gradual development of cuneiform writing. Cuneiform characters were originally simplified drawings (pictograms), but later became completely abstract, based on a combination of horizontal, vertical and diagonal wedges.

steam. Writing had been preceded by the invention of cylinder seals, on which little pictures were incised to be rolled on to clay; pottery may have degenerated, but these seals were one of the great Mesopotamian artistic achievements. The earliest writings are in the form of pictograms or simplified pictures (a step towards non-representative communication), on clay tablets usually baked after they had been inscribed with a reed stalk. The earliest are in Sumerian and it can be seen that they are memoranda, lists of goods, receipts; their emphasis is economic and they cannot be read as continuous prose. The writing on these early notebooks and ledgers evolved slowly towards cuneiform, a way of arranging impressions stamped on clay by the wedge-like section of a chopped-off reed. With this the break with the pictogram form is complete. Signs and groups of signs come at this stage to stand for phonetic and possibly

syllabic elements and are all made up of combinations of the same basic wedge shape. It was more flexible as a form of communication by signs than anything used hitherto and Sumer reached it soon after 3000 BCE.

HOW WRITING WAS USED

A fair amount is known about the Sumerian language. A few of its words have survived to this day; one of them is the original form of the word "alcohol", which is suggestive. But its greatest interest is its appearance in written forms. Literacy must have been both unsettling and stabilizing. On the one hand it offered huge new possibilities of communicating; on the other it stabilized practice because the consultation of records became possible. It made much easier the complex operations of irrigating lands, harvesting and storing crops, which were fundamental to a growing society. Writing made for more efficient exploitation of resources. It also immensely strengthened government and emphasized its links with the priestly castes who at first monopolized literacy. Interestingly, one of the earliest uses of seals appears to be connected with this, since they were used somehow to certify the size of crops at their receipt in the temple. Perhaps they record at first the operations of an economy of centralized redistribution, where people brought their due produce to the temple and received there the food or materials they themselves needed.

THE EPIC OF GILGAMESH

The invention of writing opens more of the past to historians. Not only can they study administrative records, but they can at last begin to deal in hard currency when talking about mentality because writing preserves literature. The oldest story in the world is the Epic of Gilgamesh. Its most complete version, it is true, goes back only to the seventh century BCE, but the tale itself appears in Sumerian times and is known to have been written down soon after 2000 BCE.

Gilgamesh was a real person, ruling at Uruk. He became also the first individual and hero in world literature, appearing in other poems, too. He is the first person whose name must appear in this book. To a modern reader the most striking part of the Epic is the coming of a great flood which obliterates humankind except for a favoured family who survive by building an ark; from them springs a new race to people the world after the flood has subsided. This was not part of the Epic's oldest versions, but a separate poem telling a story which turns up in many Near Eastern forms, though its incorporation is easily understandable. Lower Mesopotamia must always have had much trouble with flooding which would undoubtedly put a heavy strain on the fragile system of irrigation on which its prosperity depended. Floods were the type, perhaps, of general disaster, and must have helped to foster the pessimistic fatalism which some scholars have seen as the key to Sumerian religion.

This sombre mood dominates the Epic. Gilgamesh does great things in his restless search to assert himself against the iron laws of the gods which ensure human failure, but they triumph in the end. Gilgamesh, too, must die:

The image on this stamp depicts Gilgamesh overpowering a buffalo.

The heroes, the wise men, like the new moon have their waxing and waning. Men will say, "Who has ever ruled with might and with power like him?" As in the dark month, the month of shadows, so without him there is no light. O Gilgamesh, this was the meaning of your dream. You were given the kingship,

The legend of Gilgamesh

The Epic of Gilgamesh consists of a series of mythical verses concerning the Sumerian hero Gilgamesh, King of Uruk, who lived around 2700 BCE. The verses were written down on early earthenware tablets and were eventually collated to form a complete story.

According to the legend, Gilgamesh ruled in the city of Uruk more than 4,000 years ago. As time passed he became a tyrant and his subjects appealed to the gods to keep him in check. The gods created Enkidu, the wild man of the woods, to confront the king. Hearing of Enkidu's existence, Gilgamesh sent a prostitute out to tempt the wild man into the city. In the city, Enkidu and Gilgamesh began to fight but eventually became friends. They decided to combine their strengths to combat the dragon of the woods. The goddess Ishtar, who was infatuated with Gilgamesh, was very jealous of his friendship with Enkidu. Gilgamesh, however, rejected Ishtar, and Enkidu even reproached the goddess for her whimsical nature. Ishtar and the gods could not

forgive Enkidu for this insult and killed him. Gilgamesh was stunned – he had lost his friend and he had been made aware of human mortality. He decided to search for the fountain of eternal youth and set off to find Utnapishtim, the sole survivor of the Great Flood. On his journey, Gilgamesh met Sidri. She asked him, "Why are you searching for the fountain of eternal youth? The gods say that the fate of men is to die ... enjoy your days and nights, because that too is man's fate."

Gilgamesh continued his journey until he found Utnapishtim, but came to realize that immortality was impossible. Gilgamesh then returned to his city and resigned himself to the inevitability of death.

This 8th-century BCE Assyrian bas-relief from Jorabad shows Gilgamesh wrestling with a lion.

These images of men in prayer (see above and right) are typical of much Sumerian statuary. Most such figurines were made between 3000 and 2500 BCE and are shown wearing Sumerian sheepskin skirts.

such was your destiny; everlasting life was not your destiny.

Apart from this mood and its revelation of the religious temperament of a civilization, there is much information about the gods of ancient Mesopotamia in the Epic. But it is hard to get at history through it, let alone relate it to the historical Gilgamesh. In particular, attempts to identify a single, cataclysmic flood by archaeological means have not been convincing, though plentiful evidence of recurrent flooding is available. From the water eventually emerges the land: perhaps, then, what we are being given is an account of the creation of the world, of genesis. In the Hebrew Bible earth emerges from the waters at God's will and this account was the one which was to satisfy most educated Europeans for a thousand years.

It is fascinating to speculate that we may owe so much of our own intellectual ancestry to a mythical reconstruction by the Sumerians of their own prehistory when farming land had been created out of the morass of the Mesopotamian delta. But it is only speculation; caution suggests we remain satisfied merely to note the undeniable close parallels between the Epic and one of the best of the Bible stories, that of Noah's Ark.

THE DIFFUSION OF THE EPIC

The story of Gilgamesh hints at the possible importance of the diffusion of Sumerian ideas in the Near East long after the focus of its history had moved away to upper Mesopotamia. Versions and parts of the Epic – to stick to that text alone for a moment – have turned up in the archives and relics of many peoples who dominated parts of this region in the second millennium BCE. Though later to be lost to sight until rediscovery in modern times, Gilgamesh was for two thousand years or so a name to which literature in many languages could knowingly refer, somewhat in the way, say, that European authors until recently could take it for granted that an allusion to classical Greece would be understood by their readers. The Sumerian language lived on for centuries in temples and scribal schools, much as Latin lived on for the learned in the muddle of vernacular cultures in Europe after the collapse of the western classical world of Rome. The comparison is suggestive, because literary and linguistic tradition embodies ideas and images which impose, permit and limit different ways of seeing the world; they have, that is to say, their own historic weight.

SUMERIAN RELIGION

PROBABLY THE MOST important ideas kept alive by the Sumerian language were religious. Cities like Ur and Uruk were the seedbed of ideas which, after transmutation into other religions in the Near East during the first and second millennia BCE, were four thousand years later to be influential world-wide, albeit in almost unrecognizably different forms. There is, for example, in the Gilgamesh Epic an ideal creature of nature, the man Enkidu; his Fall from his innocence is sexual, a seduction by a harlot, and thereafter, though the outcome for him is civilization, he loses his happy association with the natural world. Literature makes it possible to observe such hints at the mythologies of other and later societies. In literature, the writers begin to make explicit the meanings earlier hidden in obscure relics of sacrificial offerings, clay figures and the ground plans of shrines and temples. In earliest Sumer these already reveal an organization of human discourse with the supernatural much more complex and elaborate than anything elsewhere at so early a date. Temples had been the focus of the early cities and they grew bigger and more splendid (in part, because of a tradition of building new ones on mounds enclosing their

predecessors). Sacrifices were offered in them to ensure good crops. Later their cults elaborated, temples of still greater magnificence were built as far north as Assur, three hundred miles away up the Tigris, and we hear of one built with cedars brought from the Lebanon and copper from Anatolia.

No other ancient society at that time gave religion quite so prominent a place or diverted so much of its collective resources to its support. It has been suggested that this was because no other ancient society left humans feeling so utterly dependent on the will of the gods. Lower Mesopotamia in ancient times was a flat, monotonous landscape of mudflats, marsh, water. There were no mountains for the gods to dwell in, only

The biblical myth of the Tower of Babel is probably based on the terraced temples of Mesopotamia, the ziggurats. The Dur-Kurigalzu ziggurat, pictured below, was built for a Kassite king in the 14th century BCE. Early explorers mistook it for the ruins of the Tower of Babel.

This statue, called the Goddess of the Flowing Cup, was found at Mari. It represents a goddess of fertility, who was believed to provide the fields with water.

the empty heavens above, the remorseless summer sun, the overturning winds against which there was no protection, the irresistible power of flood-water, the blighting attacks of drought. The gods dwelt in these elemental forces, or in the "high places" which alone dominated the plains, the brick-built towers and ziggurats remembered in the biblical Tower of Babel. The Sumerians, not surprisingly, saw themselves as a people created to labour for the gods.

THE SUMERIAN GODS

By about 2250 BCE a pantheon of gods more or less personifying the elements and natural forces had emerged in Sumer. It was to be the backbone of Mesopotamian religion. This is the beginning of theology. Originally, each city had its particular god. Possibly helped by political changes in the relations of the cities, they were in the end organized into a kind of

hierarchy which both reflected and affected people's views of human society. The gods of Mesopotamia in the developed scheme are depicted in human form. To each of them was given a special activity or role; there was a god of the air, another of the water, another of the plough. Ishtar (as she was later known under her Semitic name) was the goddess of love and procreation, but also of war. At the top of the hierarchy were three great male gods, whose roles are not easy to disentangle, Anu, Enlil and Enki. Anu was father of the gods. Enlil was at first the most prominent; he was "Lord Air", without whom nothing could be done. Enki, god of wisdom and of the sweet waters that literally meant life to Sumer, was a teacher and life-giver, who maintained the order Enlil had shaped.

These gods demanded propitiation and submission in elaborate ritual. In return for this and for living a good life they would grant prosperity and length of days, but not more. In the midst of the uncertainties of Mesopotamian life, some feeling that a possible access to protection existed was essential. Human beings depended on the gods for reassurance in a capricious universe. The gods – though no Mesopotamian could have put it in these terms – were the conceptualization of an elementary attempt to control environment, to resist the sudden disasters of flood and dust-storm, to assure the continuation of the cycle of the seasons by the repetition of the great spring festival when the gods were again married and the drama of Creation was re-enacted. After that, the world's existence was assured for another year.

Discovered in the ancient city of Nippur, this relief depicts an offering ceremony being carried out in honour of Enlil, god of earth and air, who is seated on the bottom right. The figure's size symbolizes the god's great importance.

DEATH AND THE AFTERLIFE

One of the great demands which humans later came to make of religion was that it should help them to deal with the inevitable horror of death. The Sumerians and those who inherited their religious ideas can hardly have derived much comfort from their beliefs, in so far as we can apprehend them; they seem to have seen the world of life after death as a gloomy, sad place. It was "The house where they sit in darkness, where dust is their food and clay their meat, they are clothed like birds with wings for garments, over bolt and door lie dust and silence." In it lies the origin of the later notions of Sheol, of Hell. Yet at least one ritual involved virtual suicide, for a Sumerian king and queen of the middle of the third millennium were followed to their tombs by their attendants who were then buried with them, perhaps after taking some soporific drink. This could suggest that the dead were going somewhere where a great retinue and gorgeous jewellery would be as important as on earth.

RELIGION AND POLITICS

There were important political aspects to Sumerian religion. All land belonged ultimately to the gods; the king, probably a king-priest as much as a warrior-leader in origin, was but their vicar. No human tribunal, of course, existed to call him to account. The vicariate also meant the emergence of a priestly class, specialists whose importance justified economic privilege which could permit the cultivation of special skills and knowledge. In this respect, too, Sumer was the origin of a tradition, that of the seers, soothsayers, wise men of the East. They also had charge of the first organized system of education, based on memorizing and copying in the cuneiform script.

SUMERIAN ART

Among the by-products of Sumerian religion were the first true likenesses of human beings in art. In particular at one religious centre,

Ziggurats were erected in many Mesopotamian cities. They consisted of brick platforms, built one on top of the other and linked by stairways, and were crowned by a temple. The first ziggurats were built by Ur Nammu (2112–2095 BCE), founder of the third dynasty of Ur. The above illustration is a reconstruction of the Ur ziggurat, based on its remains.

This plaster statuette, which was found in the Temple of Inanna in Nippur, shows a Sumerian couple in an affectionate pose.

shoulder. The men are often, but not always, clean-shaven. Soldiers wear the same costume and are only distinguishable because they carry weapons and sometimes wear a pointed leather cap. Luxury seems to have consisted in leisure and possessions other than dress, except for jewellery, of which quantities have survived. Its purpose often seems to be the indication of status and it symptomizes a society of growing complexity. There survives, too, a picture of a drinking-party; a group of men sit in armchairs with cups in their hands while a musician entertains them. At such moments Sumer seems less remote.

MARRIAGE

Sumerian marriage had much about it which would have been familiar to later societies. The crux of the matter was the consent of the bride's family. Once arranged to their satisfaction, a new monogamous family unit was established by the marriage which was recorded in a sealed contract. Its head was the patriarchal husband, who presided over both his relatives and his slaves. It is a pattern which was until very recently observable in most parts of the world. Yet there are interesting nuances. Legal and literary evidence suggest that even in early times Sumerian women were less down-trodden than their sisters in many later

Mari, there seems to have been something of a fondness for portraying human figures engaged in ritual acts. Sometimes they are grouped in processions; thus is established one of the great themes of pictorial art. Two others are also prominent: war and the animal world. Some have detected in the early portraiture of the Sumerians a deeper significance. They have seen in them the psychological qualities which made the astonishing achievements of their civilization possible, a drive for pre-eminence and success. This, again, is speculative. What we can also see for the first time in Sumerian art is much of a daily life in earlier times hidden from us. Given the widespread contacts of Sumer and its basic similarity of structure to other, neighbouring peoples, it is not too much to infer that we can begin to see something of life much as it was lived over a large area of the ancient Near East.

Seals, statuary and painting reveal a people often clad in a kind of furry – goatskin or sheep-skin? – skirt, the women sometimes throwing a fold of it over one

A Sumerian statuette portraying a man with a shaved head. He is wearing the long sheep-skin skirt that was typical of Sumerian dress.

Near-Eastern societies. Semitic and non-Semitic traditions may diverge in this. Sumerian stories of their gods suggest a society very conscious of the dangerous and even awe-inspiring power of female sexuality; the Sumerians were the first people to write about passion.

WOMEN IN SUMER

It is not always easy to relate attitudes to institutions, but Sumerian law (whose influence can be traced in post-Sumerian times well past 2000 BCE) gave women important rights. A woman was not a mere chattel; even the slave mother of a free man's children had rights which could be protected at law. Divorce arrangements provided for women as well as men to seek separations and for the equitable treatment of divorced wives. Though a wife's adultery was

This plaster representation of a woman's head was found in Mari next to the Temple of Ishtar.

punishable by death, while a husband's was not, this difference is to be understood in the light of concern over inheritance and property. It was not until long after Sumerian times that Mesopotamian law began to emphasize the importance of virginity and to impose the veil on respectable women. Both were signs of a hardening and more cramping role for them.

TECHNOLOGY

The Sumerians demonstrated great technical inventiveness. Other peoples would owe much to them. It was they who laid the foundations of mathematics, establishing the technique of expressing number by position as well as by sign (as we, for example, can reckon the figure 1 as one, one-tenth, ten or several other values, according to its relation to the decimal point), and they arrived at a

The Standard of Ur, a mosaic made of shell and lapis lazuli and depicting scenes of war and peace, was found in one of the royal tombs. In this detail, the Sumerian army's foot soldiers and charioteers are shown going into battle.

The Ur ziggurat after being partially reconstructed. It was originally built in the 21st century BCE.

The city of Ur (today called Tell al-Muqayyar) was one of the most important cities in Sumer. Because it was located close to what was then the coast, Ur was a major port.

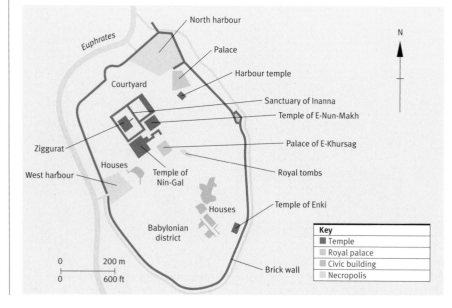

method of dividing the circle into six equal segments. They knew about the decimal system, too, but did not exploit it.

By the end of their history as an independent civilization they had learnt to live in big groups; one city alone is said to have had thirty-six thousand males. This made big demands on building skill, and even more were made by the large monumental structures. Lacking stone, southern Mesopotamians had first built in reeds plastered with mud, then with bricks made from the mud and dried in the sun. Their brick technology was advanced enough by the end of the Sumerian period to make possible very large buildings with columns and terraces; the greatest of its monuments, the Ziggurat of Ur, had an upper stage over a hundred feet high and a base two hundred feet by a hundred and fifty. The earliest surviving potter's wheel was found at Ur; this was the first way in which use was made of rotary motion and on it rested the large scale production of pottery which made it a man's trade and not, like earlier pottery, a woman's. Soon, by 3000 BCE, the wheel was being used for transport. Another invention of the Sumerians was glass, and specialized craftsmen were casting in bronze early in the third millennium BCE.

TRADE

Sumerian innovation raises further questions: where did the raw material come from? There is no metal in southern Mesopotamia.

Moreover, even in earlier times, during the Neolithic, the region must have obtained from elsewhere the flint and obsidian it needed to produce the first agricultural implements. Clearly a widespread network of contacts abroad is in the background, above all with the Levant and Syria, huge distances away, but also with Iran and Bahrein, down the Persian Gulf. Before 2000 BCE Mesopotamia was obtaining goods – though possibly indirectly – from the Indus valley. Together with the evidence of documentation (which reveals contacts with India before 2000 BCE), it makes an impression of a dimly emerging international trading system already creating important patterns of interdependence. When, in the middle of the third millennium, supplies of tin from the Near East dried up, Mesopotamian bronze weapons had to give way to unalloyed copper ones.

AGRICULTURE

The whole economy was sustained on an agriculture which was from an early date complicated as well as rich. Barley, wheat, millet and sesame were grains grown in quantity; the first may have been the main crop, and no doubt explains the frequent evidence of the presence of alcohol in ancient Mesopotamia. In the easy soil of the flood beds iron tools were not needed to achieve intensive cultivation; the great contribution of technology here was in the practice of irrigation and the growth of government. Such skills accumulated slowly; the evidence of Sumerian civilization was left to us by fifteen hundred years of history.

This bull's head, made of gold and lapis lazuli, once adorned a lyre.

MESOPOTAMIAN HISTORY

SO FAR THIS HUGE stretch of time has been discussed almost as if nothing happened during it, as if it were an unchanging whole. Of course it was not. Whatever reservations are made about the slowness of change in the ancient world and though it may now seem to us very static, these were fifteen centuries of great change for the Mesopotamians – history, in the true sense. Scholars have recovered much of the story, but this is not the place to set it out in detail, especially as much of it is still debated, much of it remains obscure and even its dating is for much of the time only approximate. All that is needed here is to relate the first age of Mesopotamian civilization to its successors and to what was going on elsewhere at the same time.

Three broad phases can be marked out in the history of Sumer. The first, lasting from about 3360 BCE to 2400 BCE, has been called its archaic period. Its narrative content is a matter of wars between city states, their waxings and wanings. Fortified cities and the application of the wheel to military technology in clumsy four-wheeled chariots are some of the evidence of this. Towards the middle of this nine-hundred-year phase, local dynasties begin to establish themselves with some success. Originally, Sumerian society seems to have had some representative, even democratic basis, but a growth of scale led to the emergence of kings distinct from the first priestly rulers; probably they began as warlords appointed by cities to command

Many tombs from the 26th and 25th centuries BCE have been unearthed in Ur. Of these, 17 are thought to have been created for royalty because of their elaborate design and precious contents. This statue of a male goat is made from gold, lapis lazuli, silver and shell. It was found in a tomb where a retinue of 74 people were sacrificed to accompany their lord and master in death.

This head, made of cast copper, was found in Nineveh and is thought to represent Naram Sin (2254–2218 BCE), the grandson of Sargon of Akkadia.

their forces who did not give up their power when the emergency which called them forth had passed. From them stemmed dynasties which fought one another. The sudden appearance of a great individual then opens a new phase.

SARGON I

Rimush, the son and heir of Sargon, had his military victories recorded on a stele, of which this is a fragment.

Sargon I was a king of the Semitic city of Akkad who conquered the Sumerian cities between 2400 and 2350 BCE and inaugurated an Akkadian supremacy. There exists a sculpted head which is probably of him; if it is, it is one of the first royal portraits. He was the first of a long line of empire-builders; he has been thought to have sent his troops as far as Egypt and Ethiopia. His rule was not based on the relative superiority of one city state to another; he set up a unified empire integrating the cities into a whole. His people were among those which for thousands of years pressed in on the civilizations of the river valleys from outside. They took over from its

culture what they wanted but imposed themselves by force and left behind a new style of Sumerian art marked by the theme of royal victory.

THE AKKADIAN EMPIRE

The Akkadian empire was not the end of Sumer but its second main phase. Though itself an interlude, it was important as an expression of a new level of organization. By Sargon's time a true state has appeared. The division between secular and religious authority which had appeared in old Sumer was fundamental. Though the supernatural still interpenetrated daily life at every level, lay and priestly authority had diverged. The evidence is physically apparent in the appearance of palaces beside the temples in the Sumerian cities; the authority of the gods lay behind their occupants, too.

Obscure though the turning of the notables of early cities into kings remains, the evolution of professional soldiery probably played a part in it. Disciplined infantry, moving in a phalanx with overlapping shields and levelled spears, appear on monuments from Ur. In Akkadia there is something of a climax to early militarism. Sargon, it was boasted, had 5,400 soldiers eating before him in his palace. This, no doubt, was the end of a process which built power on power; conquest provided the resources to maintain such a force. But the beginnings may again have lain originally in the special challenges and needs of Mesopotamia. As population rose, one chief duty of the ruler must have been to mobilize labour for big works of irrigation and flood control. The power to do this could also provide soldiers and as weapons became more complex and expensive, professionalism

would be more likely. One source of Akkadian success was that they used a new weapon, the composite bow made of strips of wood and horn.

The Akkadian hegemony was relatively short. After two hundred years, under Sargon's great-grandson, it was overthrown, apparently by mountain peoples called Gutians, and the last phase of Sumer, called "neo-Sumerian" by scholars, began. For another two hundred years or so, until 2000 BCE, hegemony again passed to the native Sumerians. This time its centre was Ur and, though it is hard to see what it meant in practice, the first king of the Third Dynasty of Ur who exercised this ascendancy called himself King of Sumer and Akkad. Sumerian art in this phase showed a new tendency to exalt the power of the prince; the tradition of popular portraiture of the archaic period almost vanished. The temples were built again, bigger and better, and the kings seem to have sought to embody their grandeur in the ziggurats. Administrative documents show that the Akkadian legacy was strong, too; neo-Sumerian culture shows many Semitic traits and perhaps the aspiration to wider kingship

reflects this inheritance. The provinces which paid tribute to the last successful kings of Ur stretched from Susa, on the frontiers of Elam on the lower Tigris, to Byblos on the coast of Lebanon.

Prisoners are shown being led naked and bound in this detail from the stele of Sharrumkin, King of Akkadia. Sharrumkin, the Sargon of the Bible, was the founder of the first empire to include all Mesopotamia. He is thought to have reigned during the 24th century BCE.

THE SUMERIAN LEGACY

This was the sunset of the first people to achieve civilization. Of course they did not disappear, but their individuality was about to be merged in the general history of Mesopotamia and the Near East. Their great creative era was behind them and has focused our attention on a relatively small area; the horizons of history are about to expand. Enemies abounded on the frontiers. In about 2000 BCE, the Elamites came and Ur fell to them. Why, we do not know. There had been intermittent hostility between the peoples for a thousand years and some have seen in this the outcome of a struggle to control the routes of Iran which could guarantee access to the highlands where lay minerals the Mesopotamians needed. At all events, it was the end of Ur. With it disappeared the distinctive Sumerian tradition, now merged in the swirling currents of a world of more than one civilization. It would now be only visible from time to time in patterns made by others.

For fifteen centuries or so Sumer had built up the subsoil of civilization in Mesopotamia, just as its precivilized forerunners had built up the physical subsoil on which it itself rested. It left behind writing, monumental buildings, an idea of justice and legalism and the roots of a great religious tradition. It is a considerable record and the seed of much else. The Mesopotamian tradition had a long life ahead of it and every side of it was touched by the Sumerian legacy.

NEW PEOPLES IN THE NEAR EAST

While the Sumerians had been building up their civilization, their influence had contributed to changes elsewhere. All over the Fertile Crescent new kingdoms and peoples had been appearing. They were stimulated or taught by what they saw in the south and by the empire of Ur, as well as by their own needs. The diffusion of civilized ways was already rapid. This makes it very hard to

In the inner courtyard of the grand palace of Mari, fragments of paintings dating from the beginning of the 28th century BCE have been discovered. This section probably represents a sacrificial scene. The gigantic figure – only his arm and the bottom of his clothes can be seen – is thought to be the king.

delineate and categorize the main processes of these centuries in a clear-cut way. Worse still, the Near East was for long periods a great confusion of peoples, moving about for reasons we often do not understand. The Akkadians themselves had been one of them, pushing up originally from the great Semitic reservoir of Arabia to finish in Mesopotamia.

This 19th-century BCE bronze statuette depicts Warad-Sin, sovereign of Larsa, carrying a basket. For centuries this was the traditional style for votive figures, which were buried in the foundations of the temples.

The Gutians, who took part in the Akkadians' overthrow, were Caucasians. The most successful of all of these peoples were the Amorites, a Semitic stock which had spread far and wide and joined the Elamites to overthrow the armies of Ur and destroy its supremacy. They had established themselves in Assyria, or upper Mesopotamia, in Damascus, and in Babylon in a series of kingdoms which stretched as far as the coast of Palestine. Southern Mesopotamia, old Sumer, they continued to dispute with the Elamites. In Anatolia their neighbours were the Hittites, an Indo-European people which crossed from the Balkans in the third millennium. At the edges of this huge confusion stood another old civilization, Egypt, and the vigorous Indo-European peoples who had filled up Iran. The picture is a chaos; the area is a maelstrom of races pushing into it from all sides. Patterns grow hard to distinguish.

THE BABYLONIAN EMPIRE

ONE CONVENIENT LANDMARK is provided by the appearance of a new empire in Mesopotamia, one which has left behind a famous name: Babylon. Another famous name is inseparably linked to it, that of one of its kings, Hammurabi. He would have a secure place in history if we knew nothing of him except his reputation as a law-giver; his code is the oldest statement of the legal principle of an eye for an eye. He was also the first ruler to unify the whole of Mesopotamia, and though the empire was short-lived the city of Babylon was to be from his time the symbolic centre of the Semitic peoples of the

Many statues have been found of Gudea, who was king of Lagash in the 21st century BCE. Gudea ruled during the neo-Sumerian age, which followed the decline of the Akkadian empire.

south. It began with the triumph of one Amorite tribe over its rivals in the confused period following the collapse of Ur. Hammurabi may have become ruler in 1792 BCE; his successors held things together until sometime after 1600 BCE, when the Hittites destroyed Babylon and Mesopotamia was once more divided between rival peoples who flowed into it from all sides.

At its height the first Babylonian empire ran from Sumeria and the Persian Gulf north to Assyria, the upper part of Mesopotamia. Hammurabi ruled the cities of Nineveh and Nimrud on the Tigris, Mari high on the Euphrates, and controlled that river up to the point at which it is nearest to Aleppo. Seven hundred or so miles long and about a hundred miles wide, this was a great state, the greatest, indeed, to appear in the region up to this time, for the empire of Ur had been a looser, tributary affair.

HAMMURABI'S CODE OF LAWS

The empire had an elaborate administrative structure, and Hammurabi's code of laws is justly famous, though it owes something of its pre-eminence to chance. As probably happened to earlier collections of judgements and rules which have only survived in fragments, Hammurabi's was cut in stone and set up in the courtyard of temples for the public to consult. But at greater length and in a more ordered way than earlier collections it assembled some 282 articles, dealing comprehensively with a wide range of questions: wages, divorce, fees for medical attention and many other matters. This was not legislation, but a declaration of existing law, and to speak of a "code" may be misleading unless this is remembered. Hammurabi assembled rules already current; he did not create those laws *de novo*. This body of "common law" provided one of the major continuities of Mesopotamian history.

The family, land and commerce seem to be the main concerns of this compilation of rules. It gives a picture of a society already far beyond regulation by the ties of kindred, local community and the government of village headmen. By Hammurabi's time the judicial process had emerged from the temple and non-priestly courts were the rule. In them sat the local town notables and from them appeals lay to Babylon and the king himself. Hammurabi's stele (the stone pillar on which his code was carved) stated that its aim was to assure justice by publishing the law:

Let the oppressed man who has a cause
Come into the presence of my statue
And read carefully my inscribed stele.

This diorite bust shows a headdress typical of those worn by Mesopotamian kings at the beginning of the 2nd millennium BCE.

The first written laws

The oldest known system of laws was created by King Hammurabi of Babylonia and dates from the 18th century BCE. It is thought that the articles are based on a common law tradition that began during the Sumerian period. The laws were engraved on a monolith that is now kept in the Louvre museum in Paris. Its articles regulate a number of issues, including property, slavery, family, trade, prices and wages, loans and the payment of interest, and crimes and their punishments. At the top of the monolith on which the Laws of Hammurabi are engraved, the King added his own image. He is depicted listening respectfully to Shamash, the god of justice, who is seated on his throne with the attributes of power held in his right hand and flames blazing around his shoulders. Shamash is ordering Hammurabi to carry out his wishes, in much the same way as Moses receives instructions from Yahweh in the Bible.

A detail from the stone monolith on which the Laws of Hammurabi are inscribed.

Sadly, perhaps, its penalties seem to have harshened, by comparison with older Sumerian practice, but in other respects, such as the laws affecting women, Sumerian tradition survived in Babylon.

SLAVERY AND LUXURY

The provisions of Hammurabi's code in respect of property included laws about slaves. Babylon, like every other ancient civilization and many of modern times, rested on slavery. Very possibly the origin of slavery is conquest; certainly slavery was the fate which probably awaited the loser of any of the wars of early history and his women and children, too. But by the time of the first Babylonian empire, regular slave-markets existed and there was a steadiness of price which indicates a fairly regular trade. Slaves from certain districts were especially prized for their reliable qualities. Though the master's hold on the slave was virtually absolute, some Babylonian slaves enjoyed remarkable independence, engaging in business and even owning slaves on their own account. They had legal rights, if narrow ones.

It is hard to assess what slavery meant in practice in a world lacking the assumption which we take for granted that chattel slavery cannot be justified. Generalities dissolve in the light of evidence about the diversity of things slaves might do; if most lived hard lives, then so, probably, did most people who were free. Yet it is hard to feel anything but pity for the lives of captives being led away to slavery before conquering kings on scores of memorials from the "golden standard" of Ur in the middle of the third millennium to the stone reliefs of Assyrian conquests fifteen hundred years later. The ancient world rested civilization on a great exploitation of man by man; if it was not felt to be very cruel, this is only to say that no other possible way of running things was conceivable.

Babylonian civilization in due time became a legend of magnificence. The survival of one of the great images of city life – the worldly, wicked city of pleasure and consumption – in the name "Babylon" was a legacy which speaks of the scale and richness of its civilization, though it owes most to a later period. Yet enough remains, too, to see the reality behind this myth, even for the first Babylonian empire. The great palace of Mari is an outstanding example; walls in places forty feet thick surrounded courtyards, three hundred or so rooms forming a complex drained by bitumen-lined pipes running thirty feet deep. It covered an area measuring 150 by over 200 yards and is the finest evidence of the authority the monarch had come to enjoy. In this palace, too, were found great quantities of clay tablets whose writing reveals the business and detail which government embraces by this period.

CULTURE AND SCIENCE

Many more tablets survive from the first Babylonian empire than from its predecessors or immediate successors. They provide the

The city of Mari (today Tell Hariri, Syria) was founded beside the Euphrates River nearly 5,000 years ago. Mari was deserted after it was sacked by Hammurabi in the 18th century BCE.

positions of the apparently fixed stars. This was a scientific tradition reflected in Babylonian mathematics, which has passed on to us the sexagesimal system of Sumer in our circle of 360 degrees and the hour of sixty minutes. The Babylonians also worked out mathematical tables and an algebraic geometry of great practical utility.

BABYLONIAN RELIGION

Astronomy began in the temple, in the contemplation of celestial movements announcing the advent of festivals of fertility and sowing, and Babylonian religion held close to the Sumerian tradition. Like the old cities, Babylon had a civic god, Marduk; gradually he elbowed his way to the front among his Mesopotamian rivals. This took a

Numerous clay plaques evoke different aspects of life in Mesopotamia almost 4,000 years ago. Here a carpenter is depicted at work.

detail which enables us to know this civilization better, it has been pointed out, than we know some European countries of a thousand years ago. They contribute evidence of the life of the mind in Babylon, too. It was then that the Epic of Gilgamesh took the shape in which we know it. The Babylonians gave cuneiform script a syllabic form, thus enormously increasing its flexibility and usefulness. Their astrology pushed forward the observation of nature and left another myth behind, that of the wisdom of the Chaldeans, a name sometimes misleadingly given to the Babylonians. Hoping to understand their destinies by scanning the stars, the Babylonians built up a science, astronomy, and established an important series of observations which was another major legacy of their culture. It took centuries to accumulate after its beginnings in Ur but by 1000 BCE the prediction of lunar eclipses was possible and within another two or three centuries the path of the sun and some of the planets had been plotted with remarkable accuracy against the

In this clay plaque a musician is shown strumming a harp.

long time. Hammurabi said (signi-
ficantly) that Anu and Enlil, the
Sumerian gods, had conferred the
headship of the Mesopotamian
pantheon upon Marduk, much
as they had bidden him to
rule over all men for their
good. Subsequent vicissitudes
(sometimes accompanied by
the abduction of his statue
by invaders) obscured
Marduk's status, but after
the twelfth century BCE it
was usually unquestioned.
Meanwhile, Sumerian tradition
remained alive well into the first
millennium BCE in the use of
Sumerian in the Babylonian
liturgies, in the names of the
gods and the attributions they
enjoyed. Babylonian cosmogony
began, like that of Sumer, with
the creation of the world from
watery waste (the name of one
god meant "silt") and the
eventual fabrication of humans
as the slaves of the gods. In
one version, gods turned people
out like bricks, from clay
moulds. It was a world picture
suited to absolute monarchy,
where kings exercised power
like that of gods over the slaves
who toiled to build their
palaces and sustained a hierarchy of officials and great
men which mirrored that of
the heavens.

This statue depicts Ishtulilum, who
ruled Mari in the year 2100 BCE.
The expression on his face is
noticeably stern.

THE FALL OF BABYLON

The achievement of Hammurabi did not long
survive him. Events in northern Mesopotamia

indicated the appearance of a new power
even before he formed his empire.
Hammurabi had overthrown an
Amorite kingdom which had established itself in Assyria at the end of
the hegemony of Ur. This was a
temporary success. There followed nearly a thousand years
during which Assyria was to
be a battleground and prize,
eventually overshadowing a
Babylon from which it was
separated; the centre of gravity
of Mesopotamian history had
decisively moved northwards
from old Sumer. The Hittites,
who were establishing themselves in Anatolia in the last
quarter of the third millennium
BCE, were pushing slowly forwards in the next few centuries;
during this time they took
up the cuneiform script, which
they adapted to their own
Indo-European language. By
1700 BCE they ruled the lands
between Syria and the Black
Sea. Then, one of their kings
turned southwards against a
Babylonia already weakened
and shrunken to the old
land of Akkad. His successor
carried the advance to
completion; Babylon was
taken and plundered and
Hammurabi's dynasty and
achievement finally came to
an end. But then the Hittites withdrew and
other peoples ruled and disputed
Mesopotamia for a mysterious four centuries of which we know little except
that during them the separation of Assyria
and Babylonia which was to be so important
in the next millennium was made final.

In 1162 BCE the statue of Marduk was again taken away from Babylon by Elamite conquerors. By that time, a very confused era has opened and the focus of world history has shifted away from Mesopotamia. The story of the Assyrian empire still lies ahead, but its background is a new wave of migrations in the thirteenth and twelfth centuries BCE which involve other civilizations far more directly and deeply than the successors of the Sumerians. Those successors, their conquerors and displacers, none the less built on the foundations laid in Sumer. Technically, intellectually, legally, theologically, the Near East, which by 1000 BCE was sucked into the vortex of world politics – the term is by then not too strong – still bore the stamp of the makers of the first civilization. Their heritage would pass in strangely transmuted forms to others in turn.

Excavations at Ebla, Syria, have revealed temples, palaces and walls dating from 2600 to 1600 BCE. The most important find was that of the palace archives. Thousands of tablets remained intact, having been baked during the fire that destroyed most of the city.

3 ANCIENT EGYPT

ESOPOTAMIA WAS NOT the only great river valley to cradle a civilization, but the only early example to rival it in the antiquity and staying-power of what was created was that of Egypt. For thousands of years after it had died, the physical remains of the first civilization in the Nile valley fascinated people and stirred their imaginations; even the Greeks were bemused by the legend of the occult wisdom of a land where gods were half human, half beast, and people still waste their time trying to discern a supernatural significance in the arrangement of the pyramids. Ancient Egypt has always been our greatest visible inheritance from antiquity.

The palette of King Narmer, found in Hieraconpolis in 1898 CE, dates from 5,000 years ago. At the top of the palette, the king's name appears in hieroglyphics, framed by two humanized cows' heads representing the goddess Hathor. Below this, the king, wearing the crown of Lower Egypt, inspects a battlefield.

MESOPOTAMIAN INFLUENCE

The richness of its remains is one reason why we know more about Egyptian than about much of Mesopotamian history. In another way, too, there is an important difference between these civilizations: because Sumerian civilization appeared first, Egypt could benefit from its experience and example. Exactly what this meant has been much debated. Mesopotamian contributions have been seen in the motifs of early Egyptian art, in the presence of cylinder seals at the outset of Egyptian records, in similar techniques of monumental building in brick and in the debt of hieroglyph, the pictorial writing of Egypt, to early Sumerian script. That there were important and fruitful connexions between early Egypt and Sumer seems incontestable, but how and when the first encounter of the Nile peoples with Sumer came about will probably never be known. It seems at least likely that when it came, Sumerian influence was transmitted by way of the peoples of the delta and lower Nile. In any case, these influences operated in a setting which always radically differentiated Egyptian experience from that of any other centre of civilization. This was provided by the Nile itself, the heart of Egypt's prehistory, as of its history.

THE ROLE OF THE NILE

Egypt was defined by the Nile and the deserts which flanked it; it was the country the river watered, one drawn-out straggling oasis. In prehistoric times it must also have been one great marsh, six hundred miles long, and, except in the delta, never more than a few miles wide. From the start the annual floods of the river were the basic mechanism of the economy and set the rhythm of life on its banks. Farming gradually took root in the beds of mud deposited higher and higher year by year, but the first communities must have been precarious and their environment semi-aquatic; much of their life has been irrecoverably swept away to the delta silt-beds. What remain of the earliest times are things made and used by the peoples who lived on the edge of the flood areas or on occasional rocky projections within it or at the valley sides. Before 4000 BCE they began to feel the impact of an important climatic change. Sand drifted in from the deserts and desiccation set in. Armed with elementary agricultural techniques, these people could move down to work the rich soils of the flood-plain.

The river was, therefore, from the start the bringer of life to Egypt. It was a benevolent deity whose never-failing bounty was to be thankfully received, rather than the dangerous, menacing source of sudden, ruinous

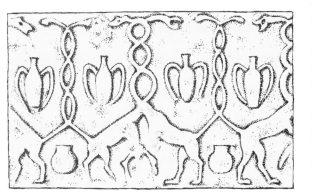

inundations, amid which the people of Sumer struggled to make land out of a watery waste. It was a setting in which agriculture (though it established itself later than in the Levant or Anatolia) gave a quick and rich return and perhaps made possible a population "explosion" which released its human and natural resources. Although, as signs of contact in the fourth millennium BCE show, Sumerian experience may have been available as a fertilizing element, it cannot be said that it was decisive; there always existed a potential for civilization in the Nile valley and it may have needed no external stimulus to discharge it. It is at least obvious, when Egyptian civilization finally emerged, that it is unique, unlike anything we can find elsewhere.

This drawing represents the markings on a Sumerian cylinder. The appearance of similar Mesopotamian subjects on King Narmer's palette indicates Mesopotamia's cultural influence on the early Egyptian civilization.

In the middle of the desert, the Nile valley forms a long and narrow oasis. In ancient Egypt, as there were no bridges over the main section of the river, ferries constantly crossed the water, linking communities on opposite banks. Larger sail and rowing boats travelled north and south, linking Lower and Upper Egypt.

Shallow Egyptian ships, such as the one depicted on this pre-dynastic pottery vase, were powered by oars or by sail, depending on the direction of the journey. Because the wind in Egypt blew consistently from the north, sail could only be used on the Nile to travel southwards.

There are no obstacles to shipping on the Nile from its mouth to what ancient Egyptians called "the first waterfall" (a stretch of cataracts, or rapids, that marked the traditional border between Egypt and Nubia).

THE NEOLITHIC HAMITIC PEOPLES

The deepest roots of this civilization have to be pieced together from archaeology and later tradition. They reveal Hamitic peoples in Upper Egypt (the south, that is, up the Nile) in Neolithic times. From about 5000 BCE such peoples were hunting, fishing, gathering crops and finally embarking on purposeful cultivation in the valley. They lived in villages grouped round market centres and seem to

have belonged to clans which had animals as symbols or totems; these they copied on their pottery. This was the basis of the eventual political organization of Egypt, which began with the emergence of clan chiefs controlling the regions inhabited by their followers.

At an early stage these peoples already had several important technological accomplishments to their credit, though they do not seem such advanced farmers as those of other parts of the ancient Near East. They knew how to make papyrus boats, how to work hard materials such as basalt, and how to hammer copper into small articles for daily use. They were, that is to say, pretty accomplished well before the dawn of written record, with specialist craftsmen and, to judge by their jewels, well-marked distinctions of class or status. Then, somewhere about the middle of the fourth millennium BCE, there is an intensification of foreign influences, apparent first in the north, the delta. Signs of trade and contact with other regions multiply,

notably with Mesopotamia, whose influence is shown in the art of this era. Meanwhile, hunting and occasional farming give way to a more intense cultivation. In art, the bas-relief appears which is to be so important later in the Egyptian tradition; copper goods become more plentiful. Everything seems suddenly to be emerging at once, almost without antecedents, and to this epoch belongs the basic political structure of the future kingdom.

UPPER AND LOWER EGYPT

At some time in the fourth millennium BCE there solidified two kingdoms, one northern, one southern, one of Lower and one of Upper Egypt. This is interestingly different from Sumer; there were no city states. Egypt seems to move straight from pre-civilization to the government of large areas. There was no era of city states. Egypt's early "towns" were the market-places of agriculturalists; the agricultural communities and clans coalesced into groups which were the foundation of later provinces. Egypt was to be a united political whole seven hundred years before Mesopotamia, and even later she would have only a restricted experience of city life.

Of the kings of the two Egypts we know little until about 3200 BCE, but we may guess that they were the eventual winners in centuries of struggles to consolidate power over larger and larger groups of people. It is about the same time that the written record begins and because writing is already there at the beginning of the Egyptian story, a much more historical account of the development of its civilization can be put together than in the case of Sumer. In Egypt writing was used from its first appearance not merely as an administrative and economic convenience but to record events on monuments and relics intended to survive.

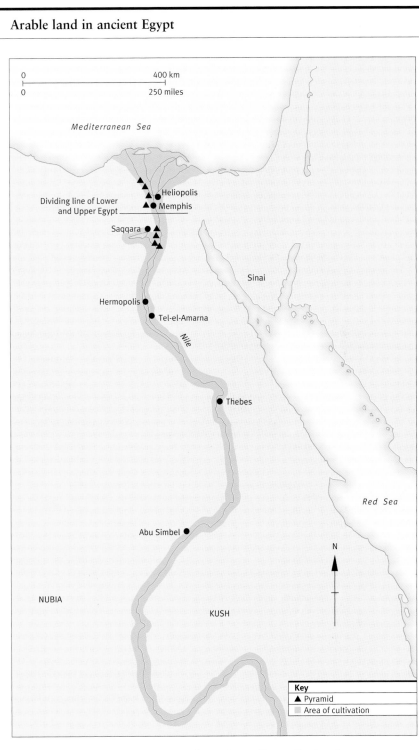

Arable land in ancient Egypt

The above map shows the location of arable land in ancient Egypt. Land that could be cultivated was limited to areas that could be watered from the River Nile – a long narrow strip of land in Upper Egypt and a wide triangular area in the delta region in Lower Egypt. During the summer months, the Nile, swelled by rainwater in the south, swept northwards, flooding the plains. When it receded, it left behind a rich belt of fertile silt, which was capable of sustaining two successive crops each year.

A verse from King
Narmer's palette,
in which the king,
wearing the crown of
Upper Egypt, prepares
to strike down an
enemy. To the right,
the hawk god Horus,
symbol of royalty, holds
a hieroglyph represen-
ting the territory of the
delta. The scene refers
to the battles that
preceded the unification
of Egypt.

UNIFICATION

In about 3200 BCE, the records tell us, a great
king of Upper Egypt, Menes, conquered the
north. Egypt was thus unified in a huge state
six hundred miles long, running up the river
as far as Abu Simbel. It was to be even bigger
and to extend even further up the great river
which was its heart, and it was also to
undergo disruption from time to time, but
this is effectively the beginning of a civilization which was to survive into the age of
classical Greece and Rome. For nearly three
thousand years – one and a half times the life
of Christianity – Egypt was a historical entity,
for much of it a source of wonder and focus
of admiration. In so long a period much
happened and we by no means know all of it.
Yet it is the stability and conservative power
of Egyptian civilization which is the most
striking thing about it, not its vicissitudes.

CHRONOLOGY

Roughly speaking, that civilization's greatest
days were over by about 1000 BCE. Before
that date, Egyptian history can most easily be
visualized in five big divisions. Three of these
are called respectively the Old, Middle and
New Kingdoms; they are separated by two
others called the First and Second
Intermediate periods. Very roughly, the three
"kingdoms" are periods of success or at least
of consolidated government; the two intermediate stages are interludes of weakness and
disruption from external and internal causes.
The whole scheme can be envisaged as a kind
of layer cake, with three tiers of different
flavours separated by two layers of somewhat
formless jam.

This is by no means the only way of
understanding Egyptian history, nor for all
purposes the best. Many scholars use an alternative way of setting out ancient Egyptian
chronology in terms of more than thirty
dynasties of kings, a system which has the
great advantage of being related to objective
criteria; it avoids perfectly proper but awkward disagreements about whether (for
example) the first dynasties should be put in
the "Old Kingdom" or distinguished as a separate "archaic" period, or about the line to be
drawn at the beginning or end of the intermediate era. None the less, a five-part scheme, if
we also distinguish an archaic prelude, is sufficient to make sense of ancient Egyptian
history, as set out in the accompanying table.

In the first millennium BCE, as in
Mesopotamian history, there is something of
a break as Egypt is caught up in a great series
of upheavals originating outside its own
boundaries to which the overworked word
"crisis" can reasonably be applied. True, it is
not until several more centuries have passed
that the old Egyptian tradition really comes
to an end. Some modern Egyptians insist on a

continuing sense of identity among Egyptians since the days of the pharaohs. None the less, somewhere about the beginning of the first millennium BCE is one of the most convenient places at which to break the story, if only because the greatest achievements of the Egyptians were by then behind them.

THE MONARCHICAL STATE

EGYPT'S GREAT ACHIEVEMENTS were above all the work of and centred in the monarchical state. The state form itself was the expression of Egyptian civilization. It was focused first at Memphis whose building was

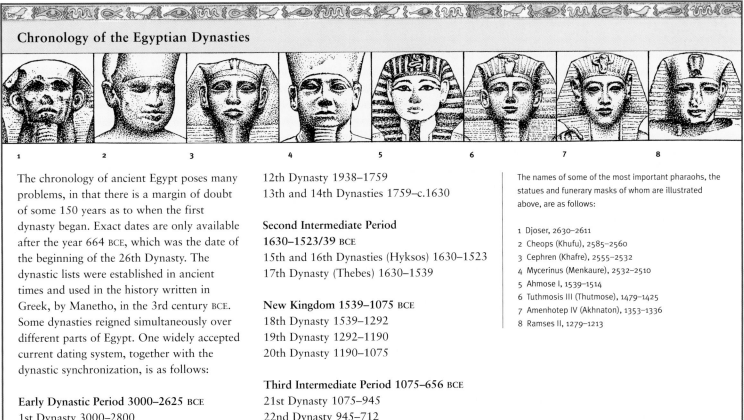

Chronology of the Egyptian Dynasties

The chronology of ancient Egypt poses many problems, in that there is a margin of doubt of some 150 years as to when the first dynasty began. Exact dates are only available after the year 664 BCE, which was the date of the beginning of the 26th Dynasty. The dynastic lists were established in ancient times and used in the history written in Greek, by Manetho, in the 3rd century BCE. Some dynasties reigned simultaneously over different parts of Egypt. One widely accepted current dating system, together with the dynastic synchronization, is as follows:

Early Dynastic Period 3000–2625 BCE
1st Dynasty 3000–2800
2nd Dynasty 2800–2675
3rd Dynasty 2675–2625

Old Kingdom 2625–2130 BCE
4th Dynasty 2625–2500
5th Dynasty 2500–2350
6th Dynasty 2350–2170
7th and 8th Dynasties 2170–2130

First Intermediate Period 2130–1980 BCE
9th and 10th Dynasties (Heracleopolis)
    2130–1980
11th Dynasty (Thebes) 2081–1938

Middle Kingdom 1980–1630 BCE
11th Dynasty (all Egypt) 2040–1991

12th Dynasty 1938–1759
13th and 14th Dynasties 1759–c.1630

**Second Intermediate Period
1630–1523/39** BCE
15th and 16th Dynasties (Hyksos) 1630–1523
17th Dynasty (Thebes) 1630–1539

New Kingdom 1539–1075 BCE
18th Dynasty 1539–1292
19th Dynasty 1292–1190
20th Dynasty 1190–1075

Third Intermediate Period 1075–656 BCE
21st Dynasty 1075–945
22nd Dynasty 945–712
23rd Dynasty 838–712
24th Dynasty (Saïs) 727–712
25th Dynasty (Nubian) 760–756

Late Period 664–332 BCE
26th Dynasty 664–525
27th Dynasty (Persian) 525–405
28th Dynasty 409–399
29th Dynasty 399–380
30th Dynasty 381–343
31st Dynasty (Persian) 343–332

Hellenistic Period 332–30 BCE
32nd Dynasty (Macedonian) 332–305
33rd Dynasty (Ptolemaic) 305–30

The names of some of the most important pharaohs, the statues and funerary masks of whom are illustrated above, are as follows:

1 Djoser, 2630–2611
2 Cheops (Khufu), 2585–2560
3 Cephren (Khafre), 2555–2532
4 Mycerinus (Menkaure), 2532–2510
5 Ahmose I, 1539–1514
6 Tuthmosis III (Thutmose), 1479–1425
7 Amenhotep IV (Akhnaton), 1353–1336
8 Ramses II, 1279–1213

This sculpture was discovered in the temple built for King Mycerinus of the 4th Dynasty. The king is shown with the goddess Hathor on his right and the personification of a province on his left.

begun during the lifetime of Menes and which was the capital of the Old Kingdom. Later, under the New Kingdom, the capital was normally at Thebes, though there were also periods of uncertainty about where it was. Memphis and Thebes were great religious centres and palace complexes; they did not really progress beyond this to true urbanism.

The absence of cities earlier was politically important, too. Egypt's kings had not emerged like Sumer's as the "big men" in a city-state community which originally deputed them to act for it. Nor were they simply men who like others were subject to gods who ruled all men, great or small. The tension of palace with temple was missing in Egypt and when Egyptian kingship emerges it is unrivalled. The pharaohs were to be gods, not servants of gods.

THE PHARAOHS

It was only under the New Kingdom that the title "pharaoh" came to be applied personally to the king. Before that it indicated the king's residence and his court. None the less, at a much earlier stage Egyptian monarchs already had the authority which was so to impress the ancient world. It is expressed in the size with which they are depicted on the earliest monuments. This they inherited ultimately from prehistoric kings who had a special sanctity because of their power to assure prosperity through successful agriculture. Such powers are enjoyed by some African rainmaker-kings even today; in ancient Egypt they focused upon the Nile. The pharaohs were believed to control its annual rise and fall: life itself, no less, to the riparian communities. The first rituals of Egyptian kingship which are known to us are concerned with fertility, irrigation and land reclamation. The earliest representations of Menes show him excavating a canal.

Under the Old Kingdom the idea appears that the king is the absolute lord of the land. Soon he is venerated as a descendant of the gods, the original lords of the land. He becomes a god, Horus, son of Osiris, and takes on the mighty and terrible attributes of the divine maker of order; the bodies of his enemies are depicted hanging in rows like dead gamebirds, or kneeling in supplication lest (like less fortunate enemies) their brains be ritually dashed out. Justice is "what Pharaoh loves", evil "what Pharaoh hates"; he is divinely omniscient and so needs no code of law to guide him. Later, under the New Kingdom, the pharaohs were to be depicted with the heroic stature of the great warriors of other contemporary cultures; they are shown in their chariots, mighty men of war, trampling down their enemies and confidently slaughtering beasts of prey. Perhaps a measure of secularization can be inferred in this change, but it does not remove Egyptian kingship from the region of the sacred and awesome. "He is a god by whose dealings one lives, the father and mother of all men, alone by himself, without an equal", wrote one of

the chief civil servants of the pharaoh as late as about 1500 BCE. Until the Middle Kingdom, only he had an afterlife to look forward to. Egypt, more than any other Bronze Age state, always stressed the incarnation of the god in the king, even when that idea was increasingly exposed by the realities of life in the New Kingdom and the coming of iron. Then, the disasters which befell Egypt at the hands of foreigners would make it impossible to continue to believe that Pharaoh was god of all the world.

BUREAUCRACY

Long before the New Kingdom, the Egyptian state had acquired another institutional embodiment and armature, an elaborate and

The heroic image of a pharaoh in his war chariot, shooting arrows at the enemy, often appears in Egyptian art. In this case, Tutankhamon is shown leading his troops in an attack against an Asian army.

impressive hierarchy of bureaucrats. At its apex were viziers, provincial governors and senior officials who came mainly from the nobility; a few of the greatest of these were buried with a pomp that rivalled that of the pharaohs. Less eminent families provided the thousands of scribes needed to staff and service an elaborate government directed by the chief civil servants. The ethos of this bureaucracy can be sensed through the literary texts which list the virtues needed to succeed as a scribe: application to study, self-control, prudence, respect for superiors, scrupulous regard for the sanctity of weights, measures, landed property and legal forms. The scribes were trained in a special school at Thebes, where not only the traditional history and literature and command of various scripts were taught, but, it seems, surveying, architecture and accountancy also.

and was increasingly mastered by irrigation techniques established in a pre-dynastic period; these were probably one of the earliest manifestations of the unsurpassed capacity to mobilize collective effort which was to be one of the hallmarks of Egyptian government. Vegetables, barley, emmer were the main crops of the fields laid out along the irrigation channels; the diet they made possible was supplemented by poultry, fish and game (all of which figure plentifully in Egyptian art). Cattle were in use for traction and ploughing at least as early as the Old Kingdom. With little change this agriculture remained the basis of life in Egypt until modern times; it was sufficient to make her the granary of the Romans.

MONUMENTAL BUILDINGS IN EGYPT

AGRICULTURE

The bureaucracy directed a country most of whose inhabitants were peasants. They cannot have lived wholly comfortable lives, for they provided both the labour for the great public works of the monarchy and the surplus upon which a noble class, the bureaucracy and a great religious establishment could subsist. Yet the land was rich

On the surplus of this agriculture there also rested Egypt's own spectacular form of conspicuous consumption, a range of great public works in stone unsurpassed in antiquity. Houses and farm buildings in ancient Egypt were built in the mud brick already used before dynastic times: they were not meant to outface eternity. The palaces, tombs and memorials of the pharaohs were a different matter; they were

This 5th-dynasty seated scribe is one of the finest surviving examples of Egyptian sculpture.

built of the stone abundantly available in some parts of the Nile valley. Though they were carefully dressed with first copper and then bronze tools and often elaborately incised and painted, the technology of utilizing this material was far from complicated. Egyptians invented the stone column, but their great building achievement was not so much architectural and technical as social and administrative. What they did was based on an unprecedented and almost unsurpassed concentration of human labour. Under the direction of a scribe, thousands of slaves and sometimes regiments of soldiers were deployed to cut and manhandle into position the huge masses of Egyptian building. With only such elementary assistance as was available from levers and sleds – no winches, pulleys, blocks or tackle existed – and by the building of colossal ramps of earth, a succession of still-startling buildings was produced.

THE PYRAMIDS

The first were put up under the Third Dynasty. The most famous are the pyramids, the tombs of kings, at Saqqara, near Memphis. One of these, the "Step Pyramid", was the masterpiece of the first architect whose name is recorded, Imhotep, chancellor to the king. His work was so impressive that he was later to be deified – as the god of medicine – as well as being revered as astronomer, priest and sage. The beginning of building in stone was attributed to him and it is easy to believe that the building of something so unprecedented as the two-hundred-foot-high pyramid was seen as evidence of godlike power. It and its companions rose without peer over a civilization which until then lived only in dwellings of mud. A century or so later, blocks of stone of fifteen tons apiece were used for the Pyramid of Cheops, and it

This wooden statue dates from the 5th Dynasty. The Egyptian workers who found it in 1860 CE, amazed at its realism, nicknamed it "the town mayor" (Sheik el-beled). The statue stands over 3 ft (1 m) tall and can be seen in the Museum of Egypt in Cairo.

was at this time (during the Fourth Dynasty) that the greatest pyramids were completed at Giza. Cheops' pyramid was twenty years in the building; the legend that 100,000 men were employed upon it is now thought an exaggeration but many thousands must have been and the huge quantities of stone (between five and six million tons) were brought from as much as 500 miles away. This colossal construction is perfectly orientated and its sides, 750 feet long, vary by less than eight inches – only about 0.09 per cent. It is not surprising that the pyramids later figured among the Seven Wonders of the World, nor that they alone from those Wonders survive. They were the greatest evidence of the power and self-confidence of the pharaonic state. Nor, of course, were they the only great monuments of Egypt. Each of them was only the dominant feature of a great complex of buildings which made up together the residence of the king after death. At other sites there were great temples, palaces, the tombs of the Valley of the Kings.

TECHNOLOGICAL LIMITATIONS

These huge public works were in both the real and figurative sense the biggest things the Egyptians left to posterity. They make it less surprising that the Egyptians were later also

On a low plateau above the Nile valley, near Cairo, the spectacular Giza funeral buildings can be seen. The group is made up of the pyramids of three 4th-dynasty pharaohs and other secondary buildings. Built at the feet of the great pyramids of Cheops (Khufu), Cephren (Khafre) and Mycerinus (Menkaure) were funereal temples, which were linked by a series of pathways to other temples in the valley.

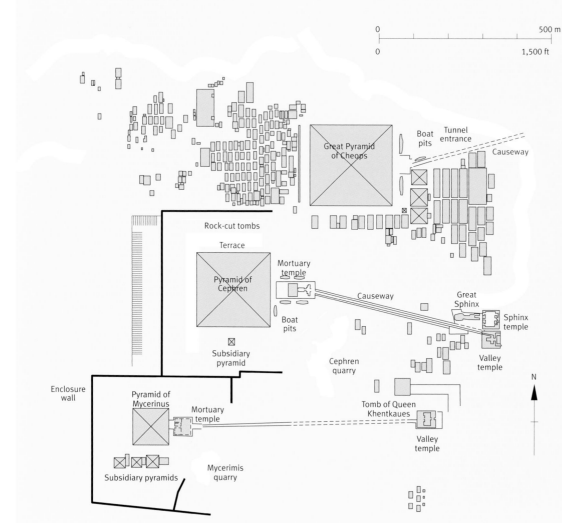

to be reputed to have been great scientists: people could not believe that these huge monuments did not rest on the most refined mathematical and scientific skill. Yet this is invalid as an inference as well as in fact untrue. Though Egyptian surveying was highly skilled, it was not until our own day that a more than elementary mathematical skill became necessary to engineering; it was certainly not needed for the erection of the pyramids. What was requisite was outstanding competence in mensuration and the manipulation of certain formulae for calculating volumes and weights, and this was as far as Egyptian mathematics went, whatever later admirers believed. Modern mathematicians do not think much of the Egyptians' theoretical achievement and they certainly did not match the Babylonians in this art. They worked with a decimal numeration which at first sight looks modern, but it may be that their only significant contribution to later mathematics was the invention of unit fractions.

EGYPTIAN ASTRONOMY

No doubt a primitive mathematics is a part of the explanation of the sterility of the Egyptians' astronomical endeavours – another field in which posterity, paradoxically, was to credit them with great things. Their observations were accurate enough to permit the forecasting of the rise of the Nile and the ritual alignment of buildings, it is true, but their theoretical astronomy was valueless. Here again they were left far behind by the Babylonians. The inscriptions in which Egyptian astronomical science was recorded were to command centuries of respect from astrologers, but their scientific value was low and their predictive quality relatively short-term. The one solid work which rested on the Egyptians' astronomy was the calendar. They were the first people to establish the solar year of 365¼ days and they divided it into twelve months, each of three "weeks" of ten days, with five extra days at the end of the year. This arrangement, it may be remarked, was revived in 1793 CE when the French revolutionaries sought to replace the Christian calendar by one more rational.

The calendar, though it owed much to the observation of stars, must have reflected also in its remoter origins observation of the great pulse at the heart of Egyptian life, the flooding of the Nile. This gave the Egyptian farmer a year of three seasons, each of approximately four months, one of planting, one of flood, one of harvest. But the Nile's endless cycle also influenced Egypt at deeper levels.

RELIGION

THE STRUCTURE AND SOLIDITY of the religious life of ancient Egypt greatly struck other peoples. Herodotus believed that the Greeks had acquired the names of their gods from Egypt; he was wrong, but it is interesting that he should have thought so.

Later, the cults of Egyptian gods were seen as a threat by the Roman emperors; they were forbidden, but the Romans had eventually to tolerate them, such was their appeal. Mumbo-jumbo and charlatanry with an Egyptian flavour could still take in cultivated Europeans in the eighteenth century CE; a more amusing and innocent expression of the fascination of the myth of ancient Egypt can still be seen in the rituals of the Shriners, the secret fraternities of respectable American businessmen who parade about the streets of small towns improbably attired in fezzes and baggy trousers on great occasions. There was, indeed, a continuing vigour in Egyptian religion which, like other sides of Egyptian civilization, long outlived the political forms that had sustained and sheltered it.

Yet it remains something with which it is peculiarly difficult to come to grips. Words like "vigour" can be misleading; religion in ancient Egypt was much more a matter of an

Egyptian religion

The numerous archaeological remains and written documents that have been preserved make the Egyptian religion one of the best-documented ancient religions. The many Egyptian gods were often personified by animals such as a hawk (Horus), or by natural elements, including the sky (Nut). However, some aspects of Egyptian religion point towards the belief in a superior god. This is noticeable in the fundamental role that Osiris played in the afterlife, essential for the Egyptians. State gods also existed, associated with successive capital cities. Amon, for example, was the ram god of Thebes, who during the New Kingdom united with the sun god Re (supreme god of the Old Kingdom) to become Amon-Re. The religious head of the Egyptians was the pharaoh, son of Re, identified as Horus. Beneath him there was a hierarchical class of priests.

The grand temple of Abu Simbel, which houses statues of several Egyptian gods, is designed in such a way that twice a year it is illuminated by the rays of the rising sun.

all-pervasive framework, as much taken for granted as the circulatory system of the human body, than of an independent structure such as what later came to be understood as a church. It was not consciously seen as a growing, lively force: it was, rather, one aspect of reality, a description of an unchanging cosmos. But this, too, may be a misleading way of putting it. An important book about the world outlook of early Mesopotamians and Egyptians has the suggestive title *Before Philosophy*; we have to remember that concepts and distinctions which we take for granted in assessing (and even talking about) the mentalities of other ages did not exist for the people whose minds we seek to penetrate. The boundary between religion and magic, for example, hardly mattered for the ancient Egyptian, though he might be well aware that each had its proper efficacy. It has been said that magic was always present as a kind of cancer in Egyptian religion; the image is too evaluative, but expresses the intimacy of the link. Another distinction lacking in ancient Egypt was the one most of us make automatically between the name and the thing. For the ancient Egyptian, the name was the thing; the real object we separate from its designation was identical with it. So might be other images. The Egyptians lived in symbolism as fishes do

in water, taking it for granted, and we have to break through the assumptions of a profoundly unsymbolic age in order to understand them.

DEATH AND BURIAL RITUALS

A whole world view is involved in appreciating the meaning and role of religion in ancient Egypt. At the outset there is overwhelming evidence of its importance; for almost the whole duration of their civilization, the ancient Egyptians show a remarkably uniform tendency to seek through religion a way of penetrating the variety of the flow of ordinary experience so as to reach a changeless world most easily understood through the life the dead lived there. Perhaps the pulse of the Nile is to be detected here, too; each year it swept away and made new, but its cycle was ever recurring, changeless, the embodiment of a cosmic rhythm. The supreme change threatening people was death, the greatest expression of the decay and flux which was their common experience. Egyptian religion seems from the start obsessed with it: its most familiar embodiments, after all, are

Dating from the 12th Dynasty, this is one of the splendid sarcophagi in which the mummies of important Egyptians were placed.

the mummy and the grave-goods from funeral chambers preserved in our museums. Under the Middle Kingdom it came to be believed that all Egyptians, not just the king, could expect life in another world. Accordingly, through ritual and symbol, through preparation of the case they would have to put to their judges in the afterworld, people might prepare for the afterlife with a reasonable confidence that they would achieve the changeless well-being it offered in principle. The Egyptian view of the afterlife was, therefore, unlike the gloomy version of the Mesopotamians; people could be happy in it.

The struggle to assure this outcome for so many people across so many centuries gives Egyptian religion a heroic quality. It is the explanation, too, of the obsessively elaborate care shown in preparing tombs and conducting the deceased to his eternal resting-place. Its most celebrated expression is the

building of the pyramids and the practice of mummification. It took seventy days to carry out the funerary rites and mummification of a king under the Middle Kingdom.

The Egyptians believed, it appears, that after death people could expect judgement before Osiris; if the verdict was favourable, they would live in Osiris' kingdom, if not, they were abandoned to a monstrous destroyer, part crocodile, part hippopotamus. This did not mean, though, that in life human beings need do no more than placate Osiris, for the Egyptian pantheon was huge. About two thousand gods existed and there were several important cults. Many of them originated in the prehistoric animal deities. Horus, the falcon god, was also god of the dynasty and probably arrived with the mysterious invaders of the fourth millennium BCE. These animals underwent a slow but incomplete humanization; artists stick their animal heads on to human bodies. These totemlike creatures were rearranged in fresh patterns as the pharaohs sought through the consolidation of their cults to achieve political ends. In this way the cult of Horus was consolidated with that of Amon-Re, the sun-god, of whom the pharaoh came to be regarded as the incarnation. This was the official cult of the great age of pyramid-building and by no means the end of the story.

Horus was later to undergo another transformation, to appear as the offspring of Osiris, the central figure of a national cult, and his consort Isis. This goddess of creation and love was probably the most ancient of all – her origins, like those of other Egyptian deities, go back to the pre-dynastic era, and she is one development of the ubiquitous mother-goddess of whom evidence survives from all over the Neolithic Near East. She was long to endure, her image, the infant Horus in her arms, surviving into the Christian iconography of the Virgin Mary.

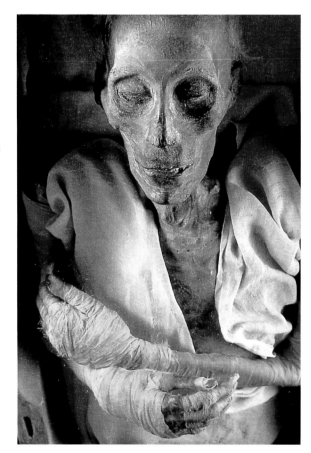

Medical examinations carried out on the mummy of Ramses II, the powerful pharaoh of the 19th Dynasty, have revealed that he suffered from heart disease, dental problems and arthritis.

RELIGIOUS DIVERSITY AND THE PRIESTLY CLASS

The theme of Egyptian religion is immensely complicated. Different places had different cults and there were even occasional variations of a doctrinal and speculative kind. The most famous of these was the attempt of a fourteenth-century pharaoh to establish the cult of Aton, another manifestation of the sun, in which has been discerned the first monotheistic religion. Yet there is a recurring sense of a striving after synthesis, even if it is often the expression of dynastic or political interest. Much of the history of Egyptian religion must be, if we could only decipher it, the story of ebbings and flowings about the major cults: politics, in fact, rather than religion.

Not only the pharaohs were interested in religious issues. The institutions which maintained these beliefs were in the hands of a hereditary priestly class, initiated into the rituals to whose inner sancta the ordinary worshipper almost never penetrated. The cult statues at the shrine of the temple were rarely seen except by the priests. As time passed, they acquired important vested interests in the popularity and well-being of their cults.

EGYPTIAN ART

The gods loom large in the subject-matter of ancient Egyptian art, but it contains much more besides. It was based on a fundamental naturalism of representation which, however restrained by conventions of expression and gesture, gives two millennia of classical Egyptian art at first a beautiful simplicity and later, in a more decadent period, an endearing charm and approachability. It permitted a realistic portrayal of scenes of everyday life.

The rural themes of farming, fishing and hunting are displayed in them; craftsmen are shown at work on their products and scribes at their duties. Yet neither content nor technique is in the end the most striking characteristic of Egyptian art, but its enduring style. For some two thousand years, artists were able to work satisfyingly within the same classical tradition. Its origins may owe something to Sumer and it showed itself later able to borrow other foreign influences yet the strength and solidity of the central and native tradition never wavers. It must

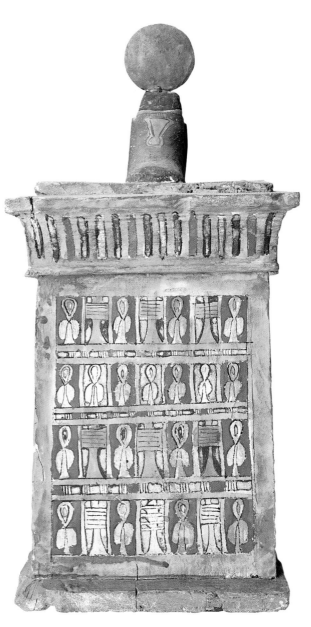

A large amount of ancient Egyptian furniture – such as this painted wooden funeral cask – has been preserved. This is due to the dry atmosphere of the tombs.

Queen Ahmose, from the 18th Dynasty, shown in a bas-relief at the Temple of Hatshepsut, in Deir-el-Bahari.

have been one of the most impressive visual features of Egypt to a visitor in ancient times; what he saw was all of a piece. If we exempt the work of the Upper Palaeolithic, of which we know so very little, it is the longest and strongest continuous tradition in the whole history of art.

It did not prove to be transplantable. Perhaps the Greeks took the column from ancient Egypt, where it had its origins in the mud-plastered bundle of reeds of which a reminiscence survives in fluting. What is clear apart from this is that although the monuments of Egypt continuously fascinated artists and architects of other lands, the result, even when they exploited them successfully for

their own purposes, was always superficial and exotic. Egyptian style never took root anywhere else; it pops up from time to time down the ages as decoration and embellishment – sphinxes and serpents on furniture, an obelisk here, a cinema there. Only one great integral contribution was made by Egyptian art to the future, the establishment for the purposes of the huge incised and painted figures on the walls of tombs and temples of the classical canons of proportion of the human body which were to pass through the Greeks to western art. Artists were still to be fascinated by these as late as Leonardo, although by now the contribution was theoretical, not stylistic.

HIEROGLYPHIC WRITING

Another great artistic achievement confined to Egypt, though exceptionally important there, was calligraphy. It seems that Egyptians deliberately took the Sumerian invention of representing sounds rather than things, but rejected cuneiform. They invented, instead, hieroglyphic writing. Instead of the device of arranging the same basic shape in different ways which had been evolved in Mesopotamia, they deliberately chose lifelike little pictures or near-pictures. It was much more decorative than cuneiform, but also much harder to master. The first hieroglyphs appear before 3000 BCE; the last example of which we know was written in 394 CE. Nearly 4,000 years is an impressively long life for a calligraphy. But the uninitiated could still not read it for another fourteen and a half centuries after its disappearance, until a French scholar deciphered the inscription on the "Rosetta stone" brought back to France after its discovery by scientists accompanying a French army in Egypt. None of the classical writers of antiquity who wrote about Egypt ever learnt to read hieroglyph, it seems, though enormous interest was shown in it. Yet it now seems likely that hieroglyph had importance in world as well as in Egyptian history because it was a model for Semitic scripts of the second millennium BCE and thus came to be a remote ancestor of the modern Latin alphabet, which has spread round the world in our own times.

THE INVENTION OF PAPYRUS

In the ancient world the ability to read hieroglyph was the key to the position of the priestly caste and, accordingly, a closely guarded professional secret. From pre-dynastic times it was used for historical record and

Hieroglyphic writing in a wall painting from a tomb in the Valley of the Kings. Below the hieroglyphs, Prince Amon-hir-Khopshep, son of Ramses II, is depicted.

as early as the First Dynasty the invention of papyrus – strips of reed-pith, laid criss-cross and pounded together into a homogeneous sheet – provided a convenient medium for its multiplication. Here was a real contribution to the progress of humankind. This invention had much greater importance for the world than hieroglyph; cheaper than skin (from which parchment was made) and more convenient (though more perishable) than clay tablets or slates of stone, it was the most general basis of correspondence and record in the Near East until well into the Common Era, when the invention of paper reached the Mediterranean world from the Far East (and even paper took its name from papyrus). Soon after the appearance of papyrus, writers began to paste sheets of it together into a long roll: thus the Egyptians invented the book, as well as the material on which it could first be written and a script which is an ancestor of

on for two thousand years before she adopted the well-sweep, by then long in use to irrigate land in the other river valley.

Perhaps the weight of routine was insuperable, given the background of the unchanging reassurance provided by the Nile. Though Egyptian art records workmen organized in teams for the subdivision of manufacturing processes down to a point which faintly suggests the modern factory, many important devices came to Egypt only much later than elsewhere. There is no definite evidence of the presence of the potter's wheel before the Old Kingdom; for all the skill of the goldsmith and coppersmith, bronze-making does not appear until well into the second millennium BCE and the lathe has to wait for the Hellenistic age. The bow-drill was almost the only tool for the multiplication and transmission of energy available to the mass of Egyptian craftsmen.

A papyrus vignette from the Book of the Dead of Nakhte, an important scribe. The dead man and his wife stand before the god Osiris in the garden of their house. Abundant sycamore trees and date palms surround the garden pool.

our own. It may be our greatest debt to the Egyptians, for a huge proportion of what we know of antiquity comes to us directly or indirectly via papyrus.

EGYPTIAN ACHIEVEMENT

Undoubtedly, the rumoured prowess of her religious and magical practitioners and the spectacular embodiment of a political achievement in art and architecture largely explain Egypt's continuing prestige. Yet if her civilization is looked at comparatively, it seems neither very fertile nor very responsive. Technology is by no means an infallible test – nor one easy to interpret – but it suggests a people slow to adopt new skills, reluctant to innovate once the creative jump to civilization had been made.

Stone architecture is the only major innovation for a long time after the coming of literacy. Though papyrus and the wheel were known under the First Dynasty, Egypt had been in contact with Mesopotamia for getting

Reconstruction of a bow drill, similar to the ones used by Egyptian carpenters.

MEDICINE

Only in medicine is there indisputable originality and achievement and it can be traced back at least as far as the Old Kingdom. By 1000 BCE Egyptian pre-eminence in this art was internationally and justifiably recognized. While Egyptian medicine was never wholly separable from magic (magical prescriptions and amulets survive in great numbers), it had an appreciable content of rationality and pure empirical observation. It extended as far as a knowledge of contraceptive techniques. Its indirect contribution to subsequent history was great, too, whatever its efficiency in its own day; much of our knowledge of drugs and of plants furnishing *materia medica* was first established by the Egyptians and passed from them, eventually, through the Greeks to the scientists of medieval Europe. It is a considerable thing to have initiated the use of a remedy as long effective as has been castor oil. Here Egypt left Mesopotamia far behind.

What can be concluded about the health of the ancient Egyptians is another matter. They do not seem to have been so worried about alcoholic over-indulgence as the Mesopotamians, but it is not easy to infer anything from that. Some scholars have said there was an exceptionally high rate of infant mortality and hard evidence of a negative kind exists for some diseases of adults; whatever the explanation, the many mummified bodies surviving reveal no instance of cancer, rickets, or syphilis. On the other hand, the debilitating disease called schistosomiasis, carried by blood flukes and so prevalent in

Egypt today, seems to have been prevalent there already in the second millennium BCE. Of course, none of this throws much light on ancient Egyptian medical practice. Such evidence as we have of prescriptions and recommended cures suggests that these were a mixed bag, no better and no worse than most of those deployed in other great centres of civilization at any time before the present. Considerable preservative skill was attributed to the practitioners of mummification, though unjustifiably. Curiously, the products of their art were later themselves regarded as of therapeutic value; powdered mummy was for centuries a sovereign cure for many ills in Europe and possessed other properties as well, as is suggested to readers of *Othello*.

A large number of labourers were expected to serve their master in the afterlife as they had done in real life, as is shown in the paintings and engravings in Egyptian tombs.

PEASANT LIFE

Most Egyptians were peasants, a consequence of Egypt long remaining non-urbanized as Mesopotamia did not. The picture of Egyptian life presented by its literature and art reveals a population living in the countryside, using little towns and temples as service centres rather than dwelling places. Egypt was for most of antiquity a country of a few great cult and administrative centres such as Thebes or Memphis and the rest nothing more than villages and markets. Life for the poor was hard, but not unremittingly so. The major burden must have been conscript labour services. When these were not exacted by Pharaoh, then peasants would have considerable leisure at those times when they waited for the flooding Nile to do its work for them. The agricultural base was rich enough, too, to sustain a complex and variegated society with a wide range of craftsmen. About their activities we know more than of those of their Mesopotamian equivalents, thanks to stone-carvings and paintings. The great division of this society was between the educated, who could enter the state service, and the rest. Slavery was important, but, it appears, less fundamental an institution than elsewhere in the ancient Near East.

A ncient Egyptian field workers are depicted in this tomb painting.

Detail of a woman gathering flax in a painting in Thebes.

Daily life in ancient Egypt

The Egyptians believed firmly in the afterlife and hoped to enjoy the same pleasures there as they had in real life. To this end, they placed symbolic images of servants and objects in their tombs. Because such objects have been excellently preserved by the dry atmosphere, they have provided archaeologists with a vast collection of images. Thanks to them, we are able to visualize daily life in the Egypt of the pharaohs with much greater precision than we can that of any other ancient civilization. We can see peasants working the land or tending their livestock, craftsmen at work, servants serving their masters and musicians and dancers performing. However, in Egyptian burial paintings everything is made to appear perfect, which tends to give an over-idealized impression of Egyptian life. It also is interesting to note that the average life expectancy for ancient Egyptians was just 20 years.

This 18th-dynasty sculpture from Thebes shows a married couple, who clearly wished to depict themselves as united for eternity.

A painting from a 7th-dynasty tomb. This youth, who is depicted smelling a flower, is wearing Middle Kingdom-style dress: a close-fitting white tunic with braces. True to the conventions of Egyptian art, the figure's torso and shoulders are shown front-on while the face is shown in profile.

THE STATUS OF WOMEN

Tradition in later times remarked upon the seductiveness and accessibility of Egyptian women. With other evidence it helps to give an impression of a society in which women were more independent and enjoyed higher status than elsewhere. Some weight must be given to an art which depicts court women clad in the fine and revealing linens which the Egyptians came to weave, exquisitely coiffured and jewelled, wearing the carefully applied cosmetics to whose provision Egyptian commerce gave much attention. We should not lean too strongly on this, but our impression of the way in which women of the Egyptian ruling class were treated is important, and it is one of dignity and independence. The pharaohs and their consorts – and other noble couples – are sometimes depicted, too, with an intimacy of mood found nowhere else in the art of the ancient Near East before the first millennium BCE and suggestive of a real emotional equality; it can hardly be accidental that this is so.

The beautiful and charming women who appear in many of the paintings and sculptures may reflect also a certain political importance for their sex which was lacking elsewhere. The throne theoretically and often in practice descended through the female line. An heiress brought to her husband the right of succession; hence there was much anxiety about the marriage of princesses. Many royal marriages were of brother and sister, without apparently unsatisfactory genetic effects; some pharaohs married their daughters, but perhaps to prevent anyone else marrying them rather than to ensure the continuity of the divine blood. Such a standing must have made royal women influential personages in their own right. Some exercised important power and one even occupied the throne, being willing to appear ritually bearded and in a man's clothes, and taking the title of Pharaoh. True, it was an innovation which seems not to have been wholly approved.

There is also much femininity about the Egyptian pantheon, notably in the cult of Isis, which is suggestive. Literature and art stress a respect for the wife and mother which goes beyond the confines of the circle of the notabilities. Both love stories and scenes of family life reveal what was at least thought to be an ideal standard for society as a whole and it emphasizes a tender eroticism, relaxation and informality, and something of an emotional equality of men and women. Some women were literate and there is even an Egyptian word for a female scribe, but there were, of course, not many occupations open to women except those of priestess or prostitute. If they were well-off, however, they could own property and their legal rights seem in most respects to have been akin to those of women in the Sumerian tradition. It is not easy to generalize over so long a period as

A scene from an 18th-dynasty tomb in Thebes. Servants, wearing only belts and costly jewels, attend to the guests at a banquet. The guests, dressed in the transparent, pleated tunics that were typical of New Kingdom high society, are being entertained by dancers and musicians.

A painting from Sobketpe's tomb depicts Syrians arriving at the Egyptian court to present tributes.

that of Egyptian civilization but such evidence as we have from ancient Egypt leaves an impression of a society with a potential for personal expression by women not found among many later peoples until modern times.

THE OLD KINGDOM

So impressive is the solidity and material richness of Egyptian civilization in retrospect, so apparently unchanging, that it is even more difficult than in the case of Mesopotamia to keep in perspective what were its relations with the world outside or the ebb and flow of authority within the Nile valley. There are huge tracts of time to

account for – the Old Kingdom alone, on the shortest reckoning, has a history two and a half times as long as that of the United States – and much happened under the Old Kingdom. The difficulty is to be sure exactly what it was that was going on and what was its importance. For nearly a thousand years after Menes, Egypt's history can be considered in virtual isolation. It was to be looked back upon as a time of stability when pharaohs were impregnable. Yet under the Old Kingdom there has been detected a decentralization of authority; provincial officers show increasing importance and independence. The pharaoh, too, still had to wear two crowns and was twice buried, once in Upper and once in Lower Egypt; this

division was still real. Relations with neighbours were not remarkable, though a series of expeditions was mounted against the peoples of Palestine towards the end of the Old Kingdom. The First Intermediate period which followed saw the position reversed and Egypt was invaded, rather than the invader. No doubt weakness and division helped Asian invaders to establish themselves in the valley of the lower Nile; there is a strange comment that "the high born are full of lamentation but the poor are jubilant ... squalor is throughout the land ... strangers have come into Egypt". Rival dynasties appeared near modern Cairo; the grasp of Memphis flagged.

THE MIDDLE KINGDOM

The next great period of Egyptian history was the Middle Kingdom, effectively inaugurated by the powerful Amenemhet I who reunified the kingdom from his capital at Thebes. For about a quarter-millennium after 2000 BCE, Egypt enjoyed a period of recovery whose repute may owe much to the impression (which comes to us through the records) of the horrors of the Intermediate period. Under the Middle Kingdom there was a new emphasis on order and social cohesion. The divine status of the pharaoh subtly changes: not only is he God, but it is emphasized that he is descended from gods and will be followed by gods. The eternal order will continue unshaken after bad times have made men doubt. It is certain, too, that there was expansion and material growth. Great reclamation work was achieved in the marshes of the Nile. Nubia, to the south, between the first and third cataracts, was conquered and its gold-mines fully exploited. Egyptian settlements

were founded even farther south, too, in what was later to be a mysterious kingdom called Kush. Trade leaves more elaborate traces than ever before and the copper mines of the Sinai were now exploited again. Theological change also followed – there was something of a consolidation of cults under the god Amon-Re which reflected political consolidation. Yet the Middle Kingdom ended in political upheaval and dynastic competition.

The Second Intermediate period of roughly two hundred years was marked by another and far more dangerous incursion of foreigners. These were the Hyksos, possibly a Semitic people, who used the military advantage of the iron-fitted chariot to establish themselves in the Nile delta as overlords to whom the Theban dynasties paid tribute. Not much is known about them. Seemingly, they took over Egyptian conventions and methods, and even maintained the existing bureaucrats at first, but this did not lead to assimilation. Under the Eighteenth Dynasty the Egyptians evicted the Hyksos in a war of

A group of painted wooden soldiers from a tomb in Asyut, probably from the 12th Dynasty. This was the period in which the conquest of Nubia drove the pharaohs to organize permanent military units. The most commonly used weapons were bows, spears, axes and shields. War chariots were introduced in Egypt later by foreign invaders, the Hyksos.

This statue of the 18th-dynasty queen Hatshepsut shows her holding two vases containing offerings of wine and milk. The statue was found in Hatshepsut's mortuary temple and dates from c.1490–70 BCE.

peoples; this was the start of the New Kingdom, whose first great success was to follow up victory in the years after 1570 BCE by pursuing the Hyksos into their strongholds in south Canaan. In the end, the Egyptians occupied much of Syria and Palestine.

THE NEW KINGDOM

The New Kingdom in its prime was so successful internationally and has left such rich physical memorials that it is difficult not to think that the Hyksos domination must have had a cathartic or fertilizing effect. There was under the Eighteenth Dynasty almost a renaissance of the arts, a transformation of military techniques by the adoption of Asiatic devices such as the chariot, and, above all, a huge consolidation of royal authority. During it a female, Hatshepsut, for the first time occupied the throne in a reign notable for the expansion of Egyptian commerce, or so her mortuary temple seems to show. The next century or so brought further imperial and military glory, her consort and successor, Tuthmosis III, carrying the

Imperial expansion began in the 18th Dynasty, drawing Egypt into a conflict over power in the Near East. Great battles were fought in Nubia, to the south, and in Syria and Palestine, to the northeast. In this painting, Nubian and Syrian envoys prostrate themselves before the Egyptian pharaoh.

limits of Egyptian empire to the Euphrates. Monuments recording the arrival of tribute and slaves or marriages with Asiatic princesses testify to an Egyptian pre-eminence matched at home by a new richness of decoration in the temples and the appearance of a sculpture in the round which produced busts and statues generally regarded as the peak of Egyptian artistic achievement. Foreign influences also touched Egyptian art at this time; they came from Crete.

THE END OF ISOLATION

Towards the end of the New Kingdom, the evidence of multiplied foreign contacts begins to show something else: the context of Egyptian power had already changed importantly. The crucial area was the Levant coast which even Tuthmosis III had taken seventeen years to subdue. He had to leave unconquered a huge empire ruled by the Mitanni which dominated eastern Syria and northern Mesopotamia. His successors changed tack. A Mitanni princess married a pharaoh and to protect Egyptian interests in this area the New Kingdom came to rely on the friendship of her people. Egypt was being forced out of the isolation which had long protected her. But the Mitanni were under growing pressure from the Hittites, to the north, one of the most important of the peoples whose ambitions and movements break up the world of the Near East more and more in the second half of the second millennium BCE.

We know a lot about the preoccupations of the New Kingdom at an early stage in this process because they are recorded in one of the earliest collections of diplomatic correspondence, for the reigns of Amenhotep III and IV (c.1400–1362 BCE). Under the first of these kings, Egypt reached its peak of prestige and prosperity. It was the greatest era of Thebes. Amenhotep was fittingly buried there in a tomb which was the largest ever prepared for a king, though nothing of it remains but the fragments of the huge statues the Greeks later called the colossi of Memnon (a legendary hero, whom they supposed to be Ethiopian).

THE REIGN OF AKHNATON

Amenhotep IV succeeded his father in 1379 BCE. He attempted a religious revolution, the substitution of a monotheistic cult of the sun-god Aton for the ancient religion. To mark his seriousness, he changed his name to Akhnaton and founded a new city at Amarna, 300 miles north of Thebes, where a temple with a roofless sanctuary open to the sun's rays was the centre of the new religion.

Although there can be no doubt of Akhnaton's seriousness of purpose and personal piety, his attempt must have been doomed from the start, given the religious conservatism of Egypt, but there may have been political motives for his persistence. Perhaps he was trying to recover power usurped by the priests of Amon-Re. Whatever the explanation, the opposition Akhnaton provoked by this religious revolution helped to cripple him on other fronts. Meanwhile, Hittite pressure was producing clear signs of strain in the Egyptian dependencies; Akhnaton could not save the Mitanni who lost all their lands west of the Euphrates to the Hittites in 1372 BCE and dissolved in civil war which foreshadowed their kingdom's

Akhnaton and his wife Nefertiti depicted with their daughters, under the beneficial rays of Aton. During this period, Egyptian art departed from many of its conventions and showed figures in relaxed postures. This strongly contrasted with the rigid style that had been the norm, and which would later become common practice once again.

disappearance thirty years or so later. The Egyptian sphere was crumbling. There were other motives, perhaps, than religious outrage for the later exclusion of Akhnaton's name from the official list of kings.

TUTANKHAMON

A relief from a stele depicting servants presenting gifts of gold to the 18th-dynasty ruler Ay (1352–1348 BCE) as a token of Akhnaton's esteem. The stele was found in the tomb built for Ay at Al-Amarmah.

Akhnaton's successor bore a name which is possibly the most famous to descend to us from ancient Egypt and a significant one: Amenhotep IV had changed his to Akhnaton because he wished to erase the reminiscence of the cult of the old god Amon; his successor and son-in-law changed his name from Tutankhaton to register the restoration of the old cult of Amon and the overthrow of the attempted religious reform. It may have been gratitude for this that led to the magnificent burial in the Valley of the Kings which was given to Tutankhamon after only a short and otherwise unremarkable reign.

THE DECLINE OF EGYPT

When Tutankhamon died, the New Kingdom had two centuries of life ahead, but their atmosphere is one of only occasionally inter-rupted and steadily accelerating decline. Symptomatically, Tutankhamon's widow arranged to marry a Hittite prince (though he was murdered before the ceremony could take place). Later kings made efforts to recover lost ground and sometimes suc-ceeded; the waves of conquest rolled back and forth over Palestine and at one time a pharaoh took a Hittite princess as a bride as his predecessors had taken princesses from

other peoples. But there were yet more new enemies appearing; even a Hittite alliance was no longer a safeguard. The Aegean was in uproar, the islands "poured out their people all together" and "no land stood before them", say the Egyptian records. These sea peoples were eventually beaten off, but the struggle was hard.

At some time during these turbulent years a small Semitic people, called by the Egyptians "Hebrews", left the delta and (according to their later tradition) followed their leader Moses out of Egypt into the deserts of Sinai. From about 1150 BCE the signs of internal disorganization, too, are plentiful. One king, Ramses III, died as a result of a conspiracy in the harem; he was the last to achieve some measure of success in offsetting the swelling tide of disaster. We hear of strikes and economic troubles under his successors; there is the ominous symptom of sacrilege in a generation of looting of the royal tombs at Thebes. The pharaoh is losing his power to priests and officials and the last of the Twentieth Dynasty, Ramses XI, was in effect a prisoner in his own palace. The age of Egypt's imperial power was over. So, in fact, was that of the Hittites, and of other empires of the end of the second millennium. Not only Egypt's power, but the world which was the setting of her glories, was passing away.

THE EGYPTIAN LEGACY

Undoubtedly, it is in changes affecting the whole ancient world that much of the explanation of the decline of Egypt must be sought, yet it is impossible to resist the feeling that the last centuries of the New Kingdom expose weaknesses present in Egyptian civilization from the beginning. These are not easy to discern at first sight; the spectacular heritage of Egypt's monuments and a history counted not

A fragment from a bas-relief in the temple of Abu Simbel, depicting the battle of Qadesh between Ramses II and Muwatallis, King of the Hittites.

in centuries but in millennia stagger the critical sense and stifle scepticism. Yet the creative quality of Egyptian civilization seems, in the end, strangely to miscarry. Colossal resources of labour are massed under the direction of men who, by the standards of any age, must have been outstanding civil servants, and the end is the creation of the greatest tombstones the world has ever seen. Craftsmanship of exquisite quality is employed, and its master-pieces are grave-goods. A highly literate elite utilizing a complex and subtle language and a material of unsurpassed convenience uses them copiously, but has no philosophical or religious idea comparable to those of Greek or Jew to give to the world. It is difficult not to sense an ultimate sterility, a nothingness, at the heart of this glittering *tour de force*.

In the other scale must be placed the sheer staying-power of ancient Egyptian civilization; after all, it worked for a very long time, a spectacular fact. Though it underwent at least two phases of considerable eclipse, it recovered from them, seemingly unchanged.

A painted, stuccoed, wooden stele dating from the 21st or 22nd Dynasty. A musician strums his harp in respect for Re-Harakhty, god of Heliopolis, who is depicted with a hawk's head crowned by a sun disk. He is holding a staff and a whip, both of which are symbols of Egyptian royalty.

Survival on such a scale is a great material and historical success; what remains obscure is why it should have stopped there. Egypt's military and economic power in the end made little permanent difference to the world. Her civilization was never successfully spread abroad. Perhaps this is because its survival owed much to its setting. If it was a positive success to create so rapidly institutions which with little fundamental change could last so long, this could probably have been done by any ancient civilization enjoying such a degree of immunity from intrusion. China was to show impressive continuity, too.

It is important also to remember once more how slow and imperceptible all social and cultural change was in early times. Because we are used to change, we must find it difficult to sense the huge inertia possessed by any successful social system (one, that is, which enables people to grapple effectively with their physical and mental environment) in almost any age before the most recent.

In the ancient world the sources of innovation were far fewer and far more occasional than now. The pace of history is rapid in ancient Egypt if we think of prehistoric times; it seems glacially slow if we reflect how little daily life must have changed between Menes and Tuthmosis III, a period of more than fifteen hundred years and therefore comparable to that which separates us from the end of Roman Britain. Marked change could only come from sudden and overwhelming natural disaster (and the Nile was a reliable safeguard), or invasion or conquest (and Egypt long stood at the edge of the battleground of peoples in the Near East, affected only occasionally by their comings and goings). Only very slowly could technology or economic forces exert such pressures for change as we take for granted. As for intellectual stimuli, these could hardly be strong in a society where the whole apparatus of a cultural tradition was directed to the inculcation of routine.

Speculation about the nature of Egyptian history tends always to revert to the great natural image of the Nile. It was always present to the Egyptian eyes, so prominent, perhaps, that it could not be seen for the colossal and unique influence it was, for no context broader than its valley needed consideration. While in the background the incomprehensible (but in the end world-making) wars of the Fertile Crescent rage across the centuries, the history of Old Egypt goes on for thousands of years, virtually a function of the remorseless, beneficent flooding and subsidence of the Nile. On its banks a grateful and passive people gathers the richness it bestows. From it could be set aside what they thought necessary for the real business of living: the proper preparation for death.

The last journey: a boat carrying the sarcophagus of a dead Egyptian sails along the Nile.

4 INTRUDERS AND INVADERS: THE DARK AGES OF THE ANCIENT NEAR EAST

ESOPOTAMIA AND EGYPT are the foundation-stones of written history. For a long time the first two great centres of civilization dominate chronology and may conveniently be dealt with more or less in isolation. But obviously their story is not the whole story of the ancient Near East, let alone that of the ancient world. Soon after 2000 BCE the movements of other peoples were already breaking it up into new patterns. A thousand years later, other centres of civilization were in existence elsewhere and we are well into the historical era.

Unfortunately for the historian, there is no simple and obvious unity to this story even in the Fertile Crescent, which for a long time continued to show more creativity and dynamism than any other part of the world. There is only a muddle of changes whose beginnings lie far back in the second millennium and which go on until the first of a new succession of empires emerges in the ninth century BCE. The sweeping political upheavals which stud this confusion are hard even to map in outline, let alone to explain; fortunately, their details do not need to be unravelled here. History was speeding up and civilization was providing human beings with new opportunities. Rather than submerge ourselves in the flood of events, it is worth while to try to grasp some of the change-making forces at work.

A COMPLICATING WORLD

The most obvious change-making force remains the great migrations of peoples. Their fundamental pattern does not change much

Assyrian bas-reliefs show many scenes of cities under siege. In this bas-relief from the palace of Nimrud (Kalaj), the Assyrians are depicted using an armour-plated siege tower mounted on wheels. The siege tower has a battering ram attached, which would have been used to breach the enemy walls.

for a thousand years or so after 2000 BCE nor does the ethnic cast of the drama. The basic dynamic was provided by the pressure of Indo-European peoples on the Fertile Crescent from both east and west. Their variety and numbers grow greater; their names need not be remembered here but some of them bring us to the remote origins of Greece. Meanwhile, Semitic peoples dispute with the Indo-Europeans the Mesopotamia valley; with Egypt and the mysterious "Peoples of the Sea" they fight over Sinai, Palestine and the Levant. Another branch of the Indo-European race is established in Iran – and from it will eventually come the greatest of all the empires of the ancient past, that of sixth-century Persia. Still another branch pushes out into India. These movements must explain much of what lies behind a shifting pattern of empires and kingdoms stretching across the centuries. By standards of modern times some of them were quite long-lived; from about 1600 BCE a people called Kassites from Caucasia ruled in Babylon for four and a half centuries, which is a duration comparable to that of the entire history of the British empire. Yet, by the standards of Egypt, such polities are the creatures of a moment, born today and swept away tomorrow.

MILITARY TECHNIQUES

It would indeed be surprising if the old empires and kingdoms had not proved fragile in the end, for many other new forces were

also at work which multiplied the revolutionary effects of the wanderings of peoples. One of them which has left deep traces is improvement in military technique. Fortification and, presumably, siege-craft had already reached a fairly high level in Mesopotamia by 2000 BCE. Among the Indo-European peoples who nibbled at the civilization these skills protected were some with recent nomadic origins; perhaps for that reason they were able to revolutionize warfare in the field, though they long remained unskilled in siege-craft. Their introduction of the two-wheeled war chariot and the cavalryman transformed operations in open country. The soldiers of Sumer are depicted trundling about in clumsy four-wheeled carts, drawn by asses; probably these

Four warriors in a two-wheeled Assyrian war chariot. Mounted warriors began to take part in battles in the Near East during the 2nd millennium BCE.

Time chart (2200 BCE–562 BCE)				
	2000 BCE Knossos Palace built in Crete	1700–1200 BCE Hittite Empire	965–928 BCE Reign of Solomon	883–859 BCE Reign of Ashurnasirpal, Assyrian emperor
2000 BCE		1500 BCE	1000 BCE	500 BCE
2200 BCE Minoan civilization in Crete		1600 BCE Mycenaean civilization		604–562 BCE Reign of Nebuchadnezzar II of Babylon

were simply a means of moving generals about or getting a leader into the mêlée, so that spear and axe could be brought to bear. The true chariot is a two-wheeled fighting vehicle drawn by horses, the usual crew being two, one man driving, the other using it as a platform for missile weapons, especially the composite bow formed of strips of horn. The Kassites were probably the first people to exploit the horse in this way and their rulers seem to have been of Indo-European stock. Access to the high pastures to the north and east of the Fertile Crescent opened to them a reserve of horses in the lands of the nomads. In the river valleys horses were at first rare, the prized possessions of kings or great leaders, and the barbarians therefore enjoyed

a great military and psychological superiority. Eventually, though, chariots were used in the armies of all the great kingdoms of the Near East; they were too valuable a weapon to be ignored. When the Egyptians expelled the Hyksos, they did so by, among other things, using this weapon against those who had conquered them with it.

THE USE OF CAVALRY

Warfare was changed by riding horses. A cavalryman proper not only moves about in the saddle but fights from horseback; it took a long time for this art to be developed, for managing a horse and a bow or a spear at the same time is a complex matter. Horse-riding came from the Iranian highlands, where it may have been practised as early as 2000 BCE. It spread through the Near East and Aegean well before the end of the next millennium. Later, after 1000 BCE, there appeared the armoured horseman, charging home and dominating foot-soldiers by sheer weight and impetus. This was the beginning of a long era in which heavy cavalry were a key weapon, though their full value could only be exploited centuries later, when the invention of the stirrup gave the rider more control.

THE IMPORTANCE OF IRON

During the second millennium BCE chariots came to have parts made of iron; soon they had hooped wheels. The military advantages of this metal are obvious and it is not surprising to find its uses spreading rapidly through the Near East and far beyond, in spite of attempts by those who had iron to restrict it. At first, these were the Hittites. After their decline iron-working spread rapidly, not only because it was a more effective metal for making arms, but because iron ore, though scarce, was more plentiful than copper or tin. It was a great stimulus to economic as well as military change. In agriculture, iron-using peoples could till heavy soils which had remained impervious to wood or flint. But there was no rapid general transfer to the new metal; iron supplemented bronze, as bronze and copper had supplemented stone and flint in the human tool-kit, and did so in some places more rapidly than others. Already in the eleventh century BCE iron was used for weaponry in Cyprus (some have argued that steel was produced there, too) and from that island iron spread to the Aegean soon after 1000 BCE. That date can serve as a rough division between the Bronze and Iron Ages, but is

no more than a helpful prop to memory. Though iron implements became more plentiful after it, parts of what we may call the "civilized world" long went on living in a Bronze Age culture. Together with the "Neolithic" elsewhere, the Bronze Age lives on well into the first millenium BCE, fading away only slowly like the smile on the face of the Cheshire cat. For a long time, after all, there was very little iron to go round.

LONG-DISTANCE TRADE

Metallurgical demand helps to explain another change, a new and increasingly complex inter-regional and long-distance trade. It is one of those complicating inter-reactions

From copper to iron

The natural resources of copper and gold, which were easy to work, were the first metals to be used in western Asia. The discovery that it was possible to extract metals from various minerals using heat appears to have been made in western Asia and southeastern Europe in the 7th millennium BCE and in eastern Asia in the 3rd millennium BCE. Bronze, made from an alloy of copper and tin, was discovered in the 4th millennium BCE in western Asia and in the 3rd millennium BCE in eastern Asia. It was widely used for producing weapons and tools. Iron, which was more difficult to work, was used in western Asia from the beginning of the 2nd millennium BCE. Iron gradually replaced bronze for making weapons and tools – it was in plentiful supply and, when coal was added to the metal compound, it produced weapons that could be sharpened. Very high temperatures are needed to forge iron, a practice which started in China during the 6th century BCE. In the rest of the world, however, cast iron continued to be used for another 1,000 years.

Assyrian bronze and iron mace heads dating from around the 9th century BCE.

which seem to be giving the ancient world a certain unity just before its disruption at the end of the second millennium BCE. Tin, for example, had to be brought from Mesopotamia and Afghanistan, as well as Anatolia, to what we should now call "manufacturing" centres. The copper of Cyprus was another widely-traded commodity and the search for more of it gave Europe, at the margins of ancient history though she was, a new importance. Mine-shafts in what is now the Federal Republic of Yugoslavia were sunk sixty and seventy feet below ground to get at copper even before 4000 BCE. Perhaps it is not surprising that some European peoples later came to display high levels of metallurgical skill, notably in the beating of large sheets of bronze and in the shaping of iron (a much more difficult material to work than bronze until temperatures high enough to cast it were available).

NEW METHODS OF TRANSPORT

THE GROWTH of long-range commerce depends on transport. At first, the carriage of goods was a matter of asses and donkeys; the domestication of camels in the middle of the second millennium BCE made possible the caravan trade of Asia and the Arabian peninsula which was later to seem to be of ageless antiquity, and opened an environment hitherto almost impenetrable, the desert. Except among nomadic peoples, wheeled transport probably had only local importance, given the poor quality of early roads. Early carts were drawn by oxen or asses; they may have been in service in Mesopotamia about 3000 BCE, in Syria around 2250 BCE, in Anatolia two or three hundred years later and in mainland Greece about 1500 BCE.

A 7th-century BCE bas-relief from Nineveh showing an Assyrian camp outside the walls of a city. Two dromedaries are shown. These animals were probably introduced into Mesopotamia from Arabia during the latter half of the 2nd millennium BCE. Camels were used for transport, but not for combat.

A detail from the 16th-century BCE wall paintings found at the Akrotiri settlement, on the island of Thera (Santorini). A coastal city is depicted surrounded by mountains.

WATER TRANSPORT

For goods in quantity, water transport was already likely to be cheaper and simpler than transport by land in the second millennium BCE; this was to be a constant of economic life until the coming of the steam railway. Long before caravans began to bring up to Mesopotamia and Egypt the gums and resins of the south Arabian coasts, ships were carrying them up the Red Sea and merchants were moving back and forth in trading vessels across the Aegean. Understandably, it was in maritime technology that some of the most important advances in transport were made.

We know that Neolithic peoples could make long journeys by sea in dug-out canoes and there is even some evidence of navigation from the seventh millennium. The Egyptians of the Third Dynasty had put a sail on a sea-going ship; the central mast and square sail were the beginning of seamanship relying on anything but human energy. Improvements of rigging came slowly over the next two millennia. It has been thought that these made some approach to the fore-and-aft rigging which was necessary if ships were to sail closer to the wind, but for the most part the ships of antiquity were square-rigged. Because of this, the direction of prevailing winds was decisive in setting patterns of sea-borne communication. The only other source of energy was human: the invention of the oar is an early one and it provided the motive power for long sea crossings as well as for close handling. It seems likely, though, that oars were used more frequently in warships, and sail in what it is at a very early date possible to call merchantmen. By the thirteenth century BCE, ships capable of carrying more than 200 copper ingots were sailing about the eastern Mediterranean, and within a few centuries more, some of these ships were being fitted with watertight decks.

THE INVENTION OF MONEY

Even in recent times goods have been exchanged or bartered and no doubt this was what trade meant for most of antiquity. Yet a great step was taken when money was invented. This seems to have happened in Mesopotamia, where values of account were being given in measures of grain or silver before 2000 BCE. Copper ingots seem to have been treated as monetary units throughout the Mediterranean in the late Bronze Age. The first officially sealed means of exchange which survives comes from Cappadocia in the form of ingots of silver of the late third millennium BCE: this was a true metal currency. Yet though money is an important invention and one which was to spread, we have to wait until the seventh century BCE for the first coins. Refined monetary devices (and Mesopotamia had a credit system and bills of exchange in early times) may help to promote

Trading and storing goods

There is evidence to suggest that trade acquired growing importance in the Near East during the 2nd millennium BCE, although this does not mean that a real market economy operated at that time. It was only in the 7th century BCE that money began to be minted; before this, trade had been carried out by exchanging goods, including metal ingots. Bartering and the sending of diplomatic gifts or tributes were also common practices.

In Egypt, the storage of surplus cereals, controlled by the pharaohs' scribes and the temples, allowed Egyptians to survive years of bad harvests, such as those described in the biblical story of Joseph.

Scenes from an 11th-dynasty Egyptian burial painting, showing some of the processes involved in the storage of food.

trade, but they are not indispensable. Peoples in the ancient world could get along without them. The Phoenicians, a trading people of legendary skill and acumen, did not have a currency until the sixth century BCE; Egypt, a centrally controlled economy and of legendary wealth, did not adopt a coinage until two centuries after that, and Celtic Europe, for all its trade in metal goods, did not coin money until two centuries later still.

TRADING WITHOUT MONEY

Meanwhile, goods were exchanged without money, though it is hard to be sure quite what this means. Although there was an important rise in the volume of goods moved about the world, by 1000 BCE or so, not all of this was what would now be termed "trade". Economic organization in ancient times is for a long time very obscure. Any specialized function – pottery-making, for example – implies a machinery which on the one hand distributes its products and, on the other, ensures subsistence to the specialist by redistributing to him and his fellows the food they need to survive, and perhaps other goods. But this does not require "trade", even in the form of barter. Many peoples in historic times have been observed operating such distribution through their chiefs: these men presided over a common store, "owning", in a sense, everything the community possessed, and doling out such shares from it as were required to keep society working smoothly. This may

A detail from an 18th-dynasty wall painting shows Nubian envoys bearing gifts for the Egyptian pharaoh. Such gifts explain why archaeologists have discovered many objects far from their original place of manufacture, although the presence of some may be the result of long-distance trade.

be what lay behind the centralization of goods and supplies in Sumerian temples; it would also explain the importance of the recording and sealing of consignments deposited there and hence the early association of writing with accounting.

As for economic exchange between communities, confident generalization about its earliest stages is even more hazardous. Once into the era of historical record, we can see many activities going on which involve the transfer of commodities, not all of them aimed at monetary gain. Payment of tribute, symbolic or diplomatic gifts between rulers, votive offerings, were some of the forms it took. We should not rush to be over-definite; right down to the nineteenth century CE the Chinese empire conceived its foreign trade in terms of tribute from the outside world and the pharaohs had a way of translating trade with the Aegean into similar notions, to judge by tomb paintings. In the ancient world, such transactions might include the transfer of standard objects such as tripods or vessels of a certain weight or rings of uniform size which therefore present at an early date some of the characteristics of currency. Sometimes such things were useful; sometimes they were merely tokens. All that is wholly certain is that the movement of commodities increased and that much of this increase in the end took the form of the profitable exchanges we now think of as commerce.

New towns must have helped. They sprang up all over the old Near East no doubt in part because of population growth.

They register the successful exploitation of agricultural possibilities but also a growing parasitism. The literary tradition of the alienation of countrymen from the city is already there in the Old Testament. Yet city life also offered a new intensity of cultural creativity, a new acceleration of civilization.

THE ROLE OF LITERACY

One sign of accelerating civilization is the spreading of literacy. In about 2000 BCE, literacy was still largely confined to the river-valley civilizations and the areas they influenced. Cuneiform had spread throughout Mesopotamia and two or three languages were written in it; in Egypt the monumental inscriptions were hieroglyphic and day-to-day writing was done on papyrus in a simplified form called hieratic. A thousand years or so later, the picture had changed. Literate peoples were then to be found all over the Near East, and in Crete and Greece, too. Cuneiform had been adapted to yet more languages with great success; even the Egyptian government adopted it for its diplomacy. Other scripts were being invented, too. One, in Crete, takes us to the edge of modernity, for it reveals a people in about 1500 BCE whose language was Greek. With the adoption of a Semitic alphabet, the Phoenician, the medium of the first western literature was in existence by about 800 BCE, and so, perhaps, was its first surviving expression, in what were later called the works of Homer.

A lion hunt is depicted on this gold-encrusted copper dagger. The weapon was found in a Mycenaean tomb dating from the 16th century BCE.

Pictographic and alphabetic systems of writing

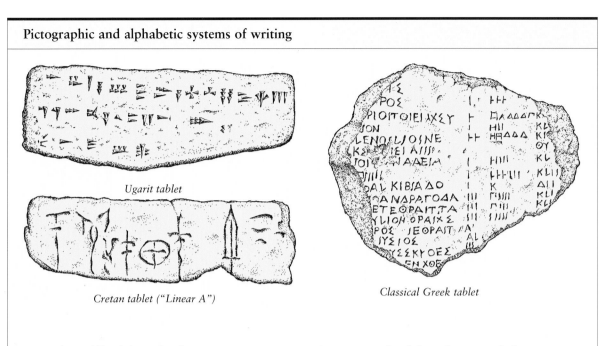

Ugarit tablet

Cretan tablet ("Linear A")

Classical Greek tablet

From the middle of the 2nd millennium BCE, writing became much more widespread in the ancient world. In Crete, in the Mediterranean, two types of pictographic writing, derived from Egyptian hieroglyphics, were used. They were called "Linear A" and "Linear B" (only the latter has so far been deciphered).

An important breakthrough came with the appearance of the first alphabetic writing, which was probably Canaanite. Other alphabetic writing systems were derived from this one, including Ugarit, on which the Greek alphabet was based, and from which Latin was later developed.

STATEHOOD AND POWER

Localized themes make nonsense of chronology; they register changes lost to sight if history is pinned too closely to specific countries. Yet individual countries and their peoples, though subject to general forces and in more and more frequent contact, also become increasingly distinct. Literacy pins down tradition; in its turn, tradition expresses communal self-consciousness. Presumably tribes and peoples have always felt their identity; such awareness is much strengthened when states take on more continuing and institutionalized forms. The dissolution of empires into more viable units is a familiar story from Sumer to modern times, but some areas emerge time and time again as enduring nuclei of tradition. Even in the second millennium BCE, states are getting more solid and show greater staying-power. They were still far from achieving that extensive and continuing control of their peoples whose possibilities have only fully been revealed in modern times. Yet even in the most ancient records there seems to be an unchecked trend towards a greater regularity in government and greater institutionalizing of power. Kings surround themselves with bureaucracies and tax-collectors find the resources for larger and larger enterprises. Law becomes a widely accepted idea; wherever it penetrates, there is a limitation, even if at first only implicit, of the power of the individual and an increase of that of the law-giver. Above all, the state expresses itself through its military power; the considerable problem of feeding, equipping and administering standing professional armies is solved by 1000 BCE.

CULTURAL DIFFERENTIATION

When states become powerful, the story of governmental and social institutions begins to escape from the general categories of early civilization. In spite of a new cosmopolitanism made possible by easier intercourse and cross-fertilizing, societies take very diverse paths. In the life of the mind, the most conspicuous expression of diversity is religion. While some have discerned in the pre-classical era a tendency towards simpler, monotheistic systems, the most obvious fact is a huge and varied pantheon of local and specialized deities, mostly coexisting tolerantly, with only an occasional indication that one god is jealous of his distinction.

There is a new scope for differentiation in other expressions of culture, too. Before civilization began, art had already established itself as an autonomous activity not necessarily linked to religion or magic (often so linked though it continued to be). The first literature has already been mentioned and of other sides of the mind we also begin to see something. There is the possibility of play; gaming-boards appear in Mesopotamia, Egypt, Crete. Perhaps people were already gambling. Kings and noblemen hunted with

A games table, made of ebony and ivory, from the tomb of the 18th-dynasty pharaoh Tutankhamon.

passion, and in their palaces were entertained by musicians and dancers. Among sports, boxing seems to go back into Bronze Age Crete, an island where a unique and probably ritualistic sport of bull-leaping was also practised.

In such matters it is more obvious than anywhere else that we need not pay much heed to chronology, far less to particular dates, even when we can be sure of them. The notion of an individual civilization is less and less helpful over the area with which we have so far been concerned, too. There is too much interplay for it to bear the weight it can do in Egypt and Sumer. Somewhere between about 1500 and 800 BCE big changes took place which ought not to be allowed to slip through the mesh of a net woven to catch the history of the first two great civilizations. In the confused, turbulent Near East and eastern Mediterranean of the centuries around 1000 BCE a new world different from that of Sumer and the Old Kingdom was in the making.

EARLY AEGEAN CIVILIZATION

A NEW INTERPLAY OF CULTURES brought many changes to peoples on the fringe of the Near East but civilization in the Aegean islands was rooted in the Neolithic as it was elsewhere. The first metal object found in Greece – a copper bead – has been dated to about 4700 BCE, and European as well as Asian stimuli may have been at work. Crete is the largest of the Greek islands. Several centuries before 2000 BCE towns with a regular layout were being built there by an advanced people which had been there through Neolithic times. They may have had contacts with Anatolia which spurred them to exceptional achievements, but the evidence

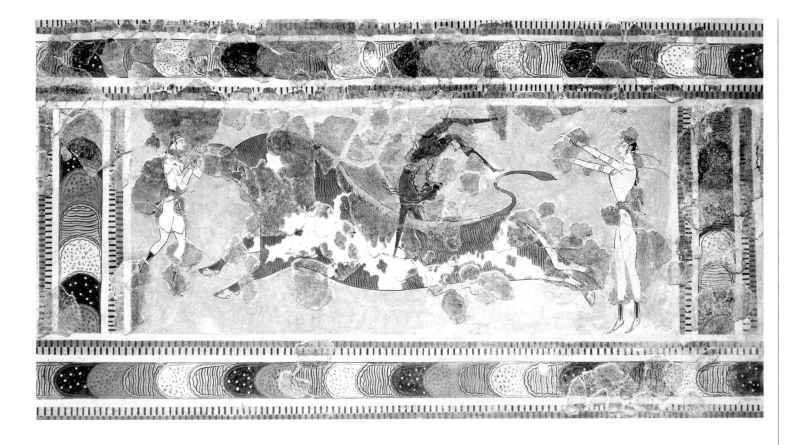

is indecisive. They could well have arrived at civilization for themselves. At any rate, for about a thousand years they built the houses and tombs by which their culture is distinguished and these did not change much in style. By about 2500 BCE there were important towns and villages on the coasts, built of stone and brick; their inhabitants practised metal-working and made attractive seals and jewels. At this stage, that is to say, the Cretans shared much of the culture of mainland Greece and Asia Minor. They exchanged goods with other Aegean communities. There then came a change. About five hundred years later they began to build the series of great palaces which are the monuments of what we call Minoan civilization; the greatest of them, Knossos, was first built about 1900 BCE. Nothing quite as impressive appears anywhere else among the islands and it exercised a cultural hegemony over more or less the whole of the Aegean.

MINOAN CRETE

Minoan is a curious name; it is taken from the name of a King Minos who, although celebrated in legend, may never have existed. Much later, the Greeks believed – or said – that he was a great king in Crete who lived at Knossos, parleyed with the gods, and married Pasiphae, the daughter of the sun. Her monstrous offspring, the Minotaur, devoured sacrificial youths and maids sent as tribute from Greece at the heart of a labyrinth eventually penetrated successfully by the hero Theseus, who slew him. This is a rich and suggestive theme and has excited scholars who believe it can throw light on Cretan civilization, but there is no proof that King Minos ever existed. It may be that, as legend suggests, there was more than one of that name, or that his name was a titular identification of several Cretan rulers. He is one of those fascinating figures who, like King

This magnificent fresco at the palace of Knossos in Crete is around 3,500 years old. It depicts the ritualistic sport of bull-leaping.

Arthur, remain just beyond the borders of history and inside those of mythology.

Minoan, then, simply means the civilization of people who lived in Bronze Age Crete; it has no other connotation. This civilization lasted some six hundred years, but only the outlines of a history can be put together. They reveal a people living in towns linked in some dependence on a monarchy at Knossos. For three or four centuries they prosper, exchanging goods with Egypt and the Greek mainland, and subsisting on a native agriculture. It may have been this which explains Minoan civilization's leap forward. Crete seems then, as today, to have been better for the production of olives and vines than either the other islands or mainland Greece. It seems likely, too, that she raised large numbers of sheep and exported wool. Whatever its precise forms, Crete experienced an important agricultural advance in late Neolithic times, which led not only to better cereal-growing but, above all, to the cultivation of the other two great staples of Mediterranean agriculture, the olive and vine. They could be grown where grains could not and their discovery changed the possibilities of Mediterranean life. Immediately they permitted a larger population. On this much else could then be built because new human resources were available, but it also made new demands, for organization and government, for the regulation of a more complex agriculture and the handling of its produce.

THE END OF MINOAN CIVILIZATION

The peak of Minoan civilization came about 1600 BCE. A century or so later, the Minoan palaces were destroyed. The mystery of this end is tantalizing. At about the same time the major towns of the Aegean islands were destroyed by fire, too. There had been earthquakes in the past; perhaps this was another of them. Recent scholarship identifies a great eruption in the island of Thera at a suitable time; it could have been accompanied by tidal waves and earthquakes in Crete, seventy miles away, and followed by the descent of clouds of ash which blighted Cretan fields. Some people have preferred to think of a rising against the rulers who lived in the palaces. Some have discerned signs of a new invasion, or postulated some great raid from the sea which carried off booty and prisoners, destroying a political power for ever by the damage it inflicted, by leaving no new settlers behind. None of these can be conclusively established. It is only possible to guess about what happened and the view which does least violence to the lack of evidence is that there was a natural cataclysm originating in Thera which broke the back of Minoan civilization.

In the 3rd millennium BCE, the Cyclades formed a bridge linking western Asia with the rest of the Greek world. Marble sculptures of naked female idols, such as the one shown here, were often made on the islands. These sculptures are remarkable for their geometrical stylization.

Whatever the cause, this was not the end of early civilization in Crete, for Knossos was occupied for another century or so by people from the mainland. Nevertheless, though there were still some fairly prosperous times to come, the ascendancy of the indigenous civilization of Crete was, in effect, over. For a time, it seems, Knossos still prospered. Then, early in the fourteenth century BCE it, too, was destroyed by fire. This had happened before, but this time it was not rebuilt. So ends the story of early Cretan civilization.

CRETAN SEA POWER

Fortunately, the salient characteristics of Cretan civilization are easier to understand than the detail of its history. The most obvious is its close relationship with the sea. More than a thousand years later, Greek tradition said that Minoan Crete was a great naval power exercising political hegemony in the Aegean through her fleet. This idea has been much blown upon by modern scholars anxious to reduce what they believe to be an anachronistic conception to more plausible proportions and it certainly seems misleading to see behind this tradition the sort of political power later exercised through their navies by such states as fifth-century Athens or nineteenth-century Great Britain. The Minoans may have had a lot of ships, but they were unlikely to be specialized at this early date and there is no hope in the Bronze Age of drawing a line between trade, piracy and counter-piracy in their employment. Probably there was no permanent Cretan "navy" in a public sense at all. Nevertheless, the Minoans felt sufficiently sure of the protection the sea gave them – and this must have implied some confidence in their ability to dominate the approaches to the natural harbours, most of which are on the north

coast – to live in towns without fortifications, built near to the shore on only slightly elevated ground. We do not have to look for a Cretan Nelson among their defenders; that would be silly. But we can envisage a Cretan Hawkins or Drake, combining trade, freebooting and protection of the home base.

The Minoans thus exploited the sea as other peoples exploited their natural environments. The result was an interchange of products and ideas which shows once more how civilization can accelerate where there is the possibility of cross-fertilization. Minoans had close connexions with Syria before 1550 BCE and traded as far west as Sicily, perhaps further. Someone took their goods up the Adriatic coasts. Even more important was

The sea was a recurring theme in the art of Minoan Crete, reflecting the important role that it played in the everyday lives of the people. Octopus motifs, such as the one shown here, were often used to decorate vases.

their penetration of Greece. The Minoans may well have been the most important single conduit through which the goods and ideas of the first civilizations reached Bronze Age Europe. Certain Cretan products begin to turn up in Egypt in the second millennium BCE and this was a major outlet; the art of the New Kingdom shows Cretan influence. There was even, some scholars think, an Egyptian resident for some time at Knossos, presumably to watch over well-established interests, and it has been argued that Minoans fought with the Egyptians against the Hyksos. Cretan vases and metal goods have been found at several places in Asia Minor: these are the things which survive, but it has been argued that a wide range of other products – timber, grapes, oil, wood, metal vases and even opium – were supplied by the Minoans to the mainland. In return, they took metal from Asia Minor, alabaster from Egypt, ostrich eggs from Libya. It was a complex trading world.

CULTURAL ACHIEVEMENTS

Together with a prosperous agriculture, trade made possible a civilization of considerable solidity, long able to recover from natural disaster, as the repeated rebuilding of the palace at Knossos seems to show. The palaces are the finest relics of Minoan civilization, but the towns were well built too, and had elaborate piped drains and sewers. This was technical achievement of a high order; early in the sequence of palaces at Knossos the bathing and lavatory provision is on a scale unsurpassed before Roman times. Other cultural achievement was less practical, though artistic rather than intellectual; Minoans seem to have taken their mathematics from Egypt and left it at that. Their religion went under with them, apparently leaving nothing to the future, but the Minoans had an important contribution to make to the style of another civilization on the Greek mainland. Art embodied Minoan civilization at its highest

Reconstruction of a chamber in the royal apartments at Knossos. The famous dolphin fresco, which decorates one of the walls, reflects a taste for joyful, colourful imagery that appears to have been typical of Minoan artists.

The palace of Knossos

Key

1	Central courtyard
2	Main floor
3	Workshop area
4	Royal domestic quarters
5	Theatre
6	Main entrance
7	Throne room
8	Procession corridor
9	Stepped causeway
10	Hall of pillars
11	Hall of the double axes

0   30 m
0   100 ft

Plan of the palace of Knossos.

For ancient Greeks, Knossos was the capital from which Minos, King of Crete, ruled. Perhaps the extensive ruins of the palace gave rise to the legend about the labyrinth and the Minotaur. Knossos was certainly the most important of all the Minoan palaces on Crete. Archaeological excavations were begun in 1900 CE by Arthur Evans and revealed large archives full of baked-clay tablets. The writing on them, called "Linear B", took 50 years to decipher. Using the information provided by the tablets, we are able to reconstruct many aspects of life in Minoan Crete. Built in about 1900 BCE on a hill which had long been inhabited, the palace reached the zenith of its splendour half a millennium later.

and remains its most spectacular legacy. Its genius was pictorial and reached a climax in palace frescoes of startling liveliness and movement. Here is a really original style, influential across the seas, in Egypt and in Greece. Through other palatial arts, too, notably the working of gems and precious metals, it was to shape fashion elsewhere.

THE MINOAN LIFESTYLE

Minoan art provides a little evidence about the Cretans' style of life because it is often representational. They seem to have dressed scantily, the women often being depicted bare-breasted; the men are beardless. There is an abundance of flowers and plants to suggest a people deeply and readily appreciative of nature's gifts; they do not give the impression that the Minoans found the world an unfriendly place. Their relative wealth – given the standards of ancient times – is attested by the rows of huge and beautiful oil-jars found in their palaces. Their concern for comfort and what cannot but be termed elegance comes clearly through the dolphins and lilies which decorate the apartments of a Minoan queen.

Archaeology has also provided evidence of a singularly unterrifying religious world, though this does not, perhaps, take us very far since we have no texts. Though we have representations of the Cretans' gods and goddesses, it is not easy to be sure who they are. Nor can we penetrate their rituals, beyond registering the frequency of sacrificial altars, double-headed axes, and the apparent centering of Minoan cults in a female figure. She is perhaps a Neolithic fertility figure such as was to appear again and again as the embodiment of female sexuality: the later Astarte and Aphrodite. In Crete she appears elegantly skirted, bare-breasted, standing between lions and holding snakes. Whether

there was a male god, too, is less clear. But the appearance of bulls' horns in many places and of frescoes of these noble beasts is suggestive if it is linked to later Greek legend (Minos' mother, Europa, had been seduced by Zeus in the shape of a bull; his wife Pasiphae enjoyed a monstrous coition with a bull from which was born the half-bull, half-man Minotaur), and to the obscure but obviously important rites of bull-leaping. It is striking that whatever it was, Cretan religion does not seem gloomy; pictures of sports and dancing or delicate frescoes and pottery do not suggest an unhappy people.

MINOAN POLITICS

The political arrangements of this society are obscure. The palace was not only a royal residence, but in some sense an economic centre – a great store – which may perhaps best be understood as the apex of an advanced form of exchange based on redistribution by the ruler. The palace was also a temple, but not a fortress. In its maturity it was the centre of a highly organized structure whose inspiration may have been Asian; knowledge of the literate empires of Egypt and Mesopotamia was available to a trading people. One source of our knowledge of what Minoan government was trying to do is a huge collection of thousands of tablets which are its administrative records. They indicate rigid hierarchy and systematized administration, but not how this worked in practice. However effective government was, the only thing the records certainly show is what it aspired to, a supervision far closer and more elaborate than anything conceivable by the later Greek world. If there are any analogies, they are again with the Asian empires and Egypt.

At present, the tablets tell us only of the last phase of Minoan civilization because

Several Cretan drinking vessels, such as this one dating from c.1500 BCE, have been found in a tomb in Vafio, near Sparta. The drinking vessels, which are evidence that there were relations between Crete and mainland Greece, depict a number of scenes in which bulls are captured using ropes and nets.

A detail from one of the frescoes at the palace of Akrotiri, on the island of Thera, dating from the middle of the 2nd millennium BCE. The style of the frescoes is reminiscent of those discovered in Minoan palaces in Crete.

many of them cannot be read. The weight of scholarly opinion now inclines to the view put forward a few years ago that the script of a great mass of them found at Knossos is used to write Greek and that they date from about 1450 to 1375 BCE. This confirms the archaeological evidence of the arrival of successful invaders from the mainland at about this time and of their supersession of the native rulers. The tablets are their documents, and the script in which they are written has been termed "Linear B". The earlier written records are found at first in hieroglyph, with some symbols borrowed from Egypt, and then in another script (not yet deciphered) termed "Linear A" and used from perhaps as early as 1700 BCE. Almost certainly it was wholly non-Greek. It seems likely that the incoming Greeks took over pre-existing Minoan administrative practice and put down records, such as were already kept, in their own tongue. The earlier tablets probably contain, therefore, information very like the later, but it is about Crete before the coming of the Greek-speaking invaders who presided over the last phase and mysterious end of Minoan civilization.

THE END OF THE CRETAN CULTURE

Successful invasion from the mainland was itself a sign that the

conditions which had made this civilization possible were crumbling away in the troubled times of the closing Bronze Age. Crete for a long time had no rival to threaten her coasts. Perhaps the Egyptians had been too busy; in the north there had long been no possible threat. Gradually, the second of these conditions had ceased to hold. Stirring on the mainland were the same Indo-European peoples who have already cropped up in so many places in this story. Some of them penetrated Crete again after the final collapse of Knossos; they were apparently successful colonists who exploited the lowlands and drove away the Minoans and their shattered culture to lonely little towns of refuge where they disappear from the stage of world history.

Ironically, only two or three centuries before this, Cretan culture had exercised something like hegemony in Greece, and Crete was always to hang about mysteriously at the back of the Greek mind, a lost and golden land. A direct transfusion of Minoan culture to the mainland had taken place through the first Achaean peoples (the name usually given to these early Greek-speakers) who came down into Attica and the Peloponnese and established towns and cities there in the eighteenth and seventeenth centuries BCE. They entered a land long in contact with Asia, whose inhabitants had already contributed to the future one enduring symbol of Greek life, the fortification of the high place of the town, or acropolis. The new arrivals were culturally hardly superior to those they conquered, though they brought

This polychrome ivory Minoan statuette was discovered in the palace of Knossos in Crete. It depicts a goddess or priestess – she is portrayed holding a snake in each hand and has a cat on her head.

with them the horse and the war chariot. They were barbarians by comparison with the Cretans, with no art of their own. More aware of the role of violence and war in society than were the islanders (no doubt because they did not enjoy the protection of the sea and had a sense of continuing pressure from the homelands from which they had come), they fortified their cities heavily and built castles. Their civilization had a military style. Sometimes they picked sites which were to be the later centres of Greek city-states; Athens and Pylos were among them. They were not very large, the biggest containing at most not more than a few thousand people. One of the most important was at Mycenae, which gave its name to the civilization that finally spread over Bronze Age Greece in the middle of the second millennium.

Cretan clay tablets bearing inscriptions.

MYCENAEAN GREECE

The Mycenaean civilization left some splendid relics, for it was very rich in gold; strongly influenced by Minoan art, it was also a true synthesis of Greek and indigenous cultures on the mainland. Its institutional basis seems to have been rooted in the patriarchal ideas found among many of the Indo-European peoples, but there is more to it than this. The bureaucratic aspiration revealed by the Knossos tablets and by others from Pylos in the western Peloponnese of about 1200 BCE suggests currents of change flowing back from conquered Crete towards the mainland. Each considerable city had a king. The one at Mycenae, presiding over a society of warrior landowners whose tenants and slaves were the aboriginal peoples, may have been at an early date the head of some sort of federation

A painted Minoan sarcophagus, from Hagia Triada in Crete. The painting depicts religious burial ceremonies. On the left, women pour wine over an altar. On the right, men present a variety of offerings to an image made in the likeness of the deceased.

of kings. There is suggestive evidence in Hittite diplomatic records which points to some political unity in Mycenaean Greece. Below the kings, the Pylos tablets show a close supervision and control of community life and also important distinctions between officials and, more fundamentally, between slave and free. What cannot be known is just what such differences meant in practice. Nor can we see much of the economic life which lay at the root of Mycenaean culture, beyond its centralization in the royal household, as in Crete.

Whatever its material basis, the culture represented most spectacularly at Mycenae had by 1400 BCE spread all over mainland Greece and to many of the islands. It was a whole, though well-established differences of Greek dialect persisted and distinguished one people from another down to classical times. Mycenae replaced the Minoan trading supremacy in the Mediterranean with its own. It had trading posts in the Levant and was treated as a power by Hittite kings. Sometimes Mycenaean pottery

exports replaced Minoan, and there are even examples of Minoan settlements being followed by Mycenaean.

The Mycenaean empire, if the term is permissible, was at its height in the fifteenth and fourteenth centuries BCE. For a while, the weakness of Egypt and the crumbling of the Hittite power favoured it; for a time a small people enriched by trade had disproportionate importance while great powers waned. Mycenaean colonies were established on the shores of Asia Minor; trade with other Asian towns, notably Troy, prospered. But there are signs of a flagging from about 1300 BCE. War seems to have been one answer; Achaeans took important parts in attacks on Egypt at the end of the century and it now seems that a great raid by them which was immortalized as the Siege of Troy took place about 1200 BCE. The troubled background to these events was a series of dynastic upheavals in the Mycenaean cities themselves.

THE DARK AGES OF THE AEGEAN

What can be called the Dark Ages of the Aegean were about to close in and they are as obscure as what was happening in the Near East at about the same time. When Troy fell, new barbarian invasions of mainland Greece had already begun. At the very end of the thirteenth century the great Mycenaean centres were destroyed perhaps by earthquakes and the first Greece broke up into disconnected centres. As an entity Mycenaean civilization collapsed, but not all the Mycenaean centres were abandoned, though their life continued at a lower level of achievement. The kingly treasures disappear, the palaces are not rebuilt. In some places the established resident peoples hung on successfully for centuries; elsewhere they were ruled as serfs or driven out by new conquerors,

Jewellery from the Treasure of Troy, discovered by Heinrich Schliemann at the end of the 19th century CE. These beautiful objects were displayed in public for the first time in April 1996 at the Pushkin Museum in Moscow.

Indo-Europeans from the north who had been on the move from about a century before the fall of Troy. It does not seem likely that these new peoples always settled the lands they ravaged, but they swept away the existing political structures and the future would be built on their kinships, not on the Mycenaean institutions. There is a picture of confusion as the Aegean Dark Age deepens; only just before 1000 BCE are there a few signs that a new pattern – the ground-plan of classical Greece – is emerging.

THE DORIANS AND IONIANS

Legendary accounts of this period attribute much to one particular group among the newcomers, the Dorians. Vigorous and bold, they were to be remembered as the descendants of Heracles. Though it is very dangerous to argue back from the presence of later Greek dialects to identifiable and compact groups of early invaders, tradition makes them the speakers of a tongue, Doric, which lived on into the classical age as a dialect setting them apart. In this case, tradition has been thought by scholars to be justified. In Sparta and Argos, Dorian communities which would be future city-states established themselves. But other peoples also helped to crystallize a new civilization in this obscure period. The most successful were those later identified as speakers of "Ionic" Greek, the Ionians of the Dark Age. Setting out from Attica (where Athens had either survived or assimilated the invaders who followed Mycenae), they took root in the

The entrance to Agamemnon's tomb, or the so-called Treasury of Atreus, seen from inside the burial place. It was built in the 13th century BCE and discovered in 1874 CE by Heinrich Schliemann, an amateur archaeologist who believed in the veracity of Homer and who set out to find the burial places of his heroes.

Agamemnon, King of Mycenae, appears in the *Iliad* as the most powerful of the Greeks. Even today, the ruins of his capital are evidence of its importance in the 15th and 14th centuries BCE. These photographs show the city walls (above) and its monumental entrance, the Gate of Lions (right).

Cyclades and Ionia, the present Turkish coast of the Aegean. Here, as migrants and pirates, they seized or founded towns, if not on islands, almost always on or near the coast, which were the future city-states of a seafaring race. Often the sites they chose had already been occupied by the Mycenaeans. Sometimes – at Smyrna, for example – they displaced earlier Greek settlers.

This is a confusing picture at best and for much of it there is only fragmentary evidence. Yet from this turmoil there would slowly re-emerge the unity of civilization enjoyed by the Bronze Age Aegean. At first, though, there were centuries of disruption and particularism, a new period of provincialism in a once cosmopolitan world. Trade flagged and ties with Asia languished. What replaced them was the physical transference of people, sometimes taking centuries to establish new settled patterns, but in the end setting out the ground-plan of a future Greek world.

DEPOPULATION IN THE AEGEAN REGION

There occurred a colossal setback in civilized life which should remind us how fragile it could be in ancient times. Its most obvious sign was a depopulation between 1100 and 1000 BCE so widespread and violent that some scholars have sought explanations in a sudden cataclysm – plague, perhaps, or a climatic change such as might have suddenly and terribly reduced the small cultivable area of the Balkan and Aegean hillsides. Whatever the cause, the effects are to be seen also in a waning of elegance and skill; the carving of hard gems, the painting of frescoes and the making of the fine pottery all come to a stop. Such cultural continuity as the age permitted must have been largely mental, a matter of songs, myths and religious ideas.

HOMERIC GREECE

Of this troubled time a very little is dimly and remotely reflected in the bardic epics later set down in writing in the *Iliad* and the *Odyssey*. They include material transmitted for generations by recitation, whose origins lie in tradition near-contemporary with the events they purport to describe, though later attributed to one poet, Homer. Exactly what is reflected, though, is much harder to agree about; the consensus has recently been that it is hardly anything for Mycenaean times, and little more for what immediately followed them. The central episode of the *Iliad*, the attack on Troy, is not what matters here, though the account probably reflects a real preponderance of Achaean initiative in the settlement of Asia Minor. What survives is a little social and conceptual information carried incidentally by the poems. Though Homer gives an impression of some special pre-eminence attributed to the Mycenaean king, this is information about the post-Mycenaean Aegean of the eighth century, when recovery from the Dark Ages begins. It reveals a society whose assumptions are those of barbarian warlords rather than those of kings commanding regular armies or supervising bureaucracies like those of Asia. Homer's kings are the greatest of great nobles, the heads of large households, their acknowledged authority tempered by the real power of truculent near-equals and measured by their ability to impose themselves; their lives are troubled and exacting. The atmosphere is individualistic and anarchic: they are more like a band of Viking leaders than the rulers commemorated by the Mycenaean tablets. Whatever reminiscences of detail may survive from earlier times (and these have sometimes been confirmed in their accuracy by excavation) and however many reflexions of later society they eventually contained, the poems only fitfully illuminate a primitive society, still in confusion, settling down

A coat of armour made of bronze and a helmet with metallic ear plates, found in a Mycenaean burial place in Dendra (c.1400 BCE). Achaean warriors wore metal plates to protect themselves and proved invincible against enemies who did not have such sophisticated armour – the *Iliad* bears testament to this.

The Trojan wars

Greek literature begins with two epic poems by Homer, the *Iliad* and the *Odyssey*. The first narrates the siege of Troy (Ilium) by the Greeks and the second the homecoming of one of the Greek heroes, Ulysses. These poems, written in the 8th century BCE (centuries after the events to which they refer had taken place), are full of legendary elements, which in turn gave rise to the idea that Troy was also merely a legend.

The first excavations took place on a mound next to the mouth of the Dardanelles straits, where Heinrich Schliemann believed Troy might have been located,

Classical Greek literature and art contain many references to the Trojan wars. On this vase, Achilles dresses the wounds of a fellow warrior.

and were begun in 1870. Schliemann found a 3rd-millennium treasure which he immediately attributed to the Trojan king Priam. Subsequent excavations have revealed that Troy was a major city throughout the 3rd and 2nd millennia BCE. On the level of excavation work known as Troy VII, traces of a fire that destroyed the city in the 13th century BCE have been discovered. The fire was probably started by the Greek invaders whose deeds were recounted by Homer. Troy was abandoned in about 1100 BCE. In 700 BCE, it regained importance as a Greek city, which also disappeared many years later.

This marble bas-relief, dating from the 8th century BCE, was found in Nimrud, Assyria. However, its design is Phoenician and depicts an unmistakably Egyptian motif: the winged sphinx with the royal headdress of the pharaohs.

perhaps, but neither so advanced as Mycenae had been, nor even dimly foreshadowing what Greece was to become.

The new civilization which was at last to emerge from the centuries of confusion owed much to the resumption of intercourse with the East. It was very important that the Hellenes (the name by which the invaders of Greece came to be distinguished from their predecessors) had spread out into the islands

and on to the Asian mainland; they provided many points of contact between two cultural worlds. But they were not the only links between Asia and Europe. Seeds of civilization were always carried about by the go-betweens of world history, the great trading peoples.

THE PHOENICIANS

One of the trading peoples, another seafaring race, had a long and troubled history, though not so long as its legends said; the Phoenicians claimed that they had arrived in Tyre in about 2700 BCE. This may be treated on a level with stories about the descent of the Dorian kings from Heracles. None the less, they were already settled on the coast of the modern Lebanon in the second millennium BCE when the Egyptians got their supplies of cedar-wood from them. The Phoenicians were a Semitic people. Like the Arabs of the Red Sea, they became seafarers because geography urged them to look outwards rather than inland. They lived in the narrow coastal strip which was the historic channel of communication between Africa and Asia. Behind them was a shallow hinterland, poor in agricultural resources, cut up by hills running down from the mountains to the sea so that the coastal settlements found it difficult to unite. There were parallels with the experience of later Greek states tempted to the sea in similar circumstances and in each case the result was not only trade but colonization.

Weak at home – they came under the sway of Hebrew, Egyptian and Hittite in turn – it cannot be entirely coincidental that the Phoenicians emerge from the historical shadows only after the great days of Egypt, Mycenae and the Hittite empire. They, too, prospered in others' decline. It was after 1000 BCE, when the great era of Minoan trade was

long past, that the Phoenician cities of Byblos, Tyre and Sidon had their brief golden age. Their importance then is attested by the biblical account of their part in the building of Solomon's Temple; "thou knowest", says Solomon, "that there is not among us any that can skill to hew timber like unto the Sidonians", and he paid up appropriately (1 Kings v, 6). This is perhaps evidence of a uniquely large and spectacular public works contract in ancient times, and there is copious later material to show the continuing importance of Phoenician enterprise. Ancient writers often stressed their reputation as traders and colonizers. They even exchanged goods with the savages of Cornwall, and must have been navigators of some skill to get so far. Phoenician dyes were long famous and much sought after down to classical times. No doubt commercial need stimulated their inventiveness; it was at Byblos (from which the Greeks were to take their name for a book) that the alphabet later adopted by the Greeks was invented. This was a great step, making a more widespread literacy possible, but no remarkable Phoenician literature survives, while Phoenician art tends to reflect their role of the middleman, borrowing and copying from Asian and Egyptian models, perhaps as the customer demanded.

PHOENICIAN TRADING STATIONS

Trade was the Phoenician occupation and did not at first require settlement overseas. Yet they came to base themselves more and more on colonies or trading stations, sometimes where Mycenaeans had traded before them. There were in the end some twenty-five of these up and down the Mediterranean, the earliest set up at Kition (the modern Larnaca) in Cyprus at the end of the ninth century BCE. Some colonies may have followed earlier

Phoenician commercial activity on the spot. They may also reflect the time of troubles which overtook the Phoenician cities after a brief phase of independence at the beginning of the first millennium. In the seventh century BCE Sidon was razed to the ground and the daughters of the king of Tyre were carried off to the harem of the Assyrian Ashurbanipal. Phoenicia was then reduced to its colonies elsewhere in the Mediterranean and little else. Yet their establishment may also have reflected anxiety at a wave of Greek colonization in the west which threatened the supply of metal, especially of British tin and Spanish silver. This could

explain the Phoenician foundation of Carthage a century earlier; it was to become the seat of a power more formidable by far than Tyre and Sidon had ever been and went on to establish its own chain of colonies. Further west, beyond the Straits of Gibraltar, Cadiz was already known to Phoenicians who called there while looking for an Atlantic trade further north.

The Phoenicians were among the most important traffickers in civilization but so, willy-nilly, had been others, the Mycenaeans by their diffusion of a culture and the Hellenes by their stirring up of the ethnic world of the Aegean. The Minoans had been something more; true originators, they not

A Phoenician war ship from the 1st millennium BCE, shown in an Assyrian bas-relief. The ship has a pointed ram, designed to make a hole in the hull of an enemy vessel. One of the two lines of oarsmen and the shields of the soldiers on board are visible. From the start of the 1st millennium BCE, Phoenician ships dominated the shipping routes of the western Mediterranean.

only took from the great established centres of culture, but remade what they took before diffusing it again. These peoples help to shape a more rapidly changing world. One important side-effect, of which little has yet been said, was the stimulation of continental Europe. The search for minerals would take explorers and prospectors further and further into that barbarian unknown. Already in the second millennium BCE there are the first signs of a complicated future; beads found at Mycenae were manufactured in Britain from Baltic amber. Trade was always slowly at work, eating away isolation, changing peoples' relations with one another, imposing new shapes on the world. But it is hard to relate this story to the stirring of the ethnic pot in the Aegean, let alone to the troubled history of the Asian mainland from the second millennium BCE.

This terracotta mask depicts the face of a Phoenician god.

THE NEAR EAST IN THE AGES OF CONFUSION

"Confusion" is a matter of perspective. For about eight hundred years from, say, the end of Knossos, the history of the Near East is indeed very confused if our standpoint is that of world history. What was essentially going on were disputes about control of the slowly-growing wealth of the best-defined agricultural region of the ancient world (the empires which came and went could not find resources in the desert and steppe area on the borders of the Near East which could justify their conquest) and in that story it is hard to find any continuing thread. Invaders came and went rapidly, some of them leaving new communities behind them, some setting up new states to replace those they overthrew. This could hardly have been grasped by those to whom these events would only have come home occasionally, and suddenly, when (for instance) their homes were burned, their wives and daughters raped, their sons carried off to slavery – or, less dramatically, when they discovered that a new governor was going to levy higher taxes. Such events would be upsetting enough – if a stronger word is not required. On the other hand, millions of people must also in those times have lived out their lives unaware of any change more dramatic than the arrival one day in their village of the first iron sword or sickle; hundreds of communities lived within a pattern of ideas and institutions unchanged for many generations. This is an important reservation. It must not be forgotten when we stress the dynamism and violence of the Near East's history during the transition from the Bronze to Iron Ages, an era already considered from the standpoint of the peoples of the Aegean.

On the mainland, wandering peoples moved about in a zone where there were well-established centres of government and population, powerful and long-lasting political structures, numerous hierarchies of specialists in administration, religion and learning. These partly explain why the coming of new peoples obliterates less of what had already been achieved than in the Aegean. Another conservative force was the long contact many of the barbarians had already had with civilization in this region. It left them wanting not to destroy it but to enjoy its fruits themselves. These two forces helped in the long run to diffuse civilization further and to produce the increasing cosmopolitanism of a large and confused, but civilized and interconnected, Near East.

THE HITTITES

The story of the civilized Near East begins very early, somewhere back towards the beginning of the second millennium BCE with the arrival in Asia Minor of the Hittites. Perhaps they belonged to the same group of peoples as the Minoans, at any rate they were established in Anatolia at about the same time that Minoan civilization was rising to its greatest triumphs. They were far from being primitive barbarians. They had a legal system of their own and absorbed much of what Babylon could teach. They long enjoyed a virtual monopoly of iron in Asia; this not only had great agricultural importance but, together with their mastery of fortification and the chariot, gave the Hittites a military superiority which was the scourge of Egypt and Mesopotamia. The raid which cut down Babylon in about 1590 BCE was something like the high-water mark of the first Hittite "empire". A period of eclipse and obscurity followed. Then, in the first half of the fourteenth century, came a renaissance of power. This second and even more splendid era saw a Hittite hegemony which stretched at one brief

The Phoenicians were quick to recognize Ibiza's strategic position in Mediterranean trade routes. One of the most outstanding examples of Ibizan architecture is the spectacular necropolis at Puig de Molin. This terracotta votive statue is one of the objects discovered at the necropolis.

moment from the shores of the Mediterranean to the Persian Gulf. It dominated all of the Fertile Crescent except Egypt

The Hittite Empire

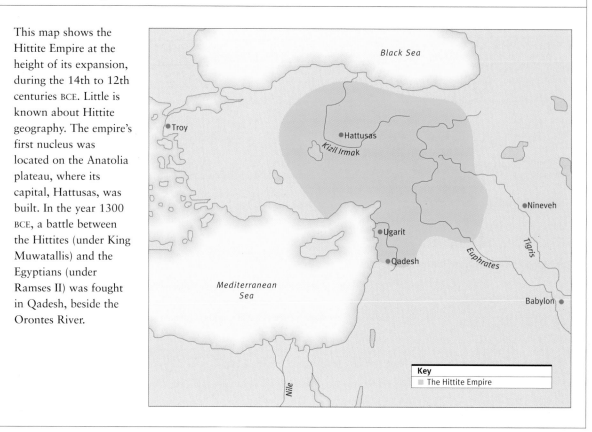

This map shows the Hittite Empire at the height of its expansion, during the 14th to 12th centuries BCE. Little is known about Hittite geography. The empire's first nucleus was located on the Anatolia plateau, where its capital, Hattusas, was built. In the year 1300 BCE, a battle between the Hittites (under King Muwatallis) and the Egyptians (under Ramses II) was fought in Qadesh, beside the Orontes River.

Black Sea

Troy

Hattusas

Kizil Irmak

Nineveh

Ugarit

Euphrates

Tigris

Qadesh

Mediterranean Sea

Babylon

Nile

Key
The Hittite Empire

---

and successfully challenged even that great military power while almost ceaselessly at war with the Mycenaeans. But like other empires it crumbled after a century or so, the end coming in about 1200 BCE.

THE END OF THE HITTITE EMPIRE

The culmination and collapse of the great organizing effort at the beginning of "dark ages" for Greece and the Aegean has two interesting features. The first is that the Hittites by this time no longer enjoyed a monopoly of iron; by about 1000 BCE it is to be found in use all over the Near East and its diffusion must surely be

part of the story of the swing of power against the Hittites. The other interesting feature is a coincidence with the rhythm of migrations, for it seems that the great diffusers of iron technology were the Indo-European peoples who from about 1200 BCE were throwing everything into turmoil. The disappearance of Troy, which never recovered from the Achaean destruction, has been thought of great strategic importance in this respect; the city seems to have played until this time a leading role in an alliance of powers of Asia

The Hittites worshipped several gods. Carved in stone, this image depicts the god of lightning.

Minor who had held the line against the barbarians from the north. After its overthrow, no other focus for resistance appeared. There is a closeness of timing which some have thought too pronounced to be merely coincidental between the collapse of the last Hittite power and the attacks of "sea peoples" recorded in the Egyptian records. The particular conquerors of the Hittites were a people from the race called the Phrygians.

THE SEA PEOPLES

The "sea peoples" were one more symptom of the great folk movements of the era. Armed with iron, from the beginning of the twelfth century BCE they were raiding the mainland of the East Mediterranean basin, ravaging Syrian and Levantine cities. Some of them may have been "refugees" from the Mycenaean cities who moved first to the Dodecanese and then to Cyprus. One group among them, the Philistines, settled in Canaan in about 1175 BCE and are commemorated still by a modern name derived from their own: Palestine. But Egyptians were the major victim of the sea peoples. Like the Vikings of the northern seas two thousand years later, sea-borne invaders and raiders plunged down on the delta again and again, undeterred by occasional defeat, at one time even wresting it from Pharaoh's control. Egypt was under great strain. In the early eleventh century, she broke apart and was disputed between two kingdoms. Nor were the sea peoples Egypt's only enemies. At one point, a Libyan fleet appears to have raided the delta, though it was drawn off. In the

A Hittite warrior depicted in the rigid and slightly rough style that is characteristic of most Hittite sculpture.

south, the Nubian frontier did not yet present a problem, but round about 1000 BCE an independent kingdom emerged in the Sudan which would later be troublesome. The tidal surge of barbarian peoples was wearing away the old structures of the Near East just as it had worn away Mycenaean Greece.

HEBREW ORIGINS

This is far enough into the welter of events to make it clear that we have entered an age both too complex and too obscure for straightforward narration. Mercifully, there soon appear two threads through the turmoil. One is an old theme renewed, that of the continuing Mesopotamian tradition about to enter its last phase. The other is quite new. It begins with an event we cannot date and know only through tradition recorded centuries later, but which probably occurred during the testing time imposed on Egypt by the sea peoples. Whenever and however it happened, a turning-point had been reached in world history when there went out of Egypt people the Egyptians called Hebrews and the world later called Jews.

For many people during many centuries, humanity's history before the coming of Christianity was the history of the Jews and what they recounted of the history of others. Both were written down in the books called the Old Testament, the sacred writings of the Jewish people, subsequently diffused world-wide in many languages by the Christian missionary impulse and the invention of printing. They were to be the first people to arrive at an abstract notion of God and to forbid his representation by images. No people has produced a greater historical impact from such comparatively insignificant origins and resources, origins so insignificant indeed that it is still difficult to be sure of very much about them in spite of huge efforts.

SEMITIC PEOPLES

Jewish origins lie among the Semitic, nomadic peoples of Arabia, whose pre-historic and historic tendency was to press into the richer lands of the Fertile Crescent nearest to their original homes. The first stage

The famous Lion Gates at the ancient Hittite capital of Hattusas (now Bogazkoy in Turkey) date from the 14th century BCE.

of their story of which history must take notice is the age of the patriarchs, whose traditions are embodied in the biblical accounts of Abraham, Isaac and Jacob. There do not seem to be good grounds for denying that men who were the origins of these gigantic and legendary figures actually existed. If they did, they lived in about 1800 BCE and their story is a part of the confusion following the end of Ur. The Bible states that Abraham came from Ur to Canaan; this is quite plausible and would not conflict with what we know of the dispersal of Amorite and other tribes in the next four hundred years. Those among them who were to be remembered as the descendants of Abraham became known in the end as "Hebrews", a word meaning "wanderer" which does not appear before Egyptian writings and inscriptions of the fourteenth or thirteenth centuries BCE, long after their first settlement in Canaan. Though this word is not wholly satisfactory, it is probably the best name to give the tribes with which we are concerned at this time. It is a better term to identify this group than "Jews", and for all the traditional associations gathered round that word by centuries of popular usage it is best to reserve it (as scholars usually do) for a much later era than that of the patriarchs.

CANAAN

It is in Canaan that Abraham's people are first distinguishable in the Bible. They are depicted as pastoralists, organized tribally, quarrelling with neighbours and kinsmen over wells and grazing, still liable to be pushed about the Near East by the pressures of drought and hunger. One group among them went down into Egypt, we are told, perhaps in the early seventeenth century BCE; it was to appear in the Bible as the family of Jacob. As the story unfolds in the Old Testament, we learn of Joseph, the great son of Jacob, rising high in Pharaoh's service. At this point we might hope for help from Egyptian records. It has been suggested that this happened during the Hyksos ascendancy, since only a period of large-scale disturbance could explain the improbable pre-eminence of a foreigner in the Egyptian bureaucracy. It may be so, but there is no evidence to confirm or disprove it. There is only tradition, as there is only tradition for all Hebrew history until about 1200 BCE. This tradition is embodied in the Old Testament; its texts only took this present form in the seventh century BCE, perhaps eight hundred years after the story of Joseph, though older elements can be and have been distinguished in them. As evidence, it stands in something like the relation to Jewish origins in which Homer stands to those of Greece.

None of this would matter very much, and certainly would not interest anyone except professional scholars, were it not for events which occurred from one to three thousand years later. Then, the destinies of the whole world were swayed by the Christian and Islamic civilizations whose roots lay in the religious tradition of a tiny, not very easily identifiable Semitic people for centuries hardly distinguishable from many similar wanderers by the rulers of the great empires of Mesopotamia and Egypt. This was because the Hebrews somehow arrived at a unique religious vision.

THE COMING OF MONOTHEISM

THROUGHOUT THE WORLD of the ancient Near East it is possible to see at work forces which were likely to make monotheistic religious views more appealing. The power

These inscriptions, which were carved into the rock of Mount Sinai during the 2nd millennium BCE, can be traced to the western Semites. Such inscriptions, later developed in Canaan, Phoenicia and Greece, form the distant roots of the Latin alphabet.

of local deities was likely to be questioned after contemplation of the great upheavals and disasters which regularly swept across the region after the first Babylonian empire. The religious innovations of Akhnaton and the growing assertiveness of the cult of Marduk have both been seen as responses to such a challenge. Yet only the Hebrews and those who came to share their beliefs were able to push the process home, transcending polytheism and localism to arrive at a coherent and uncompromising monotheism.

YAHWEH AND THE HEBREW COVENANT

The timing of the process of monotheism is very difficult to establish but its essential steps were not complete before the eighth century BCE. In the earliest times at which Hebrew religion could be distinguished it was probably polytheistic, but also monolatrous – that is to say, that like other Semitic peoples, the tribes who were the forerunners of the Jews believed that there were many gods, but worshipped only one, their own. The first stage of refinement was the idea that the people of Israel (as the descendants of Jacob

came to be called) owed exclusive allegiance to Yahweh, the tribal deity, a jealous god, who had made a covenant with his people to bring them again to the promised land, the Canaan to which Yahweh had already brought Abraham out of Ur, and which remains a focus of racial passion right down to the present. The covenant was a master idea. Israel was assured that if it did something, then something desirable would follow. This is very unlike the religious atmosphere of Mesopotamia or Egypt.

The exclusive demands of Yahweh opened the way to monotheism, for when the time came for this the Israelites felt no respect for other gods which might be an obstacle for such evolution. Nor was this all. At an early date Yahweh's nature was already different from that of other tribal gods. That no graven image was to be made of him was the most distinctive feature of his cult. At times, he appears as other gods, in an immanent dwelling place, such as a temple made with hands, or even in manifestations of nature, but, as the Israelite religion developed, he could be seen as transcendent deity:

"the LORD is in his holy temple, the LORD's throne is in heaven"
Psalm xi, 4.

says a hymn. He had created everything, but existed independently of his creation, a universal being.

"Whither shall I go from thy spirit? or whither shall I flee from thy presence?" asked the Psalmist.
Psalm cxxxix, 7.

The creative power of Yahweh was something else differentiating the Jewish from the Mesopotamian tradition. Both saw human origins in a watery chaos; "the earth was

The Hebrew rulers

The enormous influence that the Hebrew tradition, as depicted in the Bible, has had on our culture has inspired many researchers to attempt to unravel the history of that ancient nation. But the scarcity of the archaeological evidence makes it impossible to verify the historical truth of the biblical stories. We may never know for certain whether Abraham, Isaac, Jacob and Joshua really existed. Perhaps one day a palace archive will be found, which will provide concrete information about the Hebrew monarchy. At present, the chronology of the Hebrew kings before the reign of David is wholly conjectural.

Chronological table showing prophets, kings, dynasties and major events of biblical times

ABRAHAM	MOSES	SAUL	KINGDOM OF ISRAEL	•722 BCE ASSYRIAN CONQUEST OF ISRAEL	•333 BCE ALEXANDER CONQUERS PALESTINE	•63 BCE POMPEY ENTERS JERUSALEM
ISAAC	JOSHUA	DAVID				
JACOB		SOLOMON				
JOSEPH			KINGDOM OF JUDAH	•587 BCE DESTRUCTION OF JERUSALEM BY NEBUCHADNEZZAR	•168 BCE MACCABAEAN REVOLT	•70 CE DESTRUCTION OF JERUSALEM BY TITUS
			PROPHETS	•538 BCE EXILES RETURN TO JERUSALEM	HASMONAEAN DYNASTY	
			AMOS			
			JEREMIAH			JESUS OF NAZARETH
			ASHURNASIRPAL II	CONFUCIUS		
HAMMURABI	AKHNATON – RAMSES II		HOMER	BUDDHA	ARISTOTLE	AUGUSTUS

1800 BCE 1700 1600 1500 1400 1300 1200 1100 1000 900 800 700 600 500 400 300 200 100 1 CE 100

without form, and void; and darkness was upon the face of the deep", says the book of Genesis. For the Mesopotamian, no pure creation was involved; somehow, matter of some sort had always been there and the gods only arranged it. It was different for the Hebrew; Yahweh had already created the chaos itself. He was for Israel what was later described in the Christian creed, "maker of all things, by whom all things are made". Moreover, He made man in His own image, as a companion, not as a slave; man was the culmination and supreme revelation of His creative power, a creature able to know good from evil, as did Yahweh Himself. Finally, humans moved in a moral world set by Yahweh's own nature. Only He was just; laws made by humans might or might not reflect His will, but He was the only author of right and justice.

MOSES

The implications of the founding Hebrew ideas were to take centuries to clarify and millennia to show their full weight. At first, they were well wrapped up in the assumptions of a tribal society looking for a god's favour in war. Much in them reflected the special experience of a desert-dwelling people. Later Jewish tradition placed great emphasis on its origins in the exodus from Egypt, a story dominated by the gigantic and mysterious figure of Moses. Clearly, when the Hebrews came to Canaan, they were already consciously a people, grouped round the cult of Yahweh. The biblical account of the wanderings in Sinai probably reports the crucial time when this national consciousness was forged. But the biblical tradition is again all that there is to depend upon and it was only recorded much later. It is certainly credible that the Hebrews should at last have fled from harsh oppression in a foreign land – an oppression which could, for example, reflect burdens imposed by huge building operations. Moses is an Egyptian name and it is likely that there existed a historical original of the great leader who dominates the biblical story by managing the exodus and holding the Hebrews together in the wilderness. In the traditional account, he founded the Law by bringing down the Ten Commandments from his encounter with Yahweh. This was the occasion of the renewal of the covenant by Yahweh and his people at Mount Sinai, and it may be seen as a formal return to its traditions by a nomadic people whose cult had been eroded by long sojourn in the Nile delta. Unfortunately, the exact role of the great religious reformer and national leader remains impossible to define and the Commandments themselves cannot be convincingly dated until much later than the time when he lived.

THE HEBREWS ARRIVE IN CANAAN

Though the biblical account cannot be accepted as it stands, it should be treated with

A reconstruction of how the temple Solomon built in Jerusalem may have looked. According to the detailed description in the Bible, the temple was a long building at the end of which was the sanctuary containing the Ark of the Covenant. No traces of the temple remain, but the description matches the design of a number of contemporary temples that have been discovered in Syria.

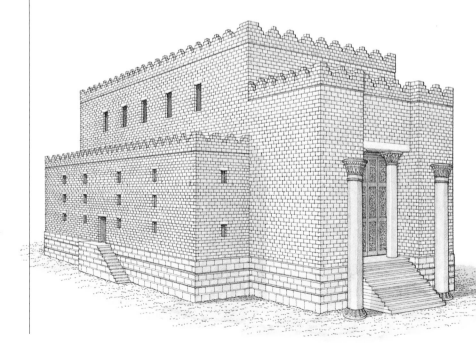

respect as our only evidence for much of Jewish history. It contains much that can be related to what is known or inferred from other sources. Archaeology comes to the historians' help only with the arrival of the Hebrews in Canaan. The story of conquest told in the book of Joshua fits evidence of destruction in the Canaanite cities in the thirteenth century BCE. What we know of Canaanite culture and religion also fits the Bible's account of Hebrew struggles against local cult practice and a pervasive polytheism. Palestine was disputed between two religious traditions and two peoples throughout the twelfth century and this, of course, again illustrates the collapse of Egyptian power, since this crucial area could not have been left to be the prey of minor Semitic peoples had the monarchy's power still been effective. It now seems likely that the Hebrews attracted

to their support other nomadic tribes, the touchstone of alliance being adherence to Yahweh. After settlement, although the tribes quarrelled with one another, they continued to worship Yahweh and this was for some time the only uniting force among them, for tribal divisions formed Israel's only political institution.

The Hebrews took as well as destroyed. They were clearly in many ways less advanced culturally than the Canaanites and they took over their script. They borrowed their building practice, too, though without always achieving the same level of town life as their predecessors. Jerusalem was for a long time a little place of filth and confusion, not within striking-distance of the level reached by the town life of the Minoans long before. Yet in Israel lay the seeds of much of the future history of the human race.

The Gebel Musa, located in the south of the Sinai peninsula, has traditionally been identified as the mountain where Moses received the Ten Commandments from Yahweh. However, we have no proof that Hebrew tribes actually went to the mountain during their exodus from Egypt.

The Twelve Tribes of Israel

The two Hebrew kingdoms and the territories of the Twelve Tribes.

When Solomon died, in about 928 BCE, only the two southernmost Hebrew tribes, Judah and Simeon, accepted his son Roboam as their king. As is shown on the above map, the Hebrew nation was thus divided into two separate kingdoms: the Kingdom of Judah in the south, whose capital was in Jerusalem, and the Kingdom of Israel in the north, whose first capital was Siquem. The Kingdom of Israel disappeared when, in about 722 BCE, the Assyrians conquered Samaria, its last capital. The Kingdom of Judah survived until 587 BCE, the year in which Jerusalem was conquered and destroyed by Nebuchadnezzar, King of Babylonia, who deported its inhabitants.

HEBREW KINGSHIP

SETTLEMENT IN PALESTINE had been essentially a military operation and military necessity provoked the next stage in the consolidation of a nation. It seems to have been the challenge from the Philistines (who were obviously more formidable opponents than the Canaanites) which stimulated the emergence of the Hebrew kingship at some time about 1000 BCE. With it appears another institution, that of the special distinction of the prophets, for it was the prophet Samuel who anointed (and thus, in effect, designated) both Saul, the first king, and his successor, David. When Saul reigned, the Bible tells us, Israel had no iron weapons, for the Philistines took care not to endanger their supremacy by permitting them. None the less, the Jews learnt the management of iron from their enemies; the Hebrew words for "knife" and "helmet" both have Philistine roots. Ploughshares did not exist, but, if they had, they could have been beaten into swords.

KING DAVID

Saul won victories, but died at last by his own hand and his work was completed by David. Of all Old Testament individuals, David is outstandingly credible both for his strengths and weaknesses. Although there is no archaeological evidence that he existed, he lives still as one of the great figures of world literature and was a model for kings for two thousand years. The literary account, confused though it is, is irresistibly convincing. It tells of a noble-hearted but flawed and all-too-human hero who ended the Philistine peril and reunited the kingdom which had split at Saul's death. Jerusalem became Israel's capital and David then imposed himself upon the neighbouring peoples. Among them were the

Phoenicians who had helped him against the Philistines, and this was the end of Tyre as an important independent state.

KING SOLOMON

David's son and successor, Solomon, was the first king of Israel to achieve major international standing. He gave his army a chariot arm, launched expeditions against the Edomites, allied with Phoenicia and built a navy. Conquest and prosperity followed.

"Solomon reigned over all kingdoms from the river [Euphrates] unto the land of the Philistines, and unto the border of Egypt . . .

and Judah and Israel dwelt safely, every man under his vine and under his fig tree, from Dan even to Beersheba, all the days of Solomon."

1 Kings iv, 21, 25.

Again, this sounds like the exploitation of possibilities available to the weak when the great are in decline; the success of Israel under Solomon is further evidence of the eclipse of the older empires and it was matched by the successes of other now-forgotten peoples of Syria and the Levant who constituted the political world depicted in the obscure struggles recorded in the Old Testament. Most of them were descendants of the old Amorite expansion. Solomon was a king of great

The image of only one Hebrew king has survived – that of Jehu, King of Israel (842–814 BCE). On the monument known as the Black Obelisk of Salmanazar, Jehu appears prostrated before the Assyrian king Salmanazar III.

energy and drive and the economic and technical advances of the period were also notable. He was an entrepreneur ruler of the first rank. The legendary "King Solomon's Mines" have been said to reflect the activity of the first copper refinery of which there is evidence in the Near East, though this is disputed. Certainly the building of the Temple (after Phoenician models) was only one of many public works, though perhaps the most important. David had given Israel a capital, thus increasing the tendency to political centralization. He had planned a temple and when Solomon built it the worship of Yahweh was given a more splendid form than ever before and an enduring focus.

THE PROPHETS

A tribal religion had successfully resisted the early dangers of contamination by the fertility rites and polytheism of the agriculturalists among whom the Hebrews had settled in Canaan. But there was always a threat of backsliding which would compromise the covenant. With success came other dangers, too. A kingdom meant a court, foreign contacts and – in Solomon's day – foreign wives who cherished the cults of their own gods. Denunciation of the evils of departing from the law by going a-whoring after the fertility gods of the Philistines had been the first role of the prophets; a new luxury gave them a social theme as well.

The prophets brought to its height the Israelite idea of God. They were not soothsayers such as the Near East already knew (though this is probably the tradition which formed the first two great prophets, Samuel and Elijah), but preachers, poets, political and moral critics. Their status depended essentially on the conviction they could generate in themselves and others, that God spoke through them. Few preachers have had such success. Israel would be remembered in the

A city under siege, a scene often repeated on Assyrian bas-reliefs such as this one. Samaria, the capital of Israel, was conquered in c.722 BCE following a long siege by Assyrian troops.

A recurring scene in Assyrian art – people being sent from their own land into exile. This is the fate that befell the inhabitants of the kingdom of Judah after Jerusalem was conquered by Nebuchadnezzar in 587 BCE.

end not for the great deeds of her kings but for the ethical standards announced by her prophets. They shaped the connexions of religion with morality which were to dominate not only Judaism but Christianity and Islam.

The prophets evolved the cult of Yahweh into the worship of a universal God, just and merciful, stern to punish sin but ready to welcome the sinner who repented. This was the climax of religious culture in the Near East, a point after which religion could be separated from locality and tribe. The prophets also bitterly attacked social injustice. Amos, Isaiah and Jeremiah went behind the privileged priestly caste to do so, denouncing religious officialdom directly to the people. They announced that all humans were equal in the sight of God, that kings might not simply do what they would; they proclaimed a moral code which was a given fact, independent of human authority. Thus the preaching of adherence to a moral law which Israel

believed was god-given became also a basis for a criticism of existing political power. Since the law was not made by a human agency it did not ostensibly emerge from that power; the prophets could always appeal to it as well as to their divine inspiration against king or priest. It is not too much to say that, if the heart of political liberalism is the belief that power must be used within a moral framework independent of it, then its taproot is the teaching of the prophets.

THE EXILE

Most of the prophets after Samuel spoke against a troubled background, which they called in evidence as signs of backsliding and corruption. Israel had prospered in the eclipse of paramount powers, when kingdoms came and went with great rapidity. After Solomon's death, Hebrew history had ups as well as

downs, but broadly took a turn for the worse. There had already been revolts; soon the kingdom split. Israel became a northern kingdom, built on ten tribes gathered together around a capital at Samaria; in the south the tribes of Benjamin and Judah still held Jerusalem, capital of the kingdom of Judah. The Assyrians obliterated Israel in 722 BCE and the ten tribes disappeared from history in mass deportations. Judah lasted longer. It was more compact and somewhat less in the path of great states; it survived until 587 BCE, when Jerusalem's walls and Temple were razed by a Babylonian army. The Judaeans, too, then suffered deportations, many of them being carried away to Babylon, to the great experience of the Exile, a period so important and formative that after it we may properly speak of "the Jews", the inheritors and transmitters of a tradition still alive and easily traced. Once more great empires had established their grip in Mesopotamia and gave its civilization its last flowering. The circumstances which had favoured the appearance of a Jewish state had disappeared. Fortunately for the Jews, the religion of Judah now ensured

that this did not mean that their national identity was doomed too.

TURMOIL IN MESOPOTAMIA

Since the days of Hammurabi, the peoples of the Mesopotamian valley had been squeezed in a vice of migratory peoples. For a long time its opposing jaws had been the Hittites and the Mitanni, but from time to time others had ruled in Assur and Babylon. When, in due course, the Hittites also crumbled, ancient Mesopotamia was the seat of no great military power until the ninth century BCE, though such a sentence conceals much. One Assyrian king briefly conquered Syria and Babylon early in the eleventh century; he was soon swept away by a cluster of pushful Semitic tribes whom scholars call Aramaeans, followers of the old tradition of expansion into the fertile lands from the desert. Together with a new line of Kassite kings in Babylon they were the awkward and touchy neighbours of the reduced kings of Assyria for two hundred years or so – for about as long as the

United States has existed. Though one of these Semitic peoples was called the Chaldees and therefore subsequently gave its name somewhat misleadingly to Babylonia, there is not much to be remarked in this story except further evidence of the fragility of the political constructions of the ancient world.

THE ASSYRIAN EMPIRE

SHAPE ONLY BEGINS to reappear in the turmoil of events in the ninth century BCE when Mesopotamia recovered. Then, the Old Testament tells us, Assyrian armies were once more on the move against the Syrian and Jewish kingdoms. After some successful resistance the Assyrians came back again and again, and they conquered. This was the beginning of a new, important and unpleasant phase of Near Eastern history. A new Assyrian empire was in the making. In the eighth century it was moving to its apogee, and Nineveh, the capital high up the Tigris, which had replaced the ancient centre of Assur, became the focus of Mesopotamian history as Babylon had once been. Assyrian empire was a unity in a way that other great empires were not; it did not rely on the vassalization of kings and the creation of tributaries. Instead, it swept native rulers away and installed Assyrian governors. Often, too, it swept away peoples. One of its characteristic techniques was mass deportation; the Ten Tribes of Israel are the best-remembered victims.

Assyrian expansion was carried forward by repeated and crushing victory. Its greatest successes followed 729 BCE, when Babylon was seized. Soon after, Assyrian armies destroyed Israel, Egypt was invaded, its kings were confined to Upper Egypt and the delta was annexed. By then Cyprus had submitted, Cilicia and Syria had been conquered. Finally, in 646 BCE, Assyria made its last important conquest, part of the land of Elam, whose kings dragged the Assyrian conqueror's chariot through the streets of Nineveh. The consequences were of great importance for the whole Near East. A standardized system of government and law spanned the whole area. Conscript soldiers and deported populations were moved about within it, sapping its provincialism. Aramaic spread widely as a common language. A new cosmopolitanism was possible after the Assyrian age.

The Assyrian Empire

The Assyrian Empire lasted for more than a millennium. Researchers have identified three stages in its development – the Old Empire, the Middle Empire and the New Empire. The Old Empire lasted from the 18th to 14th centuries BCE. The Middle Empire brought a new era of Assyrian expansion that came to an end in the 9th century BCE with the advance of the Ramians. However, the greatest moment for the Assyrian civilization came during the New Empire, founded by King Ashurnasirpal I (883–859 BCE). From the 9th to 7th centuries BCE, the Assyrians terrorized the communities of the Fertile Crescent. Assyrian military campaigns are recorded on the walls of their palaces. In about 612 BCE, the Assyrian Empire was defeated by a coalition of the Babylonians and the Medes.

A 7th-century BCE relief in the palace of Nineveh depicting the Assyrian king Ashurbanipal taking part in the regal sport of lion hunting.

ASSYRIAN MONUMENTS

The great formative power of the Assyrians is commemorated in monuments of undeniable impressiveness. Sargon II (721–705 BCE) built a great palace at Khorsabad, near Nineveh, which covered half a square mile of land and was embellished with more than a mile of sculpted reliefs. The profits of conquest financed a rich and splendid court. Ashurbanipal (668–626 BCE) also left his monuments (including obelisks carried off to Nineveh from Thebes), but he was a man with a taste for learning and antiquities and his finest relic is what survives of the great collection of tablets he made for his library. In it he accumulated copies of all that he could discover of the records and literature of ancient Mesopotamia. It is to these copies that we owe much of our knowledge of

Mesopotamian literature, among them the Epic of Gilgamesh in its fullest edition, a translation made from Sumerian.

The ideas that moved this civilization are thus fairly accessible from literature as well as from other sources. The frequent representation of Assyrian kings as hunters may be a part of the image of the warrior-king, but may also form part of a conscious identification of the king with legendary conquerors of nature who had been the heroes of a remote Sumerian past.

The stone reliefs which commemorate the great deeds of Assyrian kings also repeat, monotonously, another tale, that of sacking, enslavement, impalement, torture, and the Final Solution of mass deportation. The Assyrian empire had a brutal foundation of conquest and intimidation. It was made possible by the creation of the best army seen until

Extent of the Assyrian Empire

The decisive push for Assyrian imperial expansion took place during the reigns of Tiglathpileser III (744–727 BCE) and Sargon II (721–705 BCE). Moving outwards from the nucleus of their original settlement in the high basin of the Tigris, the Assyrians eventually controlled the whole of the Fertile Crescent. This expansion culminated in the conquest of Egypt during the reign of Ashurbanipal.

Map showing the expansion of the Assyrian Empire, 744–705 BCE.

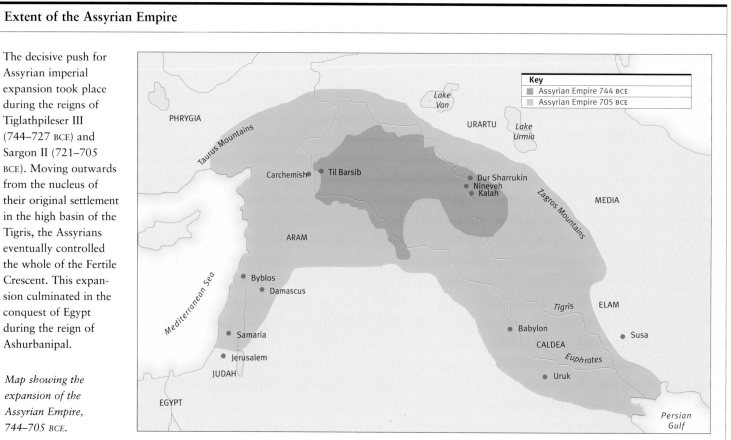

Key
- Assyrian Empire 744 BCE
- Assyrian Empire 705 BCE

that time. Fed by conscription of all males and armed with iron weapons, it also had siege artillery able to breach walls until this time impregnable, and even some mailed cavalry. It was a coordinated force of all arms. Perhaps, too, it had a special religious fervour. The god Assur is shown hovering over the armies as they go to battle and to him kings reported their victories over unbelievers.

THE ASSYRIAN EMPIRE DISAPPEARS

Whatever the fundamental explanation of Assyrian success, it quickly waned. Possibly, empire put too great a strain on Assyrian numbers. The year after Ashurbanipal died, the empire began to crumble, the first sign being a revolt in Babylon. The rebels were supported by the Chaldeans and also by a

great new neighbour, the kingdom of the Medes, now the leading Iranian people. Their entrance as a major power on the stage of history marks an important change; for a long time the Medes had been distracted by having to deal with yet another wave of barbarian invaders from the north, the Scythians, who poured down into Iran from the Caucasus (and at the same time down the Black Sea coast towards Europe). They were light cavalrymen, fighting with the bow from horseback, and it took time to come to terms with them in the seventh century. This was, in fact, the first major eruption into western Asia of a new force in world history, nomadic peoples straight from Central Asia. Like all other great invasions, the Scythian advance pushed other peoples before them (the kingdom of Phrygia was overrun by one of these). Meanwhile, the last of the political units of

The formidable Assyrian war machine combined the use of chariots, cavalry and infantry, as depicted on this bas-relief.

the Near East based on the original Caucasian inhabitants was gobbled up by Scyths, Medes or Assyrians. All this took a century and more, but amounted to a great clearing of the stage. The instability and frag- mentation of the periphery of the Fertile Crescent had long favoured Assyria; it ceased to do so when Scyths and Medes joined forces. This pushed Assyria over the edge and gave the Babylonians independence again; Assyria passes from history with the sack of Nineveh by the Medes in 612 BCE.

The sacking of Nineveh was not quite the end of the Mesopotamian tradition. Assyria's collapse left the Fertile Crescent open to new masters. The north was seized by the Medes, who pushed across Anatolia until halted at the borders of Lydia and at last drove the Scyths back into Russia. An Egyptian pharaoh made a grab at the south and the Levant, but was defeated by a Babylonian king, Nebuchadnezzar, who gave Mesopotamian civilization an Indian summer of grandeur and a last Babylonian empire which more than any other captured the imagination of posterity. It ran from Suez, the Red Sea and Syria across the border of Mesopotamia and the old kingdom of Elam

(by then ruled by a minor Iranian dynasty called the Achaemenids). If for nothing else, Nebuchadnezzar would be remembered as a great conqueror. He destroyed Jerusalem in 587 BCE after a Jewish revolt and carried off the tribes of Judah into captivity, using them as he used other captives, to carry out the embellishment of his capital, whose "hanging gardens" or terraces were to be remembered as one of the Seven Wonders of the World. He was the greatest king of his time, perhaps of any time until his own.

THE CULT OF MARDUK

The glory of the empire came to a focus in the cult of Marduk, which was now at its zenith. At a great New Year festival held each year all the Mesopotamian gods – the idols and stat- ues of provincial shrines – came down the rivers and canals to take counsel with Marduk at his temple and acknowledge his supremacy. Borne down a processional way three-quarters of a mile long (which was, we are told, probably the most magnificent street of antiquity) or landed from the Euphrates nearer to the temple, they were taken into the

This bas-relief from the palace of King Ashurbanipal shows the monarch resting under a vine arbour with the queen beside him. The royal couple are drink- ing, while the servants fan them.

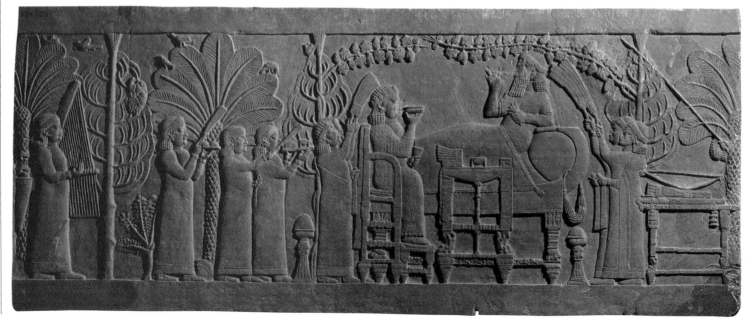

presence of a statue of the god which, Herodotus reported two centuries later, was made of two and a quarter tons of gold. No doubt he exaggerated, but it was indisputably magnificent. The destinies of the whole world, whose centre was this temple, were then debated by the gods and determined for another year. Thus theology reflected political reality. The re-enacting of the drama of creation was the endorsement of Marduk's eternal authority, and this was an endorsement of the absolute monarchy of Babylon, to which was delegated responsibility to assure the order of the world.

THE END OF INDEPENDENT MESOPOTAMIAN TRADITION

The cult of Marduk was the last flowering of the Mesopotamian tradition and was soon to end. More and more provinces were lost under Nebuchadnezzar's successors. Then came an invasion in 539 BCE by new conquerors from the east, the Persians, led by the Achaemenids. The passage from worldly pomp and splendour to destruction had been swift. The book of Daniel telescopes it in a magnificent closing scene, Belshazzar's feast. "In that night," we read, "was Belshazzar the

A detail from one of the bas-reliefs that decorated the walls of a chamber in the palace of Sargon II (721–705 BCE) in Dur Sharrukin (Jorsabad). This bas-relief depicts the transportation of wood that was used to construct the palace.

Babylon, which had been the most important city in southern Mesopotamia in the first centuries of the 2nd millennium BCE, would enjoy another moment of splendour after the fall of the Assyrian Empire. This detail is taken from a glazed brickwork wall in Nebuchadnezzar II's throne room in his Babylon palace.

king of the Chaldeans slain. And Darius the Median took the kingdom" (Daniel v, 30–31). Unfortunately, this account was only written three hundred years later and it was not quite like that. Belshazzar was neither Nebuchadnezzar's son, nor his successor, as the book of Daniel says, and the king who took Babylon was called Cyrus. None the less, the emphasis of the Jewish tradition has a dramatic and psychological truth. In so far as the story of antiquity has a turning-point, this is it. An independent Mesopotamian tradition going back to Sumer is over. We are at the edge of a new world. A Jewish poet summed it up exultantly in the book of Isaiah, where Cyrus appears as a deliverer to the Jews:

"Sit thou silent, and get thee into darkness, O daughter of the Chaldeans: for thou shalt no more be called, The lady of kingdoms."

Isaiah xlvii, 5.

A reconstruction in the Berlin Museum of glazed brickwork ornamentation from the throne room of the palace of Babylon (7th–6th centuries BCE).

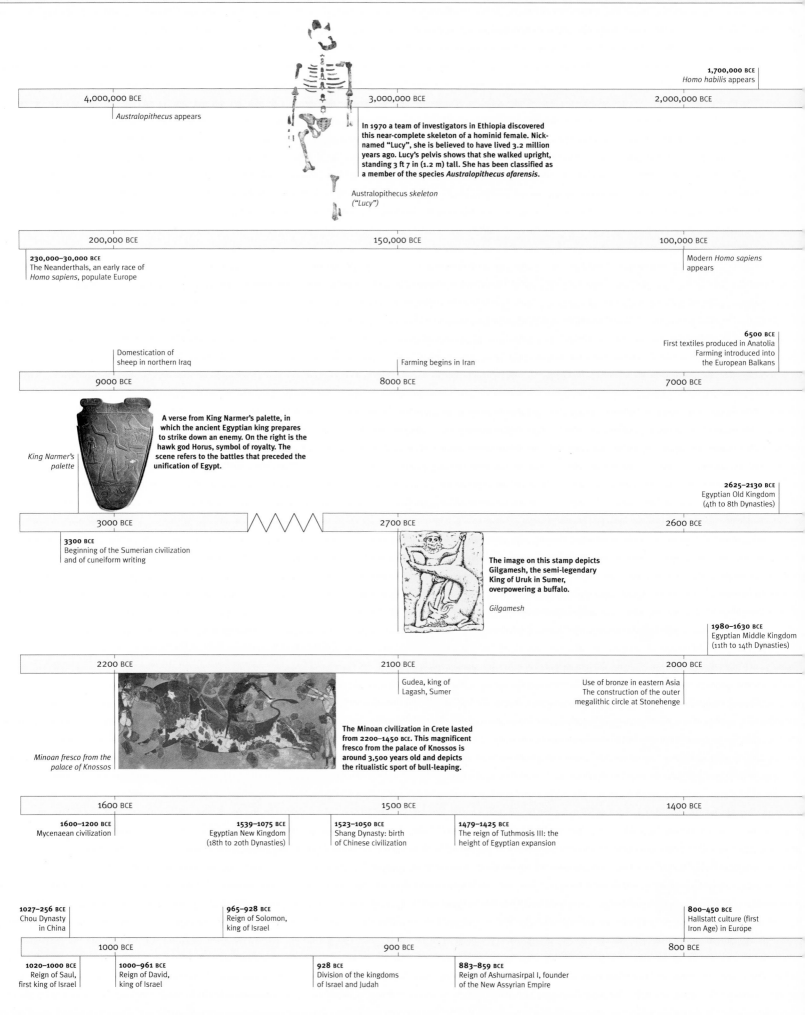

1,700,000 BCE
Homo habilis appears

4,000,000 BCE

3,000,000 BCE

2,000,000 BCE

Australopithecus appears

In 1970 a team of investigators in Ethiopia discovered this near-complete skeleton of a hominid female. Nicknamed "Lucy", she is believed to have lived 3.2 million years ago. Lucy's pelvis shows that she walked upright, standing 3 ft 7 in (1.2 m) tall. She has been classified as a member of the species *Australopithecus afarensis*.

Australopithecus *skeleton*
("Lucy")

200,000 BCE

150,000 BCE

100,000 BCE

230,000–30,000 BCE
The Neanderthals, an early race of *Homo sapiens*, populate Europe

Modern *Homo sapiens* appears

6500 BCE
First textiles produced in Anatolia
Farming introduced into the European Balkans

Domestication of sheep in northern Iraq

Farming begins in Iran

9000 BCE

8000 BCE

7000 BCE

King Narmer's palette

A verse from King Narmer's palette, in which the ancient Egyptian king prepares to strike down an enemy. On the right is the hawk god Horus, symbol of royalty. The scene refers to the battles that preceded the unification of Egypt.

2625–2130 BCE
Egyptian Old Kingdom
(4th to 8th Dynasties)

3000 BCE

2700 BCE

2600 BCE

3300 BCE
Beginning of the Sumerian civilization and of cuneiform writing

The image on this stamp depicts Gilgamesh, the semi-legendary King of Uruk in Sumer, overpowering a buffalo.

Gilgamesh

1980–1630 BCE
Egyptian Middle Kingdom
(11th to 14th Dynasties)

2200 BCE

2100 BCE

2000 BCE

Gudea, king of Lagash, Sumer

Use of bronze in eastern Asia
The construction of the outer megalithic circle at Stonehenge

Minoan fresco from the palace of Knossos

The Minoan civilization in Crete lasted from 2200–1450 BCE. This magnificent fresco from the palace of Knossos is around 3,500 years old and depicts the ritualistic sport of bull-leaping.

1600 BCE

1500 BCE

1400 BCE

1600–1200 BCE
Mycenaean civilization

1539–1075 BCE
Egyptian New Kingdom
(18th to 20th Dynasties)

1523–1050 BCE
Shang Dynasty: birth of Chinese civilization

1479–1425 BCE
The reign of Tuthmosis III: the height of Egyptian expansion

1027–256 BCE
Chou Dynasty in China

965–928 BCE
Reign of Solomon, king of Israel

800–450 BCE
Hallstatt culture (first Iron Age) in Europe

1000 BCE

900 BCE

800 BCE

1020–1000 BCE
Reign of Saul, first king of Israel

1000–961 BCE
Reign of David, king of Israel

928 BCE
Division of the kingdoms of Israel and Judah

883–859 BCE
Reign of Ashurnasirpal I, founder of the New Assyrian Empire

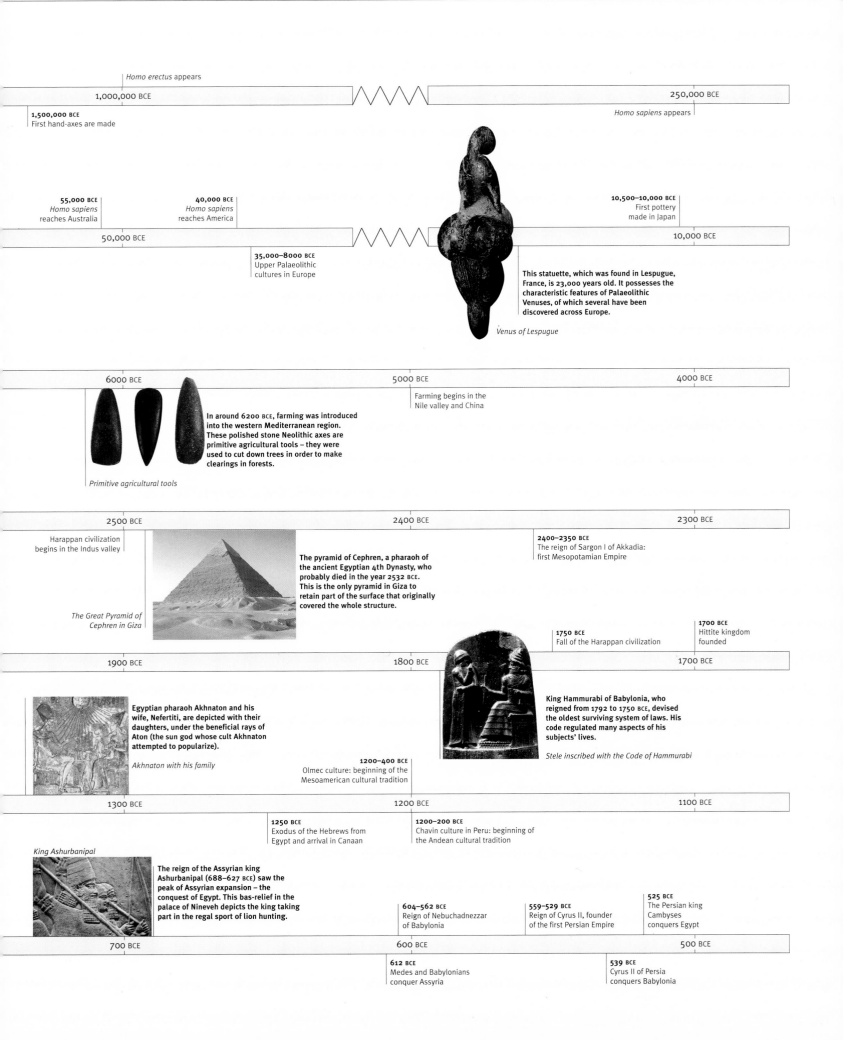

Homo erectus appears

1,000,000 BCE

250,000 BCE

1,500,000 BCE
First hand-axes are made

Homo sapiens appears

55,000 BCE
Homo sapiens
reaches Australia

40,000 BCE
Homo sapiens
reaches America

10,500–10,000 BCE
First pottery
made in Japan

50,000 BCE

10,000 BCE

35,000–8000 BCE
Upper Palaeolithic
cultures in Europe

This statuette, which was found in Lespugue, France, is 23,000 years old. It possesses the characteristic features of Palaeolithic Venuses, of which several have been discovered across Europe.

Venus of Lespugue

6000 BCE

5000 BCE

4000 BCE

Farming begins in the
Nile valley and China

In around 6200 BCE, farming was introduced into the western Mediterranean region. These polished stone Neolithic axes are primitive agricultural tools – they were used to cut down trees in order to make clearings in forests.

Primitive agricultural tools

2500 BCE

2400 BCE

2300 BCE

Harappan civilization
begins in the Indus valley

2400–2350 BCE
The reign of Sargon I of Akkadia:
first Mesopotamian Empire

The pyramid of Cephren, a pharaoh of the ancient Egyptian 4th Dynasty, who probably died in the year 2532 BCE. This is the only pyramid in Giza to retain part of the surface that originally covered the whole structure.

_The Great Pyramid of
Cephren in Giza_

1700 BCE
Hittite kingdom
founded

1750 BCE
Fall of the Harappan civilization

1900 BCE

1800 BCE

1700 BCE

Egyptian pharaoh Akhnaton and his wife, Nefertiti, are depicted with their daughters, under the beneficial rays of Aton (the sun god whose cult Akhnaton attempted to popularize).

Akhnaton with his family

1200–400 BCE
Olmec culture: beginning of the
Mesoamerican cultural tradition

King Hammurabi of Babylonia, who reigned from 1792 to 1750 BCE, devised the oldest surviving system of laws. His code regulated many aspects of his subjects' lives.

Stele inscribed with the Code of Hammurabi

1300 BCE

1200 BCE

1100 BCE

1250 BCE
Exodus of the Hebrews from
Egypt and arrival in Canaan

1200–200 BCE
Chavin culture in Peru: beginning of
the Andean cultural tradition

King Ashurbanipal

The reign of the Assyrian king Ashurbanipal (688–627 BCE) saw the peak of Assyrian expansion – the conquest of Egypt. This bas-relief in the palace of Nineveh depicts the king taking part in the regal sport of lion hunting.

604–562 BCE
Reign of Nebuchadnezzar
of Babylonia

559–529 BCE
Reign of Cyrus II, founder
of the first Persian Empire

525 BCE
The Persian king
Cambyses
conquers Egypt

700 BCE

600 BCE

500 BCE

612 BCE
Medes and Babylonians
conquer Assyria

539 BCE
Cyrus II of Persia
conquers Babylonia

VOLUME 1 Chapters and contents

BEFORE HISTORY

THE FIRST CIVILIZATIONS

Chapter 3

Ancient Egypt

Chapter 4

**Intruders and Invaders: the Dark Ages
of the Ancient Near East**

SERIES CONTENTS

Volume 1

PREHISTORY AND THE FIRST CIVILIZATIONS

Before History
The Foundations
Homo sapiens
The Possibility of
    Civilization

The First Civilizations
Early Civilized Life
Ancient Mesopotamia
Ancient Egypt
Intruders and Invaders:
    the Dark Ages of the
        Ancient Near East

Volume 2

EASTERN ASIA AND CLASSICAL GREECE

**The Beginnings of
Civilization in Eastern Asia**
Ancient India
Ancient China
The Other Worlds of
    the Ancient Past
The End of the Old World

**The Classical
Mediterranean: Greece**
The Roots of One World
The Greeks
Greek Civilization
The Hellenistic World

Volume 3

ROME AND THE CLASSICAL WEST

Rome
The Roman Achievement
Jewry and the Coming
    of Christianity
The Waning of the
    Classical West
The Elements of a Future

Volume 4

THE AGE OF DIVERGING TRADITIONS

Islam and the Re-making
    of the Near East
The Arab Empires
Byzantium and its Sphere
The Disputed Legacies of
    the Near East
The Making of Europe

Volume 5

THE FAR EAST AND A NEW EUROPE

India
Imperial China
Japan
Worlds Apart
Europe: the First
    Revolution
Europe Looks Outward

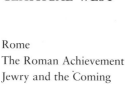

INDEX

Page references to main text in roman, to box text in **bold** and to captions in *italic*.

ACKNOWLEDGMENTS

PICTURE CREDITS

The publishers wish to thank the following for their kind permission to reproduce the illustrations in this book:

Key

b below; c centre; t top; l left; r right

AAA: Ancient Art and Architecture Collection Ltd
AGE: A.G.E. Fotostock
AISA: Archivo Iconografico SA
AKG: AKG London
AMH: Archaeological Museum, Heraklion
BAL: Bridgeman Art Library
BL: British Library, London
BM: British Museum, London
BPK: Bildarchiv Preussischer Kulturbesitz, Berlin
CSIC: Consejo Superior de Investigaciones Cientificas, Madrid
EM: Egyptian Museum, Cairo
ET: e.t. Archive
MAN: Museo Arqueológico Nacional, Madrid
NAM: National Archaeological Museum, Athens
NHPA: Natural History Photographic Agency
NMI: National Museum of India, New Delhi
RHPL: Robert Harding Picture Library
RMN: Réunion des Musées Nationaux, Paris
SPL: Science Photo Library
VM: Vorderasiatisches Museum, Berlin
WFA: Werner Forman Archive

3 BAL / Basilica San Marco, Venice
6 National Gallery, London
9 Magnum / Erich Lessing
15 AGE / Fritz Pölking
16t NHPA / Steve Robinson
18 AGE / SPL / John Reader
19t MAN
19b AGE / SPL / John Reader
23 Zardoya / Erich Lessing
26 MAN
29b AGE
29tl MAN
29tr MAN
30tl Santos Cid
30tr Santos Cid
31 Javier Trueba / Diario El Pais, SA
32 SPL / James King-Holmes
33 Comstock
34 Musée de l'homme, Paris
36 MAN
37b R.S. Soleski
37t SPL / John Reader
38 SPL / John Reader
42c MAN
42tl MAN
43 Frank Spooner / Sygma
44 Musée de l'homme, Paris
46b MAN
47t Godo-Foto
49b AGE
50 Oronoz

51b CSIC
51t CSIC
52t MAN
52b AAA / Brian Wilson
53c MAN
54tl MAN
54tc MAN
56t MAN
56b MAN
57t Zardoya / Erich Lessing
57b Magnum / Erich Lessing
58 MAN
59t MAN
59b Rätisches Museum, Chur, Switzerland
60 Sonia Halliday Photographs
61b ET / Hittite Museum, Ankara
63 AGE
65 Carmen Redondo
67 BAL / BM
68 Scala / The Iraq Museum, Baghdad
69t Godo-Foto
69b RHPL
70bl BPK / Jürgen Liepe / VM
70br AGE
71 WFA / BL
73c BAL / NMI
75 Michael Holford
76 RHPL
77b Scala / The Iraq Museum, Baghdad
78 RHPL
79t BPK / Jürgen Liepe / VM
79b Jürgen Liepe / Staatliche Museum, Berlin
81b RMN / Louvre, Paris
82tl BPK / Jürgen Liepe / VM
82b RMN / Louvre, Paris
83 Erwin Böhm
84t AAA/ G. Tortoli / BM
84b AISA
86t Scala / The Iraq Museum, Baghdad
86b AISA
87t RMN / Chuzeville / Louvre, Paris
87b Michael Holford / BM
88 RHPL / Richard Ashworth
89t Debate
89b BAL / BM
90t Scala / The Iraq Museum, Baghdad
90b RMN / Louvre, Paris
91t AAA / R. Sheridan / BM
91b RMN / Louvre, Paris
92 RMN / Louvre, Paris
93l RMN / Chuzeville / Louvre, Paris
93r BPK / Jürgen Liepe / VM
94 RMN / Louvre, Paris
95 RMN / Louvre, Paris
96 Firoexpress-Firo Foto
97t RMN / Louvre, Paris
97b RMN / Louvre, Paris
98 Hirmer Fotoarchiv
99 AAA / G.T. Garvey
100 Jürgen Liepe / EM
101b Jose Angel Gutiérrez
102t BAL / Giraudon / EM
102b Jose Angel Gutiérrez

104 Jürgen Liepe / EM
106 RHPL / John Ross / EM
107 RHPL / F.L. Kennett
108 RMN / Chuzeville / Louvre, Paris
109 AISA / EM
111 AGE
112 BAL / Stapleton Collection
113 RHPL / F.L. Kennett
114 Jose Angel Gutiérrez
115 MAN
116 Debate
117 AAA / Mary Jelliffe
118 WFA / BM
119 BAL / Giraudon
120 AKG / Erich Lessing
121 Debate
122t Jose Angel Gutiérrez / BM
122b Jose Angel Gutiérrez
123 AISA / BM
124 BAL / BM
125 Jürgen Liepe / EM
126t BAL / Giraudon / EM
126b Jose Angel Gutiérrez
127 Scala
128 BAL / Giraudon
129 AAA / Eric Hobhouse
130 RMN / Louvre, Paris
131 RMN / Chuzeville / Louvre, Paris
132 AAA / R. Sheridan / BM
133 BPK / Jürgen Liepe / VM
134 AAA / R. Sheridan
135 BM
136 BPK / Jürgen Liepe / VM
137 Magnum / Erich Lessing
138 BAL / Giraudon / EM
139 WFA / E. Strouhal
140 AAA / R. Sheridan
142 RHPL / F.L. Kennett
143 AISA
144 AAA / R. Sheridan
145 Scala / AMH
146 Jose Angel Gutiérrez
148 Scala / NAM
149 Petros M. Nomikos / Idryma Theras, Athens
150 Scala / AMH
151b Scala / AMH
152 Debate
153 AAA
154t Jose Angel Gutiérrez
154b Jose Angel Gutiérrez
155t Jose Angel Gutiérrez
155b Jose Angel Gutiérrez
156 BM
157 BAL / BM
158 ET / Archaeological Museum, Cagliari
159 MAN
160b Jose Angel Gutiérrez
161 BAL / Giraudon / Louvre, Paris
162 ET
164 Stockmarket
165 BAL / Basilica San Marco, Venice
167 AGE
169 BM

170 AISA / BM
171 Jose Angel Gutiérrez / BM
172 RMN / Chuzeville / Louvre, Paris
173 Jose Angel Gutiérrez / BM
175 Jose Angel Gutiérrez / BM
176 WFA / BM
177 AKG / Erich Lessing / BM
178 AKG / Pergamon Museum, Berlin
179 BPK / Jürgen Liepe / VM

MAPS

Maps copyright © 1998 Debate pages 20, 22, 36, 39, 40, 41, 45, 55, 66, 160, 168, 174
Maps copyright © 1998 Helicon/Debate pages 72, 103